Creativity in Education

Creativity in Education

International Perspectives

Edited by

Nicole Brown, Amanda Ince and
Karen Ramlackhan

UCLPRESS

First published in 2024 by
UCL Press
University College London
Gower Street
London WC1E 6BT

Available to download free: www.uclpress.co.uk

A CIP catalogue record for this book is available from The British Library.

ISBN: 978-1-80008-065-2 (Hbk.)
ISBN: 978-1-80008-064-5 (Pbk.)
ISBN: 978-1-80008-063-8 (PDF)
ISBN: 978-1-80008-066-9 (epub)
DOI: https://doi.org/10.14324/111.9781800080638

For teachers, trainers, coaches. In short, for educators and educationalists everywhere.
May these pages enthuse, inform, excite and inspire.
Nicole

This book is dedicated to the creativity within every one of us and to those fortunate enough to recognise, nurture and generously share their creative lives with others.
Amanda

To educators around the world who strive to make educational systems equitable and inclusive through creative capacities.

I would like to express my gratitude to those I cherish in my heart: you know who you are. Many thanks for sharing in this journey with me. Each of you, in your uniqueness, enhanced this experience. And to my husband and daughter, my deepest appreciation for your unrelenting love, unwavering encouragement and wonderful humour that light my way in darkness, give strength to persevere and show me what really matters in life. You are my inspiration. I love you two!
Karen

Contents

List of figures and tables

Figures

Tables

Notes on editors

Nicole Brown is an associate professor at UCL and director of Social Research and Practice & Education Ltd. She is known for her expertise in social research practice, a form of thinking-doing-being that interweaves practice, research and teaching. Her publications include *Making the Most of Your Research Journal, Embodied Inquiry: Research Methods,* and *Photovoice Reimagined*. Nicole shares her work at www.nicole-brown.co.uk, and she tweets as @ncjbrown and @AbleismAcademia.

Amanda Ince is an associate professor at UCL. She is programme leader for the UCL national professional qualification in early years leadership. Amanda's interest is in professional learning and the use of facilitated action research to empower professionals in their pedagogy and practices. Her publications include *A Practical Guide to Action Research and Teacher Enquiry, Towards a Child-centred Curriculum* and *Reflective Teaching in Early Education*.

Karen Ramlackhan is an assistant professor of educational leadership and policy studies at the University of South Florida. She is committed to work that engenders transformative change of unjust conditions that marginalise populations within educational contexts, with a particular focus on social justice leadership praxis, as well as culturally affirming equitable and inclusive practices. Karen's scholarly activities bridge disciplinary areas and emphasise creativity and critical thinking in problem-solving current issues of equity and justice in educational systems.

Notes on contributors

Keumhee Ahn is a professor at Gyeongin National University of Education in Korea. Having graduated from Seoul National University, she studied at the Ohio State University for her PhD in art education. She has taught art education at Jeonju National University of Education and Gyeongin National University of Education for more than 20 years. Keumhee's research subjects cover issues related to art criticism education, art history education and art museum education. Since 2018, she has been curating art exhibitions and developing educational programmes at GINUESIUM, the art gallery of Gyeongin National University of Education.

Roxana Balbontín-Alvarado holds a PhD in education from the University of Nottingham. She currently works as an academic for the School of Education and Humanities at Universidad del Bío-Bío, Chile. Roxana's research areas include teachers' identities, teachers' training, the teaching profession, school leadership, school contexts and higher education, among other areas.

Lizbeth Bullough is a lecturer at UCL and has been an educationalist for over 30 years. She works on the early years and leadership MA programmes and supports the development of knowledge exchange in international contexts. Lizbeth has worked as an academic adviser in Jordan and Myanmar for initial teacher education programmes and has led in-service initiatives for head teachers and teachers in China, Qatar and Pakistan. The primary themes in her research are related to equality of opportunity and factors that contribute to social inequalities in education.

Christiane Dalton-Puffer is a professor of English linguistics at the University of Vienna, where she is also co-opted to the teacher education programme. She has researched Medieval English in the past, but today both her teaching and research interests are in educational linguistics and language-teacher education. Christiane has authored *Discourse in Content* *and Language Integrated Learning (CLIL) Classrooms*, as well as numerous articles published in international journals. She enjoys crossing disciplinary borders and collaborating with colleagues from other fields of education. One of her missions is to convince subject educators of the relevance of language in learning.

Rosemary Davis CBE serves at IOE, UCL's Faculty of Education and Society. She was previously a teacher and a headteacher of three schools. Rosemary founded the primary postgraduate certificate of education at the IOE. In teaching teachers and trainers in southern Africa and south-east Asia, her emphasis is on the creative participatory methods of teaching for adults and children.

Sofia Eriksson Bergström works as a senior lecturer at the department of education at Mid Sweden University. She is a teacher educator mainly in play, creativity and learning environments, but also in qualitative research methods. Her research interests concern places for learning, creativity and accessibility in schools, special education, museums and science centres. Sofia has a specific interest in the agency of children and how to create circumstances with affordances that promote agency in learning environments. She leads the research group for young children, childhood and aesthetic subjects in her department.

Mengxuan Gao is a teacher assistant in Shanghai Normal University Tianhua College. She lectures students who major in early years education. Mengxuan has an MA in early childhood education from UCL and a BA from East China Normal University. She is presently a PhD student at Northern Arizona University. Her research interest is children's perspective and play pedagogy.

Klesia Garcia Andrade holds a graduate certificate in music education, MM and PhD in music education. She is a professor in the department of music education of the Federal University of Paraíba, and permanent professor in the graduate programme in music at the Federal University of Pernambuco. Klesia works mainly in the field of music education and creativity processes, and choral music education. She is a choir conductor, pianist, composer and researcher. She has authored articles in the proceedings of scientific events and specialised journals.

Maria Gross EdD is a former chemical engineer who was called into teaching while leading project-based learning activities as an elementary school volunteer. She taught middle- and high-school maths and science while serving as the maths and science department head. She has taught community college engineering and maths and graduate maths methods, and has led City University of Seattle's teacher credential programme as associate dean. Maria currently serves as a director of clinical experiences and single-subject faculty at Azusa Pacific University, focusing on diversifying the teaching profession. She is passionate about supporting teachers, teacher candidates and their students through application-based and trauma-informed teaching practices.

Sarah Knox is a lecturer in dance studies at the University of Auckland in Aotearoa New Zealand. She has had an extensive career as a performer, choreographer and teacher. Sarah's research interests include choreography, collaboration, creativity, dance pedagogies and techniques. Her research has been presented and published internationally. She holds a master's in dance studies and is a doctoral candidate at the University of Auckland. Sarah is the chair of the World Dance Alliance Asia Pacific Education and Training Network and the co-chair of the Early Career Researchers' Community – Dance.

Sirpa Lappalainen works as a professor of sociology at the University of Eastern Finland. Her expertise lies in the feminist sociology of education and qualitative methodology. Sirpa's recent publications contribute to the fields of critical race studies, critical disability studies and qualitative methodology. At the University of Eastern Finland, she co-leads the Research Community of Learning, Work and Everyday Life in Digitalised Society.

Marie Lundgren is an assistant professor at the department of education at Mid Sweden University. She works mainly with theoretical and practical issues regarding the subject of leadership in the teacher education. Marie has 30 years' experience working as a preschool teacher and she uses that experience at the university today. She is convinced that there are many opportunities to reach joyful learning when working with aesthetic subjects. Above all, she believes in supporting a sociocultural perspective to learning, where relations and genuine interest reflect a positive climate of learning.

Sibylle Menzel Kühne works as an assistant professor at the department of education at Mid Sweden University. She works mainly in music, practical leadership and preschool didactics in teacher education. Sibylle is responsible for aesthetic courses with a particular focus on music, as well as internship education. She has a background as a music teacher in the municipal music school in Sweden, and with music and theatre productions for Musik i Västernorrland. She is committed to leading and researching children's musical development and to creating conditions for music from a lifelong learning perspective.

Áine McAllister is a lecturer in languages in education and academic head of learning and teaching at UCL. As UCL public policy, policy engagement and impact fellow she works to develop engagement pathways with policymakers to reduce barriers to refugee and asylum seeker access to higher education. Áine uses dialogue to elicit poetry to uncover marginalised voices and to disrupt silencing. She draws on collaborative critical autoethnographic poetic enquiry and on applied ethnopoetic analysis to arrive at her own poetic representations and to facilitate others' poetic representations of their intercultural experiences.

Anna-Maija Niemi is a senior research fellow in the department of education, University of Turku. Her research areas include educational inclusion, both in education policy and in school's everyday practices, as well as youth studies and disability studies. Currently, Anna-Maija leads a longitudinal life-historical study focusing on belonging and agency of young adults in their educational and employment paths.

Jung Duk Ohn is a professor at Gyeongin National University of Education, Korea. Having graduated from Ewha Womans University she was awarded her PhD in curriculum and instruction at the University of Iowa. An experienced elementary school teacher, she has been teaching at university for more than 15 years, both in the United States and in Korea. Her research interests include teacher education, curriculum integration and competency-based education. She actively participates in national and local curriculum design and consultant work for elementary, middle and high school teachers.

Cristian Rivas-Morales holds a master's in education and is currently pursuing a doctorate in social sciences at Universidad Nacional de la Plata, Argentina. He works as a curriculum adviser for the School of

Education and Humanities at Universidad del Bío-Bío, Chile. His research areas include curriculum design theory, quality of education, the teaching profession, and social and educational policies, among other areas.

Manuela Schlick attained experience in the field of foreign-language teaching from both research and everyday classroom practice. Since her PhD on professional vision and collegial feedback within expert–novice groups, her research has focused on foreign-language teacher education and continuing professional development. Manuela also publishes on differentiation and material development for individualised learning settings. Currently, she is a postdoc researcher and teacher educator at the Centre for English Language Learning, Teaching and Teacher Education Research at the department of English studies of Vienna University.

Anne-Mari Souto has a PhD in social sciences and works as a senior lecturer in career guidance and counselling at the University of Eastern Finland. Her expertise is in the sociology of education, youth studies, critical race and whiteness studies, anti-racism in education, and participatory methods in qualitative research.

Carolyn Swanson (DMLS, GDipT, PGDEd, (Dis), PhD) is a senior lecturer in initial teacher education at Auckland University of Technology, New Zealand. Carrie's interests, research and teaching include science education, the use of creative pedagogies such as dramatic enquiry and mantle of the expert, curricular integration, action research and identity lenses.

Sally Windsor is an associate professor in sustainability and international education at the department of pedagogical, curricular and professional studies, the University of Gothenburg, Sweden. She currently teaches courses in education for sustainable development, international and comparative education and educational research methods. Sally's research interests include inequality and the unequal provision of school education, creative and artistic approaches to sustainability education in schools, civics and citizenship education, preservice and beginning teacher experiences, and practicum period observations and discussions.

Denise Wu is an assistant lecturer at the University of Hong Kong and a doctoral candidate at the department of curriculum and instruction, the Education University of Hong Kong. Her research interests include shadow education, children's rights and students' learning experiences.

She received her master's degree in primary education (policy and practice) from UCL. She was also previously an English primary school teacher in Hong Kong.

Ying Zhang is currently a PhD student at the faculty of education, the University of Hong Kong. She holds an MA in early childhood education from UCL and a BA from Beijing Normal University. Before her PhD studies, she developed the coding curriculum for young children in an educational technology company, and then worked as a research assistant at the Chinese University of Hong Kong. Her research interests lie in introducing computational thinking to young learners.

Jinying Zhou has been working in the education field for more than 10 years in China in a range of roles, from teaching English-related courses to children of three to 12 years old, to research on teaching methodology and provide training to teachers. She is currently designing both online and offline courses and curriculums. She obtained her master's in early years education from the IOE, UCL in 2016.

Foreword

Vlad P. Glăveanu, Dublin City University, Ireland

Creativity should be a central concern for educators worldwide. This is a commonly shared belief and an ideal that many teachers, students, parents and educational institutions are making tangible steps towards, despite some formidable challenges. The present book offers rich reflections on and illustrations of this ideal in the education of teachers and its implementation across the globe. It points to the resources that educators build on, the creative processes that they initiate and, most of all, the passion that they bring to educating future teachers *creatively* as well as *for* creativity. But there is another insight that this book makes visible; the fact that education is, in turn, central for our understanding and practice of creativity.

As a sociocultural psychologist, in my own thinking about 'creativity' I often return to the etymological roots of the term. 'To create', in Latin, means to bring into being, to bring forth, to make. Quite a contrast with the relentless emphasis on disembodied ideas and solitary minds within current creativity research. But there is something else that is interesting when considering the origin of this notion; the fact that it seems to emerge from an even older concept, *ker*, which means to grow. *Creare* or creating, in modern English, has to do with making things grow. What exactly grows as a consequence of creative processes? Ideas and things, practices, values and institutions, among other things. And yet growth is not merely about the outcome, it is about the process itself. To create means to grow as individuals, communities and societies.

This meaning, metaphorical as it might seem, is convergent with the symbolic root of education, which, in Latin again, relates to the acts of bringing up, bringing out and leading forth. Education, just like creativity, is a process of becoming, the kind of becoming in which the two realities are fundamentally intertwined. From this rather radical perspective, we cannot picture any forms of education that are actively non-creative or anti-creative as they would miss the essence of what it means – or, at least, meant – to educate. Equally, the bringing forth of creativity requires the scaffolding of transformation and growth that comes from learning, experiencing, educating.

The appeal to etymology might seem strange in a world focused on the latest research findings, on best (and next) practices, and on the uncertainty of the future. It might also be considered reductionist inasmuch as language is framed by culture and different terms carry with them specific cultural heritages that are not universal. For as insightful and deep as the connection between creativity and education seems to be in Latin, would it hold in other languages, in other cultural spaces, on different continents?

The contributions in this book suggest that it just might. We are presented, in its pages, with an impressive array of perspectives, experiences and world views around teacher education and, more specifically, creative teacher education. There is a lot to learn from the differences, gaps and tensions between each type of knowledge and each type of practice. But what makes this dialogue most productive is that it is underlined by a shared concern for creativity, by the fact that teachers of teachers across many countries do consider it important, they value it and they are ready to incorporate it in their classrooms and beyond. *Creativity in Education: International Perspectives* presents us with a polyphony of views and experiences, not a unified, single melody. It does not try to align perfectly any of these perspectives but to genuinely put them in dialogue with each other. And the marker of authentic dialogue is precisely the fact that we can never foresee what exactly it might lead to, that it is always surprising, that it does not have to end in agreement but in understanding. And, in this case, also in action, including social action for justice and equity. There is a sense, reading this book, that important steps are being made worldwide to collaborate and to develop complex and meaningful ways of thinking about and doing teacher education differently. That there is hope, despite all the constraints associated with teaching, that future teachers will not only learn about creativity but also experience it, first hand, in their own education.

If creativity means to grow things and education to bring up, then one of the most important tasks of creative education is to cultivate oneself, one's abilities, passions, interests and future possibilities. This is a process, we are reminded here, that can never take place in isolation. There are not only other teachers, other students and other schools that build up a creative ecosystem, but other cultures and other societies as well. As we engage in creative ways of growing and educating, we would do well to remember that nobody – no school, no teacher, no student – is an island. What old definitions of creativity and education are missing, at least in their Western history, is precisely this sense of togetherness. Future teachers would be well advised to remember it; luckily, they now have the present volume as a wonderful guide in how to think and do education differently, creatively and internationally.

Acknowledgements

The adage 'it takes a village to raise a child' has never been truer than in our current times of economic, environmental and societal change. Often, the major contributors in that village are teachers, trainers, coaches, leaders of learning, librarians, mentors, assistants, professional and administrative services staff, as well as support personnel working in all kinds of educational settings and contexts. We would therefore like to begin our acknowledgements section by thanking them. Without their creativity, resilience, commitment and dedication to education we would not be able to raise our children – and this book would not exist.

We are particularly grateful to all the contributors in *Creativity in Education: International Perspectives*. Although the global pandemic upended so many aspects of life, they remained steadfast in their commitment to complete this book. Their work highlights the importance of developing creative capacities and using creativity in teaching, leading and learning.

We would also like to thank the editorial and commissioning teams at UCL Press, as well as their anonymous reviewers, whose feedback was invaluable in shaping the book. Special thanks to Pat Gordon-Smith, for believing in this project and for her support in ensuring that it came to fruition.

We are indebted to Professor Frank Dolphin ARCA for giving permission to use one of his fabulous monotypes as a book cover. We are grateful for his creative insights and support for this publication. More information about Frank's work is available at Frank Dolphin at Linden Hall Studio, https://lindenhallstudio.co.uk/artists/82-frank-dolphin/works/.

Acknowledgements

Introduction

Nicole Brown, Amanda Ince and Karen Ramlackhan

The title of a book always carries with it a huge responsibility and potentially competing perspectives. Authors, editors, contributors and publishers want to make sure that the title is snappy and engaging but an accurate reflection of content, so that the cover draws the readers in. Yet, readers approach books with specific expectations and their own interpretations based on the title and their previous understandings. This is especially so when book titles consist of big terms and complex concepts. Therefore, the ultimate decision for the title of this book was not taken lightly and it is the result of a discussion that started with the book proposal submission and only finished with submission of the full manuscript. Ultimately, the title *Creativity in Education: International Perspectives* was agreed on, and with it the challenge of delivering to expectations with new and exciting innovations across international perspectives and a wide interpretation of education.

This introductory chapter outlines the aim, purpose and philosophy of this book while highlighting the conversational nature of its approach to creativity in education from international perspectives. We introduce key concepts and discussion points to explore teacher education in its broadest interpretations and philosophies underpinning theory and practice, including how creativity within the role teacher education is afforded. This is undertaken specifically from a range of international and at times completely contrasting contexts. The inclusion of 'responses to chapters' draws on voices from across the world to critique and discuss the content in relation to their own experiences, commonalities and potential lessons to be shared from each contributor in pursuit of creativity. In doing so, we aim to support readers in engaging with discussions and perspectives about creativity that might in other circumstances seem irrelevant to their context. The text provides a discussion and literature review on creativity in general terms, but more specifically looking at what creativity is, and what counts as creativity in educational contexts and fields.

Understanding teacher education

Teacher education is a deceptively simple construction. However, it is also one that excites huge variation in approach and policy. At one level it could be understood to mean the leading forth or development of teachers, relying on a more direct translation of the source of education from the Latin (*educare*, *-atum*, to rear; and *educere* from *ducere* to lead, Chambers, 1989). But that direct and historical translation has morphed into a complex set of approaches and contexts, all determined by local interpretations of policy, which in turn is informed by underpinning values and aims for education. In taking a more international perspective on creativity in teacher education, this book considers those variations, their applicability and role in supporting educators now and in the future.

Within Anglo-Western-centric contexts teacher education is commonly understood as the training of and for individuals who would like to become teachers in primary and secondary education. Usually, such education is divided into initial and then continuing or ongoing professional development, although there is a shift, particularly in Europe, to the term 'professional learning and development' (Ostinelli and Crescenti, 2021) or to 'professional learning communities' (Antinluoma *et al.*, 2018).

The terminology is contested, with many preferring the term 'initial teacher education' to 'initial teacher training' to describe the formal process of gaining Qualified Teacher Status, a legal requirement to teach in England (DfE, 2022). However, it is possible to teach in some contexts without such credentials, and they apply to the primary and secondary sectors but also to other educational contexts, such as education settings in the creative and performing arts or sport. This is where professional learning communities and professional development play a role. Professional learning and development occur through collaboration, coaching, creativity in problem-solving curricula, pedagogical and practice issues, and they often involve leadership (Lucas *et al.*, 2021) and professional services staff alongside teaching communities (Hord and Sommers, 2008; Wenner and Campbell, 2017).

Education is much broader with early years and tertiary, including further and higher education establishments, many of whom now also require specific certification and/or degrees. This links to an American import of a more technical and 'what works' approach, which potentially limits creativity within initial teacher education across all phases. It also plays into a view that education is a tool for economic improvement and a more market-driven understanding of its aims and values that might suggest that there is no place for creativity.

In China, teacher education is often seen as the remit of so-called 'normal universities' that provide initial, usually four-year degree programmes. Teachers are then required to complete further on-the-job work and a final examination to gain the teacher qualification (Song and Xu, 2019). However, with a population of approximately 1.4 billion and, since 1986, a free education system for nine years of compulsory schooling from the age of six, there is huge demand and there are schools with teachers who are unqualified in some locations (Hu *et al.*, 2014). As a countermeasure, there is now a huge policy drive to improve the situation with China's Education Modernisation 2035 plan. This aims to continue a move from capacity to quality. There is ongoing training and development that teachers must engage with throughout their careers to gain promotion and reward. China is also influenced by globalisation and economic drivers, with education a competitive marketplace, as exemplified by Gaokao, a highly competitive national examination to gain entry to the best educational establishments that drives the whole education system for parents and children (Zhou *et al.*, 2021). However, Chinese education is also tempered by the influence of Eastern philosophies such as Confucianism, Taoism and the political ideology of Communism.

These two examples of Anglo-Western and Eastern approaches to teacher education are by no means definitive or all encompassing. They do, however, highlight both similarities and differences between otherwise quite culturally diverse education systems, some of which are evident in other countries beyond these examples. But the initial education and training of teachers is just one part of a complex educational landscape – and this is explored in the next section.

Context of teacher education

Within the broader discourses of improving teaching, leading and learning, ensuring best teaching practices and guaranteeing positive student experiences, teacher education activities have entered the professional development narratives far beyond the limitations of the primary and secondary classrooms. Higher education institutions, further education colleges, nursing and medical training and sports coaching programmes are only some examples of what today constitutes training for teaching; thus, a form of teacher education (Ashwin *et al.*, 2020). Educational contexts are therefore much broader than the immediate understanding of a classroom of 30 pupils aged five to 18. Within this premise of a broader understanding of what constitutes 'teacher education', therefore, creativity and the role of creativity become even more relevant.

What is creativity?

Creativity is a complex yet universal phenomenon (Shao *et al.*, 2019). Most people feel confident in recognising creativity and what constitutes creativity, with many thinking that they are creative in some way or other. The internet is awash with quotes on creativity attributed to scientific geniuses, old masters, artistic highflyers, successful entrepreneurs and celebrities. Most famously, theoretical physicist Albert Einstein is believed to have said that 'creativity is intelligence having fun', while entrepreneur and industrial designer Steve Jobs of Apple fame and physician and psychologist Edward de Bono, most famous for his 'thinking hats', have focused on creativity as making connections or 'thinking outside of the box'. Creativity in this respect is not so much about finding something that is new, as it is about finding new ways of thinking about common occurrences. Just like Isaac Newton allegedly developed his theory of gravity as he watched an apple fall from a tree. Many people had watched apples fall from trees, but Newton started thinking about that everyday occurrence in a new way; something that everyone has the potential of doing.

However, when it comes to defining 'creativity' we seem to struggle to put into words what it is that is required to 'be' creative, how to 'do' creativity. The complexity becomes even more pronounced once the different fields of research involved with and related to creativity are included and considered. There are, of course, the disciplines such as those related to arts, design and performance, which are considered as inherently creative fields. But then there are also fields where creativity is involved that may not in themselves be inherently creative, such as in the social sciences and humanities. Shifts in what constitutes good research, how funding is allocated and how research impact is measured, have led to many social and humanist scientists drawing on creative approaches for data collection, analysis and dissemination. It is not uncommon for geographers to create poetry or for educators to curate and create bespoke photographs, as creativity is often linked to aesthetic artfulness or the processes of making (Sefton-Green and Sinker, 2000). In contemporary society, the links between the sciences and the arts are further strengthened through how museums and galleries present their work to ensure that visitors understand these powerful connections that may have been previously considered unlikely and unscientific.

Finally, there are researchers who focus specifically on creativity itself, on what creativity is, how creative thought develops in human beings and what creativity means for human understanding, communication and life more generally (Glăveanu, 2018). Each of these disciplinary vantage points brings its own interpretation, which impacts on how creativity is viewed. Though it has been defined and conceptualised in multiple ways, there is consensus among researchers that creativity comprises two attributes: originality, something unusual, novel or unique; and usefulness, something fit for purpose or appropriateness (Runco and Jaeger, 2012). In contemporary everyday life, particularly in connection with an increased interest in social media in the digital age and the resulting widening of communications via visual forms of expression being used alongside or even instead of speech, creativity also takes on a particular role. This heightened focus on creativity has in turn affected and influenced the education sector. Scholars report on the relationship between creativity, technology and education (Henriksen *et al.*, 2018), the link between creativity and environmental sustainability (Cheng, 2019), the role that school environments play regarding the development of creativity in education (Ahmadi *et al.*, 2019), and, more broadly, the relationship that creativity plays in contemporary education (e.g., Pllana, 2019; Kaplan, 2019). Research has also been undertaken to consider student and pupil experience of creativity (e.g., Fleith, 2019; Gong *et al.*, 2020; Kasirer and Shnitzer-Meirovich, 2021; Matraeva *et al.*, 2020). Within wider literature relating to educational settings, there are also numerous publications regarding creativity in primary or secondary education and even within the tertiary sector (e.g., Craft, 2010; Cremin, 2018; Desailly, 2015; Harris, 2016; Loveless and Williamson, 2013; Wegerif, 2010). Thus, over time, 'creativity' has become a buzzword across all disciplines in higher education and all phases from early years and primary, through to tertiary education.

To better understand creativity, it may therefore be helpful to delve a little further. The third draft of the Creative Thinking Framework (OECD, 2019), for example, distinguishes between what it calls 'Big C' creativity and 'little c' creativity. In this definition, 'Big C' creativity requires that 'creative thinking be paired with significant talent, deep expertise and high levels of engagement in a particular area, as well as the recognition form society that the product has value' (OECD, 2019, 8). 'Little c' creativity, by contrast, does not relate to masterpieces or genius inventions, but is the kind of 'everyday creativity [that] can be achieved by nearly all people capable of engaging in creative thinking' (OECD, 2019, 9). The framework not only recognises the value of both forms of creativity, but also emphasises that within those broad categories creative thinking skills must be distinguished further, as some people may be very creative in a specific domain, whereas others may be creative thinkers in general. This distinction is important as studies show that the previously assumed transfer of critical skills is not necessarily a given (Baer, 2015). It is therefore not quite as simple as teaching learners some creative thinking skills and then knowing that those skills can be applied elsewhere. This is where a sociocultural view of creativity proves particularly useful. According to Glăveanu *et al.* (2020, n.p.), creativity is a sociocultural phenomenon that is:

> at once, a psychological, social and material (physical and embodied) phenomenon
> . . . culturally mediated action
> . . . at all times, relational
> . . . meaningful
> . . . fundamental for society
> . . . dynamic in both its meaning and practice
> . . . situated but its expression displays both similarities and differences across situations and across domains.

It is against the backdrop of this view of creativity that this book explores the role of creativity in educational settings, where two contradicting trends can be observed: the devaluation of creativity and the revaluation of creativity. With the increasing relevance of league tables and comparison charts (e.g., the Organisation for Economic Co-operation and Development's (OECD) Programme for International Student Assessment (PISA)), curricula are being redeveloped to emphasise knowledge and attainment. This means that subjects usually associated with creative productions, such as the arts or music, become more peripheral. However, simultaneously, skills such as criticality, reflexivity and/or creative thinking among pupils in compulsory education and students in post-compulsory settings are centralised. In practice, this means that educators are required to embed the teaching of these soft skills within the delivery of their subject contents. Despite the shift towards a more embedded and integrated approach to teaching creativity in primary, secondary and higher education, the role of education programmes remains largely invisible, as publications do not tend to focus on how creativity is modelled, nurtured or taught to future teachers, who, in turn, are supposed to foster creativity among their learners. Yet, education programmes have adjusted to explore the teaching of creativity and to impart knowledge, skills and techniques that prepare trainees for a future in a creative classroom and for teaching creativity themselves (Ata-Akturk and Sevimli-Celik, 2020). It is therefore the aim of this edited book to fill this gap by presenting case studies of creativity in teacher education settings from countries across the world.

Each chapter is based on ethically conducted practice-based enquiry or other forms of empirical research. These studies provide the scholarly foundations on which a particular form or conceptualisation of what creativity is and means in the country-specific educational context. Contributors thus provide ideas that are generally applicable and relevant and are therefore transferrable to new educational settings and contexts. Each contribution is followed by responses in relation to other parts of the world. These responses are, in effect, a critical reflection and commentary discussing themes and issues to draw out commonalities and lessons that could be applied across contexts and inform future developments in creativity in education. They potentially support a social justice agenda that is inherent to education and teacher education. In philosophical-conceptual terms, social justice relates to the inherently unequal, unjust, oppressive policies and procedures that are embedded in the core of societies and cultures (Hytten and Bettez, 2011). Yet, social justice is also defined as a practice and praxis fostering strategic initiatives, experiential methods and pedagogical principles that seek to equalise and level the playing field of all stakeholders (Bell, 2016). In our current times, humanity faces significant changes from the effects of global warming, war and the resulting influx of refugees from those areas most affected. The Covid-19 pandemic both highlighted and exacerbated equity-related issues in all sectors, including in education, deepening inequalities and access to technology, resources and services. Suddenly, skills such as critical thinking, problem-solving and collaboration grounded on creative capacities became essential to help find solutions that would otherwise not have been considered (Anderson *et al.*, 2021). The immediate shift at the onset of the pandemic to remote and distance learning across all educational contexts is just one example.

While all chapters provide an insight into creativity across the world, their individual focus on country-specific contexts allows the chapters to grow and expand on their differences. These range from practical strategies within teacher education, such as the use of art exhibitions and object-work, to more philosophical approaches and teacher education.

Overview of chapters

The opening chapter by our Swedish colleagues describes a course in the final semester of the preschool teacher programme called *Playworld and Play as Phenomenon and Tool in Preschool Education*. Throughout this course the contributors work consciously with different tools to stimulate the students' meta reflection over their own learning processes and to help them see the connection between theory and practice when it comes to creativity, imagination and play. In the final exam in this course, the students write about applying theories to different cases and they are tasked with making their own process throughout the course visible. Colleagues from Austria, Aotearoa New Zealand and the United Kingdom then discuss this chapter on Sweden.

The second chapter focuses on South Korea and presents how a university, which trains elementary school teachers, has been working on a project to model how key competencies can be developed for pre-service teachers by using a resident art gallery within the university. The basic idea is to foster creativity through curriculum integration and collaboration around the exhibition. Colleagues from Chile and New Zealand respond to this chapter on South Korea.

In Chapter 3 we hear about reading initiatives and literacy practices in Qatar. The chapter presents the educational context of the Qatar National Library in Doha. Here, librarians engage in professional development aligned with typical teacher training activities to improve children's literacy and cognitive development with the help of creative reflective activities and lucky-dip story bags. Conversation with the Qatar example relates to different settings in Malawi, Mauritius and Sweden.

The next chapter reports on teacher education in Chile, where creativity-related areas are given low importance in initial teacher training. Although as part of the pedagogical courses or within the practicum immersion experiences, pre-service teachers are permitted some preparation to solve school problems and challenges from creative perspectives. However, as the chapter shows, the tools provided are not always considered sufficient, since they are only part of a formal course and are not always included. The responses for this chapter refer to education settings in Hong Kong, Botswana and Namibia.

The chapter based on the US educational context focuses on creativity in relation to social justice and equity. Through an autoethnographic lens we learn how students on a teacher education programme are not only taught culturally sustained pedagogy and critical thinking, but also focus on presenting their own understanding of social justice in creative assignments. The responses to the US chapter come from Finland and the United Kingdom.

Our colleagues from China then present their case study examining how in Shanghai Normal University TianHua college creativity is taught to future kindergarten teachers through the Kindergarten Curriculum incorporating Chinese traditional culture. The chapter outlines how the Kindergarten Curriculum course aims to develop student teachers' understanding of teaching and learning theories, practical skills and reflection capabilities. Responses to the chapter on China are from Finland and the United States.

Our last case study interrogates the teaching practice of a dance educator in dance studies at the University of Auckland. The chapter theorises dance teacher education through the creative process of dance-making. Within this chapter, the choreographic process is described and reimagined as a series of pedagogical tactics including thematic research, improvisation, movement generation, manipulating the movement language, choreographic structuring, refining, rehearsing, performance and reflection. Teaching pre-service dance teachers requires spontaneity, play, experimentation and innovative methods of response, which are also required within the creation of a new dance. The international conversations on this chapter from Aotearoa New Zealand are with colleagues from the United States and Brazil.

In the concluding chapter, we reflect on the relationship between creativity and education in the current climate. We use the contributions from the chapters and responses as a stepping stone to outline our vision for the future of creativity in education.

References

Ahmadi, N., Peter, L., Lubart, T., and Besançon, M. 2019. 'School environments: Friend or foe for creativity education and research?'. In *Creativity Under Duress in Education? Resistive theories, practices, and actions*, edited by C. A. Mullen, 255–66. Cham: Springer.

Anderson, R. C., Bousselot, T., Katz-Buoincontro, J., and Todd, J. 2021. 'Generating buoyancy in a sea of uncertainty: Teachers creativity and well-being during the COVID-19 pandemic', *Frontiers in Psychology*, 11: 614774.

Antinluoma, M., Ilomäki, L., Lahti-Nuuttila, P., and Toom, A. 2018. 'Schools as professional learning communities', *Journal of Education and Learning*, 7(5): 76–91.

Ashwin, P., Boud, D., Calkins, S., Coate, K., Hallett, F., Light, G., Luckett, K., MacLaren, I., Mårtensson, K., McArthur, J., McCune, V., McLean, M., and Tooher, M. 2020. *Reflective Teaching in Higher Education*. London: Bloomsbury Academic.

Ata-Akturk, A., and Sevimli-Celik, S. 2020. 'Creativity in early childhood teacher education: Beliefs and practices', *International Journal of Early Years Education*. Accessed 7 July 2023. https://doi.org/10.1080/09669760.2020.1754174.

Baer, J. 2015. *Domain Specificity of Creativity.* Cambridge MA: Academic Press.
Bell, L. A. 2016. 'Theoretical foundations for social justice education'. In *Teaching for Diversity and Social Justice*, edited by M. Adams and L. A. Bell, 3–26. New York: Routledge.
Cheng, V. M. 2019. 'Developing individual creativity for environmental sustainability: Using an everyday theme in higher education', *Thinking Skills and Creativity*, 33: 100567.
Craft, A. 2010. *Creativity and Education Futures: Learning in a digital age.* Stoke-on-Trent: Trentham Books Ltd.
Cremin, T. (ed.). 2018. *Creativity and Creative Pedagogies in the Early and Primary Years.* London: Routledge.
Department for Education (DfE). 2022. *Routes to qualified teacher status (QTS) for teachers and those with teaching experience outside the UK.* London: DfE.
Desailly, J. 2015. *Creativity in the Primary Classroom.* London: SAGE.
Fleith, D. D. S. 2019. 'The role of creativity in graduate education according to students and professors', *Estudos de Psicologia* (Campinas), 36.
Glăveanu, V. P. 2018. 'Educating with creativity?', *Thinking Skills and Creativity*, 27: 25–32.
Glăveanu, V. P., Hanchett Hanson, M., Baer, J., Barbot, B., Clapp, E. P., Corazza, G. E., Hennessey, B., Kaufman, J. C., Lebuda, I., Lubart, T. Monuori, A., Ness, I. J., Plucker, J., Reoter-Palmon, R., Sierra, Z., Simonton, D. K., Neves-Pereira, M. S., and Sternberg, R. J. 2020. 'Advancing creativity theory and research: A socio-cultural manifesto', *Journal of Creative Behavior*, 54(3): 741–5.
Gong, X., Zhang, X., and Tsang, M. C. 2020. 'Creativity development in preschoolers: The effects of children's museum visits and other education environment factors', *Studies in Educational Evaluation*, 67: 100932.
Harris, A. 2016. *Creativity, Education and the Arts.* London: Palgrave Macmillan.
Henriksen, D., Henderson, M., Creely, E., Ceretkova, S., Černochová, M., Sendova, E., and Tienken, C. H. 2018. 'Creativity and technology in education: An international perspective', *Technology, Knowledge and Learning*, 23(3): 409–24.
Hord, S. M., and Sommers, W. A. 2008. *Leading Professional Learning Communities: Voices from research and practice.* Thousand Oaks CA: SAGE Publications.
Hu, B. Y., Zhou, Y., Li, K., and Roberts, S. K. 2014. 'Examining program quality disparities between urban and rural kindergartens in China: Evidence from Zhejing', *Journal of Research in Childhood Education*, 28(4): 461–83.
Hytten, K., and Bettez, S. C. 2011. 'Understanding education for social justice', *Educational foundations*, 25: 7–24.
Kaplan, D. E. 2019. 'Creativity in education: Teaching for creativity development', *Psychology*, 10(2): 140–7.
Kasirer, A., and Shnitzer-Meirovich, S. 2021. 'The perception of creativity and creative abilities among general education and special education teachers', *Thinking Skills and Creativity*, 40: 100820.
Loveless, A., and Williamson, B. 2013. *Learning Identities in a Digital Age: Rethinking creativity, education and technology.* London: Routledge.
Lucas, B., Spencer, E., and Stoll, L. 2021. 'Creative leadership to develop creativity and creative thinking in English schools: A review of the evidence'. London: Mercers' Company.
Matraeva, A. D., Rybakova, M. V., Vinichenko, M. V., Oseev, A. A., and Ljapunova, N. V. 2020. 'Development of creativity of students in higher educational institutions: Assessment of students and experts', *Universal Journal of Educational Research*, 8(1): 8–16.
Organisation for Economic Co-operation and Development (OECD). 2019. *PISA 2021 creative thinking framework: Third draft.* Paris: OECD.
Ostinelli, G., and Crescentini, A. 2021. 'Policy, culture and practice in teacher professional development in five European countries: A comparative analysis', *Professional Development in Education*, 1–17.
Pllana, D. 2019. 'Creativity in modern education', *World Journal of Education*, 9(2): 136–40.
Runco, M. A., and Jaeger, G. J. 2012. 'The standard definition of creativity', *Creativity Research Journal*, 24(1): 92–6.
Sefton-Green, J., and Sinker, R. (eds). 2000. *Evaluating Creativity: Making and learning by young people.* London and New York: Routledge.
Shao, Y., Zhang, C., Zhou, J., Gu, T., and Yuan, Y. 2019. 'How does culture shape creativity? A mini-review', *Frontiers in Psychology.* Accessed 7 July 2023. https://doi.org/10.3389/fpsyg.2019.01219.

Song, H., and Xu, M. 2019. 'From external accountability to potential-oriented development: Quality assurance system building for teacher preparation in China', *ECNU Review of Education*, 2(2): 137–65. Accessed 7 July 2023. https://doi.org/10.1177/2096531119853663.
Wegerif, R. 2010. *Mind Expanding: Teaching for thinking and creativity in primary education*. Maidenhead: McGraw-Hill Education.
Wenner, J. A., and Campbell, T. 2017. 'The theoretical and empirical basis of teacher leadership: A review of the literature', *Review of Educational Research*, 87(1): 134–71.
Zhou, M., and Tan, C. K. 2021. 'Leave them kids alone- parents tire of China's world beating education system', *Nikkei China*, 4 August 2021. Accessed 7 July 2023. https://asia.nikkei.com/Spotlight/The-Big-Story/Leave-them-kids-alone-Parents-tire-of-China-s-world-beating-education-system.

1

Teach about creativity or teach creatively in Sweden: does it have to be a contradiction?

Sofia Eriksson Bergström, Sibylle Menzel Kühne and Marie Lundgren

Early childhood education in Sweden

In Sweden, preschool, after-school care and compulsory schooling from the age of five to the age of 16 are governed by national school legislation and the national curriculum. All curricula are based on a democratic set of values that are outlined before the more subject-related goals are written about. Preschool is thus part of Sweden's education system and rests on the foundations of democracy.

The National Education Act (2010, 800) states that everyone who works in a preschool must promote respect for the inviolability of human life, the freedom and dignity of the individual, the equal value of all people, equality between women and men, girls and boys, and solidarity between people. The national school system is based on democratic foundations. The Act (2010, 800) stipulates that education aims at pupils acquiring and developing knowledge and values. Education should impart and establish respect for human rights as well as the fundamental democratic values on which Swedish society is based. Everybody working in schools should also encourage respect for the intrinsic value of each person and the environment we all share. In accordance with the ethics borne by a Christian tradition and Western humanism, this is achieved by fostering a sense of justice, generosity, tolerance and responsibility in the individual. Teaching in school must be non-denominational. The task of the school is to encourage all pupils to discover their own uniqueness as individuals and thereby be able to participate in the life of society by giving their best in responsible freedom. No child shall be subjected to discrimination in preschool on the grounds of sex, transgender identity or expression, ethnicity, religion or other belief, disability, sexual orientation or age, in the child or anyone with whom the child is related, or to other abusive treatment (Swedish National Agency for Education, 2018).

Teacher education in Sweden

Teacher education is arranged through different programmes that correspond to the different ages of pupils in schools. The Swedish education system includes preschool to high school, children aged from one year to 16 years. All teacher education is run by individual colleges or universities and is regulated according to the Higher Education Act's nationally established Swedish Council of Higher Education in accordance with the Higher Education Ordinance.

These are the main programmes:

- early childhood teacher education (preschool);
- primary school teacher programme (school year 1–6, age of children 7–12);
- elementary school teacher programme (school year 7–9, age of children 13–15); and
- primary school teacher after-school centre (leisure-time teacher).

Since this chapter concerns preschool teacher education, we will explain this programme in more detail. The programme includes studies in three different areas: preschool pedagogy; educational science; and internship education. The internship education is worth 30 credits within the European Credit Transfer and Accumulation System, which equates to approximately 900 hours of study work, and which involves the student teacher, under supervision, planning and carrying out activities in a preschool.

The credits are distributed over four shorter periods throughout the programme. Preschool teacher education is vocationally oriented and aims for the student teacher to develop both a scientific and pedagogical approach, theoretical understanding, practical knowledge and personal development. In the different courses various forms of pedagogical and didactic working methods are studied; for example, by using art, music and drama. Children's linguistic and mathematical development are also studied, and in preschool play has a central role in the programme as a whole. The area of educational science contains other fields that are important for the profession. It includes, for example, preschool and school history, preschool values and curriculum theory, leadership and social relations, as well as conflict management. The programme ends with an independent paper worth 15 credits.

At Mid Sweden University, preschool teacher education is arranged according to a campus and distance model, which means that the students conduct their studies in their hometown and only spend certain weeks at the campus. The students spend four to five weeks per semester on campus and one week varies between three to five days. The teaching is thus delivered through seminars, lectures and workshops on campus and through distance learning via the internet. The campus weeks contain many different activities and elements that are important for the student teachers to be able to develop knowledge and skills for the future profession.

The role of creativity in Sweden

The creative process is often described as taking place within an interdisciplinary context and as an ability that is stimulated by collaboration (Eriksson Bergström, 2021). The aesthetic forms of expression are often mentioned in connection with creativity in the curricula. Since this chapter concerns preschool teacher education, we focus on the curriculum concerning preschool.

The curriculum for preschool (Swedish National Agency for Education, 2018) states that the children's creativity, curiosity and self-efficacy should be stimulated, along with their desire to solve problems and test their own ideas. The curriculum states that children should be stimulated, given opportunities and conditions:

> Children learn through play, social interaction, exploration and creation, but also by observing, conversing and reflecting. Children's learning can be versatile and cohesive if the didactical methods vary, and the environment is challenging and stimulating and encourages play and activity. The education should provide space for children's own initiatives, imagination and creativity. Children should be able to switch between different activities during the day, both outdoors and indoors and in varying environments. (11)

According to the preschool curriculum, children should be given the opportunity to marvel and develop their ability to explore, communicate and reflect. Education should stimulate children to take initiative and responsibility, and to enable them to work both independently and together with others. Education should encourage and challenge children to try out their own as well as other people's ideas, solve problems and translate ideas into action.

In the preschool curriculum 'play' is defined as the foundation of development, learning and wellbeing. In play, children get the opportunity to imitate, imagine and process impressions. Play stimulates imagination and empathy. Play can also challenge and stimulate children's motor skills, communication, co-operation and problem-solving, as well as their ability to think in pictures and symbols (Sutton-Smith, 1997). Therefore, it is important to give children time, space and peace to invent play, to experiment and to experience. Play should have a central and significant place in education. The right attitude of everyone involved in education and an environment that encourages play, therefore, confirms the importance of play in children's development, learning and wellbeing.

John Dewey's pragmatic theory has had a significant effect on education (Swedish National Agency for Education, 2018). Dewey often returned to the value of learners being allowed to imagine and fantasise. In his pragmatic idea of education, he allowed the democratic process to become the entity on which the entire education system was expected to rest. Today, creative skills like imagination and fantasy are often discussed in relation to the climate crisis and sustainability. 'Creativity' can be defined as actions that are based on combinatorial actions that combine and create new ones based on past experiences. 'Creativity' is considered to be discovering and creating something new based on past experiences (Vygotsky, 1995).

Caiman and Lundegard (2018) argue for the need of an education that supports and stimulates creative processes that can serve as a tool in the creation of a more sustainable world. The relationship with sustainability education is urgent and, within the framework of democracy, learners can participate creatively in the work for a fairer and more sustainable world. By creatively dissolving old beliefs and creating new thoughts, it will be possible for learners to influence how we live together. Democracy and creativity could create prerequisites for one another.

In this chapter, we define 'aesthetic learning processes' as children being both allowed to and stimulated to comment and reflect on qualities in life and the outside world using their senses and intellect. By integrating music, rhythm, dance, drama, arts and crafts in all subjects, Klerfelt and Qvarsell (2020) argue that pupils can find and use the form of expression that suits them best, and thereby they convey their thoughts and opinions and make themselves understood. In Swedish primary schools, the aesthetic subjects (e.g. music, arts and drama) have reduced space in timetables to increase the amount of time for the theoretical subjects such as mathematics. We must ask whether this is the right measure in a dynamic society, as the question of creativity needs to be broadened (Selander, 2018). In a changing modern era, a developed creative ability is an important attribute (European Commission, 2012). The development of knowledge and abilities, such as children's creativity, can have a major impact on how individuals succeed in education (Swedish National Agency for Education, 2014).

Unfortunately, you can barely find the word 'creativity' in the Swedish Higher Education Ordinance, even though student teachers must display knowledge about both practical and aesthetic learning processes to obtain their degrees. Student teachers must achieve deep understanding of how to use play and aesthetic subjects to create circumstances for every child to learn and develop. This chapter aims to discuss prerequisites and constraints regarding teaching creativity or teaching creatively in early childhood teacher education in Sweden.

Case study of teaching creativity in Sweden

> One of the biggest impressions I take with me from this course is that I have a completely different view of myself, where I have not previously seen myself as a creative person but after reading and discussing what the course literature highlights such as creativity, I have changed my former view of myself.
>
> (Jane, student)

In Sweden, early childhood teacher education has developed from being a mostly vocational profession to being, today, an academic profession. Alvestad (2018) believes that there is less room for playfulness within the university and that this is disadvantageous for the thinking person and constitutes a danger for society. According to Huizinga (1938), 'Human culture could not exist without this element of play'. The specific case in this chapter is about *Playworld and Play as Phenomenon and Tool in Preschool Education*, a course that was run for the first time in spring 2014 and was held in the penultimate semester of the programme. Early in our planning it was discussed how we could create a course that would really have an impact on student knowledge and understanding about creativity and play; a course where students would not only read about and hear about play but would also be more exposed to and affected by play. There was also an effort to create a course that, in an effective and meaningful way, would weave together theory and practice so that two aspects would emerge for the student teachers. Teaching staff on this course are teachers with aesthetic orientations such as drama, music and art, as well as teachers with a more theoretical background about imagination and creativity. The course aims for the student to develop in-depth knowledge and ability for leadership in order to plan and organise for play and learning based on the preschool curricula. During the course students must also acquire knowledge and skills in documenting and evaluating educational activities.

Based on the learning goals, we identified different content themes in the planning of the course. *Theme 1* is about play as a phenomenon. This theme deals with theories of play, different types of play, creating environments for play and play as a tool for different subjects, such as mathematics and natural sciences. *Theme 2* is about children today, modern childhood, and the role of play. In this theme, we deal with concepts such as institutionalised childhood, children's right to play, and aspects of power. *Theme 3* is about documenting, analysing and evaluating from different perspectives. This theme deals with techniques such as observation and interviews.

The case: *Playworld and Play as Phenomenon and Tool in Preschool Education*

This course can be metaphorically described as a 'weave', where the threads symbolise different tools that the student teachers can use to weave the content of the course into a completely personal pattern. The course puts great emphasis on the student teachers' own responsibilities and activities. However, it also challenges the teachers, their view of knowledge and the attitude they take towards their student teachers. The three 'threads' that run throughout the course will now be described and the text will then focus on the four elements that form the content of the weave. The four elements – workshops; input and lectures; seminars; and field studies – will act as examples of situations where the student teachers' creativity can take place and develop. The text contains quotes and documentation from 10 student teachers who have participated in the course. Below we will start to describe the three didactical threads and continue by focusing on different examples of the content in the course.

Thread 1: Teams – and roundtable conversations

With the team as a base, the student teachers immerse themselves theoretically in the course and go through the course literature, but they simultaneously raise issues related to practice to develop a didactic as well as a creative competence based on a scientific foundation and proven experience. We have chosen to work with student teacher teams because we believe that they need collaborative learning alongside individual learning. They will soon be preschool teachers who will work in teams; therefore, being able to practise and manage differences and conflicts in a team is an important part of the experience that they need to gain. From the beginning of the course, we teach the student teachers a conversation model that is inspired by action research (Rönnerman, 2010). The model allows everyone to speak and be listened to. One member of the group takes notes, and each member of the group, in turn, says what is on their mind about the subject while everyone else listens quietly. During 'the round', no one asks questions or offers comments. When everyone has spoken, the student teacher who has taken notes reads them back to the group and summarises, then questions can be asked and comments offered. All teams describe their purpose from their individual perspective as well as from a collegial perspective. They formulate an individual goal and a team goal. We use questions like the following:

- What kind of personal and collegial experience do you want?
- What is the content of the workshop?

At the end of the course, we return to the roundtable conversations to illuminate the student teachers' learning. We then use questions like the following:

- How did you reach your focus and goals?
- How did the workshop go and why do you think it went the way it did?
- What did you learn individually and in what way do you think your team worked and developed through the process?

After a while, the student teachers become familiar with the process and understand what it means when we ask them to conduct roundtable conversations in their teams.

This way of working within a team means that every semester we have student teachers who reflect on their individual development, and in this way discover how important it is to say what they think and to stand by the collegial reflections that result from the teamwork.

Thread 2: Process writing

Process writing aims to encourage student teachers to be aware of their own learning process and to be able to reflect on their own development over time. The writing contains reflections, questions and discussions about their individual development as well as the collective team development during the course. Writing makes their thoughts visible and makes it practically possible to make use of their thoughts and follow their own development.

By allowing student teachers to go back to their texts it is possible for them to reformulate plans, discover new chains of associations and move forward in thinking. Writing can also support the student teachers' thoughts about new contexts, as well as reveal what is contradictory and what lacks consistency in the text. The student teachers gain deep rather than superficial learning through writing, making writing an important learning strategy. One student teacher has stated: 'I think a lot while I'm reading . . . for me, it is absolutely necessary to write in order to remember the content and make it mine.' The student teachers write throughout the course, and we call this method of writing the 'process paper', which in other countries may be termed 'reflective journals' or 'professional portfolios'. When the course drew to a close, a number of student teachers stated that they had felt at the beginning that it was going to be more practical in nature, but had actually found that the course entailed extensive writing linked to reflection, analysis and theoretical elements.

Through process writing, both new knowledge and the student teachers' individual development are processed, thereby making their progression visible: 'Knowledge of theories and theoretical concepts affects [*sic*] my approach and how I interpret the play in a nuanced way.' Process writing is informal exploratory writing with the primary purpose of identifying and moving forward in thinking about a certain theme. More traditional academic writing usually aims to communicate and present material for readers. Throughout the course, we state some teaching content that the student teachers must write about, while simultaneously pointing out that they can write as much or as little as they wish. In the final exams the student teachers are instructed to return to their process papers and demonstrate their own development by relating it to the process writing. We see this writing as an opportunity for the student teachers to reflect on the literature read during the course. One student teacher put it this way: 'By writing diary entries and blog posts, I have seen many other thoughts and reflections that I have then been able to raise and discuss with my classmates.'

Thread 3: The literature

The literature is chosen carefully to give student teachers as much variety as possible in the field of culture, imagination, creativity and play. It provides diverse theory and practice. Some of the books are co-authored by researchers together with practitioners, some are anthologies, and one is a work by Vygotsky (1995). One student teacher expressed:

> For me, it has been a kind of liberation to read this literature and discuss it with others as it has partly changed my own view of me as a creative person but also the view that I can, for example, safely play fantasy games, as I can creatively create something new through my imagination based on previous experiences. I am grateful for this development and insight as I now realise that I can and want to play and create play worlds, both individually and together with others, both adults and children.

Having described the three different didactical threads in the course, this chapter will now focus on the content, in four parts, which can be read as examples of how and in what contexts the student teachers' creativity and playfulness takes place in this course. Thereafter, we will describe two different assessments: a practical assessment and a written examination.

Content 1: Workshops

The student teachers experience several practical workshops that focus on music, cultural heritage, drama and movement. One overall purpose of the workshops is to stimulate student teachers to gain an in-depth understanding of aesthetic learning processes and how they can work with these. During the workshops, we work consistently with the student teachers' didactic leadership. Many student teachers express that they are undergoing a major change through the course in terms of their own leadership. For example, we offer a 'playful leadership' workshop. This session aims to challenge student teachers in conversations and reflections based on imagination, creativity, play and storytelling. The focus is on the student teachers' own thoughts, fears and challenges. The following questions are the starting point for these conversations and reflections:

- What can we learn from the children?
- What are the differences and similarities in children's and adults' attitudes towards play, imagination, creativity?

- What does it take to have the courage to challenge yourself? What are the obstacles?
- Can the obstacles be overcome and how?
- How do you look upon your playful self-image?
- If not me, who? If not now, when? If not here, where?

Together with the teacher educators, student teachers are challenged to reflect on these issues that serve as support for their own development and are given the opportunity to challenge themselves.

Content 2: Input lectures

The course has four overall lectures that connect with each other. Initially, in the first lecture, student teachers receive input on play theories that they practise by applying them to observations during the internship. The second lecture deals with play and peer cultures. They are given input on how play negotiations are done between children, what can facilitate them and what can make them more difficult. This leads to the third lecture that deals with physical environments for play, such as playgrounds and environments within preschool and school. Finally, during the fourth lecture, we deal with the area of children who find it more difficult to play or to get involved in playing with other children. During this lecture, we return to the models that have been drawn during lecture 2 to understand the play negotiations, but we use them to point out what specifically makes it so difficult for some children to play. After the fourth lecture, it is common for student teachers to express that they now understand more deeply how to respond to children who have difficulty with imagination and play. The student teachers often relate this new knowledge to the image we have drawn up, they also understand exactly where the difficulties lie in the negotiation and transformation between reality and fantasy.

Content 3: Seminars

The course seminars are based on the themes described above. One example of a seminar is called 'Play, Imagination and Creativity in Childhood'. The student teachers read Vygotsky's (1995) book *Fantasy and Creativity*. They answer questions about how Vygotsky defines creativity, how he describes the relationship between imagination and creativity, and how he explains the difference between children's and adults' imaginations. The student teachers then choose a fiction book for children. Based on instructions, they carry out a literature analysis where they answer questions about how play, imagination and culture appear in the chosen book. Finally, based on their knowledge of how Vygotsky describes imagination and creativity, they make some comparisons between the fiction book they have read and their theoretical knowledge of imagination and creativity.

During the seminar, there are roundtable conversations where everyone can talk about their literature analyses, and reflect and think together about the prompt questions. This type of seminar generally supports the student teachers in a meaningful way to develop a deep understanding of the creativity theories and apply them at a societal level.

Content 4: Field studies

A field study is included in the course. During the first week, the student teachers agree, along with their teams, a phenomenon or area affecting children's play and imagination that they are particularly interested in investigating. This area of interest is followed by the teams through their field study and inspiration days.

The field study is carried out in *four steps* and after each step the student teachers write their reflections in their process paper. *Step 1* is to observe children at play. Student teachers receive instructions about what they can read in the course literature about observing, techniques to observe and other ethical questions that are good to consider before observations. The student teachers then visit a preschool and ask for permission to observe play.

In the *Step 2*, the student teachers will attempt to enter some children's playworld. They are tasked to reflect on whether they can enter the game on the children's terms and think about questions such as whether they, as adults, are trying to control the play in some way, such as using play as a tool for learning. Before this step, they receive reading instructions based on the course literature. After the student teachers have participated in the play, they reflect on a number of issues – for example:

- When you were in the same play bubble as the children, how were your conversations/negotiations expressed?
- What negotiation strategies did the children use?
- Was there power, manipulation and dominance? And if so, in what way?

In *Step 3*, the student teachers have the task of leading play with the children. The student teachers then select something from the plan that they have written for an inspiration day and try this in a group of children. After completing play, a song or a dance, they reflect on what happened in their process paper and ask questions, such as:

- How did it go? Why did it go that way?
- In what way did I, as a leader, influence the group of children?
- What can I learn from this opportunity and what can I change for the next time?

To delve into the meaning of the concepts of *child perspective* and *children's perspective*, the student teachers will interview one or two children in *Step 4* of the field studies. When all the steps have been completed, the student teachers must present orally the analysis of their field study. Their reasoning, which should be written in the process papers, should relate to relevant research and literature as well as to the texts. The student teachers should also explain what further research they would like to conduct based on what has emerged from their field study.

The practical assessment: Inspiration day

> In the dark hallway a fairy-tale portal glitters, welcoming us into an exciting and magical world. A group of ten children whisper and paw at each other, and two teachers watch them with anticipation. One preschool student teacher dressed as a giraffe suddenly emerges from the fairy-tale portal and welcomes the children to a magical jungle world. The children, who earlier in the week received a message in a bottle from the giraffe, are fully aware that they will now crawl through the fairy-tale portal to enter the jungle, where they will experience an adventure together with the giraffe.

The vignette above is one example of how creativity is developed among the student teachers in their practical assessment. The development of these workshops is a process that starts in the first week when the student teachers, together with their team, begin to formulate a vision for the creativity workshop where children are invited to our campus to participate in those workshops. This vision describes what the student teachers want the children to learn and experience during the workshops. The student teachers formulate a purpose for the workshop from an individual and a collegial perspective about what knowledge and experience they wish to achieve.

Because of the distance learning aspect, it is vital that all team members agree on the division of work and responsibilities. Together in the team the student teachers write a contract to formalise how they will meet and through which channels they will communicate. Although it is us, the teacher educators, who make the first contact with several interested preschools, it is the student teachers who are responsible for further contact. The student teachers create the invitation to a group of children in a playful way; for example, with mysterious letters, messages in bottles or maps, to create expectations among the children. In the middle of the course, we meet the student teachers in a seminar where they report on the development of their plans for the workshops. They tell each other about their planning and share something they plan to do with the children during the workshop. They will also receive feedback from teacher educators and fellow students; for example, about how the workshop has a common thread, how it ends or how the student teachers should greet the children when they arrive. The content of the written planning should be related to the course literature. These seminars aim to highlight the process for the student teachers and help to raise the their awareness of the process.

At the end of the course, the planned workshop with the children is carried out. The student teachers often spend the evening before in classrooms, transforming them into the amazing, imaginative environments. They use folding walls, light strings, fabrics and mats to fill the rooms with 'magic'. On one occasion pine and birch trees were brought into the classroom, and when there was a historical theme, antique tools were used as props, with the student teachers in period dress.

On the day of the final exams, the air is heavy with expectation. Crowds of children and preschool teachers bustle in the corridors trying to find the right way. The student teachers, dressed as pirates, witches, fairies, bears or historical figures, meet and guide the children and preschool teachers to the right rooms. Each student teacher team meets two groups of 10–12 children, aged between four and five years old, for 30 minutes. Between the two workshops, the student teachers have the opportunity to correct and redo, just in case something takes too long or too short a time or if something has not worked. At each workshop, one teacher is present to observe and offer feedback. At the completion of both workshops, there is an evaluation seminar with the teams and the teacher who participated in the workshop. This evaluation aims to foster student teachers' meta-reflection of the process and how they experienced the workshops. In this seminar we focus on questions such as:

- What went well?
- What can be developed in the workshop?
- What kind of support did you get from the course teachers?

During this evaluation, everyone gets the opportunity to think about and express their own development throughout the course and about the collegial development that has taken place in the team. This evaluation is based on the conversation model that the student teachers have internalised during the course. Everyone is given equal time to speak about what they have experienced. This seminar is important to link the entire process from start to finish.

Comments by student teachers after the process of Inspiration Day workshops:

> Our goal was achieved when we created play worlds and stimulated the imagination, according to Vygotsky.

> We challenged ourselves with facial expressions and body language, we feel more mature and strengthened after this.

The written examination: Independent writing assignment

The written assessment consists of three parts. Part 1 consists of a theoretical analysis based on the theories of play that the student teachers encountered during the play theory lecture and in the literature. In part 2, drawing on a case study, student teachers must write a text that relates to selected theoretical concepts that have been addressed during the course in teaching (lectures and workshops, as well as literature and scientific articles). In part 3, student teachers write a meta-reflection of their development over the duration of the course. Its structure should be characterised by a common thread and context. Student teachers are expected to use all the course literature to support their argument. This examination aims to connect the entire course for the student teachers. In relation to different cases, they apply the practical and theoretical knowledge and skills that they have gained. Above all, part 3 forces the student teachers to reflect on their development at a meta-level. In this part of the writing assignment, the student teachers get great help from their process writing (which they now return to), and through which they can trace their development and see the new knowledge and understanding gained through all the threads and content of the course.

Critique of the creative approach

The view of creativity has long been dominated by the fact that it is an ability attributed to individuals. However, mounting evidence shows that the creative process does not take place only in the mind of a person, according to his or her intentions and plans, but is played out in interactions with a physical and social world (Meusburger, 2009).

Researchers highlight that creative processes require a certain amount of space for improvisation, experimental thinking and innovation. One challenge is to plan for and design structures that stimulate creative processes but are within the framework of the assessment practice required by the university. Another important factor is that the assessment relates to clear learning objectives and criteria. When it comes to the final practical assessment (i.e. the inspiration workshops), the teacher educators jointly assess the student teachers' performance based on criteria such as implementation, purpose, leadership and the collegial process.

In a variety of ways, we, as teacher educators, have designed the course with some fixed structures that create a clear framework within which student teachers can act creatively and independently. According to Selander (2018), social interaction is one of the necessary conditions for human development, creativity is another. Regarding the view that creativity develops in interaction between people, we have developed a working method in this course in terms of collaborative learning.

While we want student teachers to develop independence, we also want them to experience the meaning of being shaped together with others. 'Education requires that the individual both shapes and is shaped' (Alvestad, 2018, 167), and this can happen only when the individual feels involved. This is why the student teachers belong to a team where they process literature but also take examinations together. The teams are intended to work like a space for experimental thinking and improvisation, almost like a room to play in together. Together, the student teachers take responsibility in their teams, and we encourage them to share responsibilities among themselves in a clear way so that no one hides or allows others to do the work.

The inspiration day sees the student teachers invite preschool groups, with children and preschool teachers, to the university. This is a real and intense scenario with real-life recipients, and there will be significant consequences if responsibilities are not met. Another of these structures is the writing that the student teachers must do throughout the course in the form of the process paper, which we described above as one of the threads running through the course. Brodin *et al.* (2014) believe that being stimulated to go against the usual is a prerequisite for creativity. As Alvestad (2018) argues, 'Whether students learn, what they learn, and how they learn, is dependent on self-confidence and confidence in their own learning process' (167). It is sometimes hard for the student teachers to realise that they are writing these texts for their own meta-reflection, not for traditional assessment.

Just as Alvestad (2018) describes similarities between the act and object of learning and the act and object of play, in this course we believe that there is an act and object of creativity. The process writing throughout the course works as an act of creativity, but there are difficulties with university structure that mean that these texts cannot be assessed traditionally according to the levels of knowledge achieved. Teaching about creativity or teaching creatively, as we have called this chapter, demonstrates the dynamism and duality that exists – creativity can be considered as an object when we teach about creativity; it can be considered as an act when we teach creatively.

The understanding and learning that student teachers achieve in this course are, in several ways, derived from their meta-reflection. We believe that writing the process papers creates a reflective distance, as Mark (2014) calls it. A distance that makes it possible, for example, to critically review practices.

In this course, we see the relationship between theory and practice as something especially important. One aim is that the seminars should, like Wilhelm von Humboldt's ideals, stimulate the free exchange of critical thinking. Humboldt (1767–1835) was the founder of the Humboldt University of Berlin. He was the architect of the Humboldtian model of higher education. The core idea is a holistic combination of research and study enabling students to become autonomous individuals and world citizens by developing their own reasoning powers in an environment of academic freedom. Study at the university should not provide merely professional skills through schooling along a fixed path, but rather allow students to build individual character by choosing their own way. He believed that education (*Ausbildung*) and *Bildung* are opposites in the sense that education (*Ausbildung*) works towards predetermined given knowledge goals, while *Bildung* is the result of a free development process based on personal interest. However, education (*Ausbildung*) is a prerequisite for *Bildung*: 'with the help of guidance and steering, the student learns to tolerate the freedom and loneliness in the search for knowledge that characterises bildung at the university' (Mark, 2014, 11). It is our hope that through this course we offer students the conditions for *Bildung* to take place.

Throughout the course, theoretical seminars and lectures are combined with and related to practical workshops. We require a lot from teachers, in the sense that teachers need a wide range of skills, from theoretical knowledge to practical aesthetic knowledge. With inspiration from the Humboldtian model, we have designed this course for student teachers to balance predetermined learning objects with free independent creative and critical thoughts. Through the threads of collegial learning in teams, the process paper writing and the literature, the course is not only about acquiring knowledge or abilities but also about the way in which creativity exists within students. It has been our aim through this chapter to describe how to design a course where you not only teach about creativity but also teach creatively.

Summary of key elements and recommendations

We have outlined a course where we believe in the following key elements and recommendations to create conditions for knowledge and understanding about play and creativity but, perhaps foremost, we believe that those elements give the student teachers courage to have and develop free independent critical thoughts within a university context.

- Key element 1: use assignments that promote meta-reflection.
- Key element 2: combine individual and collaborative learning.
- Key element 3: combine theoretical seminars and lectures with practical workshops.
- Key element 4: promote responsibility by assignments connected to reality.
- Recommendation 1: use process writing as a tool for meta-reflections.
- Recommendation 2: teach student teachers to collaborate by using roundtable conversations.
- Recommendation 3: there should be a combination of aesthetic and theoretical teachers leading the course.
- Recommendation 4: work with an ongoing process of one assignment that ends in a final examination at the end of the course.

References

Alvestad, T. 2018. 'Inte får vi lämna den lekande leken'. In *Samhälle, genus och pedagogik – Utbildningsvetenskapliga perspektiv*, edited by K. von Brömssen, S. Risenfors and L. Sjöberg. Borås: Stema.

Brodin, E., Carlsson, I., Hoff, E., and F, Rasulzada. 2014. *Kreativitet – Teori och praktik ur psykologiska perspektiv*. Stockholm: Liber.

Caiman, C., and Lundegard, I. 2018. *Kreativitet för hållbar utveckling*. Stockholm: Swedish National Agency for Education.

Eriksson Bergström, S. 2021. 'Glitter, flashlights and building pillows: About physical prerequisites for creativity', *European Early Childhood Education Research Journal*, 29(2): 278–92.

European Commission. 2012. *Rethinking education strategy*. Accessed 7 July 2023. http://europa.eu/rapid/press-release_IP-12-1233_en.htm.

Huizinga, J. 1955 [originally published 1938]. *Homo Ludens: A study of the play element in culture*. Boston MA: Beacon Press.

Klerfelt, A., and Qvarsell, B. (ed.). 2020. *Kultur, estetik och barns rätt i pedagogiken*. Malmo: Gleerups.

Mark, E. 2014. 'Inledning: Den akademiska bildningens praktiska sidor'. In *Bildningens praktiker*, edited by E. Mark. Göteborg: Makadam förlag.

Meusburger, P. 2009. 'Milieus of creativity: The role of places, environments, and spatial contexts', In *Milieus of Creativity*, edited by P. J. Meusburger, J. Funke and E. Wunder. Dordrecht: Springer.

National Education Act. 2010. *SFS*, 800. Stockholm: Ministry of Education.

Rönnerman, K. 2010. *Aktionsforskning i förskolan, trots att schemat är fullt*. Stockholm: Lärarförbundets förlag.

Selander, S. 2018. 'Learning-Design-Sequences – ett redskap för att designa undervisning'. In *Att bli lärare*, edited by S. Selander and E. Insulander. Stockholm: Liber förlag.

Sutton-Smith, B. 1997. *The ambiguity of play*. London: Harvard University Press.

Swedish Higher Education Ordinance. 1993. *SFS*, 100. Stockholm: Swedish Higher Education Ordinance.

Swedish National Agency for Education. 2014. *Att utmana och stimulera barns utveckling och lärande i förskolan*. Stockholm: Swedish National Agency for Education.

Swedish National Agency for Education. 2018. *Curriculum for preschool, Lpfö 18*. Stockholm: Swedish National Agency for Education.

Swedish Research Council. 2011. *Forskningsetiska principer inom humanistisk-samhällsvetenskaplig forskning*. Stockholm: Vetenskapsrådet.

Vygotsky, L.S. 1995. *Fantasi och kreativitet i barndomen*. Göteborg: Daidalos.

A response from the perspective of Austria

Manuela Schlick and Christiane Dalton-Puffer

We have approached the chapter from our vantage point as educators of teachers for the subject of English as a Foreign Language at secondary level. Even though we are at opposite ends of the teacher education spectrum in terms of our pupil age bracket, while we were a little sceptical, quite a number of aspects of the chapter resonated with us. First, we share the authors' understanding of teacher education as a journey of personal development (*Bildung*), not limited to training or education (*Ausbildung*).

One thing that we reacted to with dismay was to read that creative subjects have been removed from Swedish school timetables. Did we really understand that correctly? In Austria, despite some pressure towards reducing hours, creative subjects such as art and music are still in place. How alive and well they are, we cannot judge. Perhaps Austria's auto-stereotype as a nation of dancers and singers has something to do with it? According to a policy statement from 2009 (BMBWF, 2009), Austrian schools should be places of a 'holistic-creative learning atmosphere', in which teachers and learners alike can develop and enjoy their personal curiosity and creativity. Creativity is defined in its individual and social dimension, as it is 'not only an attitude of the individual but also the result of collaboration and communication' (BMBWF, 2009) and should thus be understood and implemented as a cross-curricular and interdisciplinary principle of Austrian school education. Accordingly, all school types in Austria include obligatory hours for music, the arts, language and at least one foreign language.

The chapter emphasises creativity in its expression as a collaborative undertaking. Perhaps the point needs to be made strongly in order to counteract the popular tendency to see creativity as a special and unusual trait of individual minds. The Inspiration Day projects described in the chapter certainly showcase the collaborative nature of creativity.

Apart from the dimension of individual versus collaborative creativity, the notion of creativity exhibits another tension. We are thinking here of the question of whether creativity is something that is particular of or restricted to the aesthetic sphere. The chapter clearly comes down on the side of the aesthetic-imaginative side of creativity. We would argue that there is also a much broader side to creativity that is crucial to being a teacher. Acting as a professional means being able to act creatively, that is openly and adaptively per definition, because pedagogical and methodological decisions are rarely straightforward. In general, professionals need to find the most appropriate answer among many possible ways of acting, as pedagogical settings are essentially defined by numerous conflicting principles and antinomies (Helsper, 2001). If we want to educate professional teachers, we must also strengthen their sense of autonomy and creativity at the level of classroom decision-making.

For this part of our comment, our perspective is that of secondary teacher education for the subject of English as a Foreign Language. We proceed from the general to the specific, commenting on Austrian curricula and stated educational goals, on practices of English language teaching in Austrian schools, and on English language teacher education, before we reflect on the potentials of adapting two formats discussed in the chapter. In the Austrian national curriculum creativity is specified as a principle of education but interestingly finds little further specification in subject-specific curricula. Standardised school-leaving exams have temporarily reduced the proportion of creative formats, but at the same time competence-based curricula have increased teachers' freedom to choose literary texts, creative tasks and methods. Reflecting on the broader teaching context in Austria, schools and pupils can also find a very broad range of extracurricular projects, activities and competitions in the field of the arts, language and music. These range from creative writing competitions staged by radio stations or magazines to video or web 2.0 competitions organised by private companies (*cf.* BMBWF, 2022).

The existing freedom of choice and the range of options need to be used and shaped by professional teachers, and we thus agree fully with our Swedish colleagues that teacher education is key to promoting creative education. In Austrian English language teacher education, student teachers study literature, culture and media studies, which can provide many options for including creative content and methods in English language teaching. Like other Austrian universities, the English department of Vienna University has its own student drama group and creative writing group. At Vienna, student teachers of English can also take creative writing classes.

As mentioned above, the rationale of the Inspiration Day resonated with us a lot. In Action Research Projects, our English language teaching student teachers at master's level independently design teaching interventions for a wide range of contexts, topics and methods (Wipperfürth and Mehlmauer-Larcher 2022), the projects being focused on their highly individual needs and interests. Student teachers can thus develop a sense of ownership of their learning and development (Rainer and Mathews 2002). It would surely be promising to encourage students more explicitly to opt for topics and methods from the aesthetic-imaginative spectrum of creative education in English language teaching (e.g. Maley and Bolitho, 2015) in their interventions. What we found particularly inspiring were the two methods of roundtable discussions and process writing. As we would argue that creativity in teaching also covers the level of pedagogical and methodological decision-making, both formats surely provide considerable room for enhancing awareness and openness for the development of the individual student teacher. We also liked that only the final meta-analysis of process writing was subject to assessment, which clearly establishes a 'safe space' for learning and exploration.

References

Bundesministerium für Bildung, Wissenschaft und Forschung (BMBWF). 2009. *Grundsatzerlass 'Ganzheitlich-kreative Lernkultur in den Schulen'*. Accessed 7 July 2023. https://www.bmbwf.gv.at/Themen/schule/schulrecht/rs/1997-2017/2009_15.html.

BMBWF. 2022. *Wettbewerbe*. Accessed 7 July 2023. https://www.bmbwf.gv.at/Themen/schule/schulpraxis/pwi/wb.html.

Helsper, W. 2001. 'Antinomien des Lehrerhandelns – Anfragen an die Bildungsgangdidaktik'. In *Bildungsgangdidaktik – Perspektiven für Fachunterricht und Lehrerbildung*, edited by U. Hericks, J. Keuffer, H. C. Kräft and I. Kunze, 83–103. Dordrecht: Springer.

Maley, A., and Bolitho, R. 2015. 'Creativity'. *ELT Journal*, 69(4): 434–6. Accessed 7 July 2023. https://doi.org/10.1093/elt/ccv036.

Rainer, J. D., and Matthews, M. W. 2002. 'Ownership of learning in teacher education', *Action in Teacher Education*, 24(1): 22–30.

Wipperfürth, M., and Mehlmauer-Larcher, B. 2022. 'Special issue introduction: Action research projects in ELT teacher education', *CELT Matters*. Accessed 7 July 2023. https://anglistik.univie.ac.at/research/departmental-publications/celt-matters/contributions/.

A response from the perspective of Aotearoa New Zealand

Sarah Knox

My three-and-a-half-year-old son is learning to spin. 'Make me dizzy!' he shouts. I worry. In my mind I see him falling and hitting his head, but I force myself to sit still and wait for him to stumble to me, laughing. It is an experiment, it's play, creativity in its most raw form. There is no right or wrong way of doing it, only a feeling. It is a life lesson of how his body works in space and time, with equal parts risk and joy. I can learn from this, I remind myself.

The chapter reminds me that play is a skill, relevant to us all, something that can be learned or re-learned and practised. I am prompted to consider the language that I use within my choreographic pedagogy. Although I use the word 'play' frequently at home with my son, I don't often use it with my dance students. However, the notion of creativity is always explicit, and playfulness is vital as a dance-making and teaching skill. The invitation to play has the same intention in both contexts: playfulness leads to creativity, discovery and relationship building. But, unlike with my son, creativity can evoke fear for my students in choreography class. 'I'm not creative', they say as they wade through their past experiences, fears and challenges, feeling doubtful that they are creative enough – whatever that might mean. 'It's just an experiment', I say as I set a new movement task, with the emphasis on the 'just' as though to minimise the pressure of the outcome. Regardless of the result, the experiment, the wrangling of movement, the exploring and stretching of a thought, is the valuable part, where new dances and methods of creative facilitation are to be found.

Within Aotearoa New Zealand, pre-service dance teachers hail from both dance training and dance education backgrounds. Dance training is considered to focus on the mastery of codified steps through processes of transmission and replication. It typically prepares students for professional careers in dance performance (Koff, 2000). Dance training usually takes place within private dance studios outside formal schooling, as well as in post-secondary dance conservatories. By contrast, dance education is broader and more holistic than dance training and encourages creativity and expressivity for all individuals, regardless of career pathway. Koff (2000) notes that self-knowledge, in context and relationship, is the primary aim of dance education. Dance education usually takes place within Aotearoa New Zealand's formal school curriculum and through dance degrees in universities. Some of the dance student teachers may have undertaken study in both areas, and others may have only pursued one pathway. The dilemma here is that teaching the dance curriculum in schools requires expertise in a range of areas such as choreography, performance, analysis and interpretation, culture and, to a lesser degree, dance techniques, not all of which feature within dance training. Much dance training does little to foster creativity or critical thinking skills. Additionally, traditional Western dance pedagogies typically engaged within dance training contexts do not necessarily encourage play. Consequently, some pre-service dance teachers beginning to teach in schools may be under prepared for the realities of their role and the necessity to approach teaching with an attitude of curiosity and play.

On reading the chapter, I question why playfulness is not a more explicit feature of my own curriculum in dance studies at the University of Auckland; especially as many of our students come to us via dance training routes. The questions that the authors propose in the section about a 'playful leadership' workshop are pertinent to a choreographic context where student choreographers are discovering how to reflect on their ideas, processes, interests and creative and teaching practices. Perhaps if used in dance-making pedagogy, these questions might do well to appease some of the pressures of the creative process – for example, time limitations, assessment criteria or perceptions of 'good' choreography. Further, the provocations to 'observe', 'gain entry' and 'influence' play might be germane to the creative process as useful steps for both teaching dance-making skills in the choreography class, but also for developing pre-service teachers' choreographic facilitation skills. Choreographic pedagogy requires careful negotiation of the moment of interjection, how to question, provoke reflection or offer feedback without telling the choreographer what to do creatively.

I was struck by the notion of a 'playful self-image' and how I could foster this more for myself within my teaching practice, as well as for my students. In addition, the idea of 'playful leadership' seems like a useful provocation for choreographers to explore broadly in dance, given the scholarship that critiques traditional and authoritarian choreographic roles that are often perpetuated within professional and educational contexts (for examples see Foster-Sproull, 2021; Gardner, 2007, 2011; Knox, 2013, 2017; Lakes, 2005).

The proposal of an 'inspiration day' presented in the chapter evokes a beautiful sense of possibility, of wonder and creation. I do think the choreographic process is akin to this; a 'Jungle Jim' of experiments, creative tasks are equipment or props. There is only so much that can be planned, and like the relational play between teacher and participant, collaboration between choreographer and dancer might only happen authentically as the process unfolds. I ponder, how is the dance studio a playground? Our bodies and ideas are the material. Music is an imaginative prompt. These are useful ideas to take with me into another year of choreographic pedagogy.

References

Foster-Sproull, S. 2021. 'A choreographic PACT: Proposing the notion of a "Prosumer-dancer" within dance education', *Journal of Dance Education*, 1–13.

Gardner, S. 2007. 'The dancer, the choreographer and modern dance scholarship: A critical reading', *Dance Research*, 25(1): 35–53.

Gardner, S. M. 2011. 'From training to artisanal practice: Rethinking choreographic relationships in modern dance', *Theatre, Dance and Performance Training*, 2(2): 151–65.

Knox, S. 2013. 'Dancer-centered dance-making: Five dancers' meanings and experiences of agency within choreographic collaboration'. Master's thesis, ResearchSpace@ Auckland.

Knox, S. 2017. '"It's all of me there, all of the time": Meanings and experiences of a holistic view of the individual within choreographic collaboration', *Journal of Emerging Dance Scholarship*.

Koff, Susan R. 2000. 'Toward a definition of dance education', *Childhood Education*, 77(1): 27–32.

Lakes, R. 2005. 'The messages behind the methods: The authoritarian pedagogical legacy in western concert dance technique training and rehearsals', *Arts Education Policy Review*, 106(5): 3–20.

A response from the perspective of the United Kingdom

Áine McAllister

This chapter sets out a preschool teacher education programme called Playworld and play as phenomenon and tool in preschool education. It analyses the programme's fitness to develop the creativity of student teachers, so that they can teach play creatively and can teach creatively through play. The chapter makes the inseparable link between collaboration and creativity and emphasises the role of meta-reflection for developing creativity and criticality. I ponder further the direct link between the introspective act of reflection and creativity and wonder how we can shine a brighter light on the criticality of creativity itself. The chapter offers a very clear blueprint for how creativity can be developed collaboratively through teamwork, well designed opportunities for roundtable discussion and for active and collaborative production between students in workshops. For me, in addition to the collaborative nature of the programme content, another strength is the field work aspect, as it facilitates student teachers to develop play pedagogy with preschool pupils and to reflect on it. On inspiration day when the preschool children are the immersed recipients of the student teachers' creative outcomes, it would be good to make more of this opportunity to actively involve the preschool children in some collaborative playfulness. Both because it would practically evidence developments in the student teachers' pedagogy and because who knows what the preschool children's collaborative and playful contribution might add to the knowledge produced.

The chapter emphasises the importance of student teachers' engagement with programme literature and theories of play. It seems to draw largely on the seminal work of Piaget and Vygotsky whose developmentalist views of the child and play are rooted in European/colonial values and norms (Tramwell, 2022). The authors highlight the influential role that Humboldtian ideals play in how they facilitate the exchange of ideas. A further dimension to the programme might be added by foregrounding other views of how one 'arrives at' knowledge and of the child as more 'equal to the adult in the co-construction of culture and knowledge' (Lindgren, 2020, 918) through play. Vygotsky tells us: 'in play a child is always above his average age, above his daily behavior; in play it is as though he were a head taller than himself' (1967, 16). For me, this supports the notion that Western humanist Cartesian notions have imposed reductive and false limits on the child, which becomes evident in the play of children. The chapter makes the connection between the teaching of creativity and societal sustainability, it explores the centrality of play in a child's learning and recognises the potentially significant role of playfulness for society and culture. I think it would be interesting to develop the link between play and societal transformation further. There might be four ways that could be done: by challenging the foundational role of the Western humanist ideals, by further exploring the concept of the child, of play and of the child at play from different (decolonial) perspectives, by going further to challenge the notion that education is about acquiring rather than creating knowledge, and by interrogating the false dichotomy between criticality and creativity.

I am a mother and languages educator in higher education in the United Kingdom. This is a system situated in the wider context of a hostile political environment for refugees and forced migrants for whom English is often an additional language. My own research reveals that the experience of these marginalised multilingual language users in higher education mirrors their wider experience in a hostile environment. Higher education in the United Kingdom fails to recognise the linguistic and cultural repertoires of 'non-standard' speakers of English and this has a silencing, exclusionary impact, oftentimes irrespective of prior qualifications or experience (McAllister *et al.*, 2021; McAllister 2022). As someone who researches translanguaging as a way of counteracting this marginalisation, I maintain a mindfulness of my own 'unknowing' in my position of relative privilege. As an unknowing adult, I often reflect on what there is to learn from children at play and I apply these reflections to both my pedagogy and an analysis of my work. Translanguaging is a stance that argues for a fluid conception of meaning construction (Tsang *et al.*, 2022) and a recognition of ways of knowing that have been pushed into the abyss through colonialism (Garcia *et al.*, 2021) – including, for example, childhood ways of knowing, such as play. Abyssal thinking also rejects childhood ways of knowing. Reading this chapter, I have further considered the implications of viewing play as a way of communicating understanding and of creating 'knowing' in the context of higher education for marginalised non-standard speakers of English who are multilingual and whose knowledge is transcultural and unrecognised:

> My child shows me the process at the park; how to participate.
> I didn't research it or show him how play works.
> He climbs the rope, turns to connect, uses his 'let me help you' dialogue.

This is an extract of a poem that I wrote as part of a collaborative autoethnographic poetic enquiry on the impact of collaboration and its relationship with creativity (McAllister, 2023). I offer this extract as a metaphor for openness and recognising ways of knowing that are not usually seen. We can unlearn abyssal thinking if we are open to the wonder offered through play.

The programme described offers a model for developing creativity and collaboration, not just in teacher education programmes but in other teaching and learning modules in higher education in the United Kingdom. For example, I think the roundtable and process writing tools are directly applicable to pedagogy in the field of languages in education, intercultural studies and refugee education. I would consider embedding elements of play in these tools to recognise ways of knowing that are otherised in this context. In roundtable discussions, is there room for role play or theatre methods? How can we facilitate intercultural dialogue that creates a space for a range of ways of expression that may be playful? In process writing, is there room for forms from different traditions that can be playful, such as song or poetry? Essentially the scaffold offered by the programme design is a sturdy one, and the chapter sparks ideas for me on how that scaffold could be dressed with more nuanced, more transformative conceptualisations of play that are more embedded in the programme content.

References

García, O., Flores, N., Seltzer, K., Wei, L., Otheguy, R., and Rosa, J. 2021. 'Rejecting abyssal thinking in the language and education of racialized bilinguals: A manifesto', *Critical Inquiry in Language Studies*. Accessed 7 July 2023. https://doi.org/10.1080/15427587.2021.1935957.

Lindgren, T. 2020. 'The figuration of the posthuman child', *Discourse: Studies in the Cultural Politics of Education*, 41(6): 914925. Accessed 7 July 2023. https://doi.org/10.1080/01596306.2019.1576589.

McAllister, A., and Brown, N. 2023. 'Competition and collaboration in higher education: an (auto)ethnographic poetic inquiry', *Qualitative Inquiry*. Accessed 7 July 2023. https://doi.org/10.1177/10778004231176278.

McAllister, A. 2022. 'Seeking access: An applied ethnopoetic analysis and poetic rendering of refugee and asylum seeker narratives of seeking access to higher education'. Belfast: BAAL Conference 2022.

McAllister, A., Zuoriki, W. A., Bektas, H. N., Katembwe, K., and Alibraheem, M. 2021. 'Seeking access: Refugees and asylum seekers seeking access to higher education: a poetic inquiry'. London: Self-published.

Trammell, A. 2022. 'Decolonizing play', *Critical Studies in Media Communication*, 39(3): 239–46. Accessed 7 July 2023. https://doi.org/10.1080/15295036.2022.2080844.

Tsang, S., Lam, C., and Cheng, L. 2022. 'Intermedia and interculturalism: Practitioners' perspectives on an interactive theatre for young ethnic minority students in Hong Kong', *Language and Intercultural Communication*, 22(2): 141–54. Accessed 7 July 2023. https://doi.org/10.1080/14708477.2021.2016789.

Vygotsky, L. S. 1967. 'Play and its role in the mental development of the child', *Soviet Psychology*, 5: 6–18.

2
Creativity and curriculum integration in the case of GINUESIUM in South Korea

Keumhee Ahn and Jung Duk Ohn

Introduction to the educational context of South Korea

South Korea has a single-track system with six years of elementary school, three years of middle school and three years of high school. Elementary and middle school education for children from seven to 15 years of age is free and compulsory. High schools for 15–18-year-olds correspond to the upper level of secondary education in many countries. They are categorised into several types such as general high school, school for special purposes, vocational high schools and high schools customised to industrial needs. South Korea has a centralised national curriculum, which is revised periodically to reflect the rising demands for education, emerging needs of a changing society and new frontiers of academic disciplines. The elementary school curriculum consists of subjects or subject clusters and creative experiential activities. Subjects or subject clusters taught include the Korean language, social studies/moral education, mathematics, science/practical arts, physical education, arts (music/fine arts) and English. For first and second grades, subjects include the Korean language, mathematics and the integrated subjects of moral life, inquiring life and pleasant life. Creative experiential activities include discretionary activities, club activities, community services and career-related activities.

The middle school curriculum also consists of subjects or subject clusters and creative experiential activities. Subjects or subject clusters include the Korean language, social studies including history/moral education, mathematics, science/technology, home economics/informatics, physical education, arts (music/fine arts), English and elective subjects. Creative experiential activities include discretionary activities, club activities, community services and career-related activities.

The high school curriculum consists of subjects or subject clusters that include general subjects and specialised subjects as well as creative experiential activities. General subjects consist of common courses and elective courses. Common courses include the Korean language, mathematics, English, Korean history, integrated social studies and integrated sciences (including science laboratory experiments). Elective courses include general elective courses and career-related elective courses. Depending on the type of school and students' choice, different combinations of common course and electives can be made for each student.

Curriculum standards in each subject serve as the basis for educational contents at each school and for textbook development.

The role of creativity in South Korea

Curriculum development in South Korea is through a centralised system. The vision of the national curriculum framework becomes the basis of teaching and learning practices in school. In the 2015 revised national curriculum, creativity was presented as a central value for education as a 'creative and integrative learner with moral character'. The ideas underlying this definition are twofold. First, a creative person creates new meaning and values; this process, as well as the product of creativity, should be ethical. Second, creativity requires integrative thinking, which refers to the ability to connect knowledge and ideas across different areas.

The idea of competence was also reflected in the 2015 revised curriculum. In South Korea, six key competencies were set as a vision of schooling, which include self-management skills, communication skills, creative thinking, knowledge-information processing skills, aesthetic-emotional competency and civic competency. Among them, creative thinking skills are defined as an ability to discover something novel by integrating knowledge, skills and experiences from diverse professional fields based on broad foundational knowledge. Aesthetic-emotional competency refers to the ability to find and appreciate the meanings and values of life, which is based on an empathetic understanding of others and cultural sensitivities (Korean Ministry of Education, 2015). Guidelines were shared so that the competencies could be developed through all learning activities.

In South Korea, elementary school teachers are trained at a special purpose university called the National University of Education. There are 11 campuses around the country and Gyeong-In National University of Education (GINUE), with which we are affiliated, is the largest. The core values of GINUE are innovation, creativity, excellence, communication and care. Over four years, our students, as pre-service teachers, learn subject knowledge and teaching skills as well as pedagogy, but learning occurs within separate courses. There are 14 specialisms under the umbrella of elementary education. Creativity is an important vision in teacher education and is cultivated throughout all courses. However, there is little integration and collaboration among specialisms and courses.

Case study of teaching creativity in South Korea

To foster creativity and show a model of how student teachers can plan learning activities for their pupils in their future classroom, in 2018 we began a project in a space called GINUESIUM, using a small gallery in the university. From 2018–20 five exhibitions with different themes were held in GINUESIUM. Two exhibitions themed 'From the Beginning' and 'Perspectives toward Environment: Imagination and Empathy' were held in 2018. In 2019 there were two exhibitions themed 'Making is Thinking: Exploring Materials and Storytelling' and 'Media Sensibilia: Sensory Communication through Media Arts'. In 2020 there was one exhibition themed 'Plastic, Plastic', with the sub-theme of plastic and art, the possibility of symbiosis and coexistence. However, due to the Covid-19 pandemic, there was very limited engagement with visitors.

Competence is holistic and dynamic, in that it develops as individuals interact with the environment and it is a product of attributes of individuals and the context in which they operate (Rychen and Salganik, 2003). This view can be found in Dewey's theory of experience and learning, which emphasises experiential learning and curriculum integration (Yoon and Ohn, 2016). Curriculum integration goes beyond correlating content and skills from various subject areas and is extended to personal and social integration through the organisation of a curriculum or programme around themes (Beane, 1997). With this in mind, we will present how GINUESIUM provided a space for curriculum integration around artworks and for collaboration among teacher educators, pre-service and in-service teachers, and pupils in local schools.

Connecting arts with other areas through interpretation and recreation

Creativity is the ability to think and create novel and relevant ideas. It can be developed when learners experience the changing of ideas and when they connect different ideas from a new perspective. In the study conducted by the Organisation for Economic Co-operation and Development (OECD) (2019), creative thinking is categorised into two types, 'Big C and 'little c'. 'Big C' means genius creativity to the extent of inventing world-class masterpieces or innovative technologies, such as we might have found in Mozart, Picasso and Einstein. 'Little c' refers to the level of creativity that can be experienced daily (OECD, 2019). The creative thinking pursued in this project is 'little c', which includes creative writing, art activities or creative thinking on issues that can be developed through learning.

The theme of the 2018 exhibition 'Perspectives toward Environment' was designed to give artists an opportunity to think about the surrounding environment, about our relationship with ourselves, and to look for various perspectives on nature and the everyday environment. The exhibition involved various activities of local youths and residents, as well as our pre-service teachers. The activities were organised to explore the relationship between the environment and oneself and to think about the role of art in life. To get away from the preconception that an art museum is a space only for artworks, we aimed at providing an educational platform that transcends views in various fields around exhibition.

For example, science and art were integrated in a programme called 'Beautiful World in Microscope'. Stereo, optical and polarising microscopes were installed in the exhibition lobby space. Elementary, middle and high school pupils observed plant cells, stone flakes and the like, and expressed the beautiful world of stones with marbling techniques. They were given enough time to decide what to see and observe with a microscope. The microscope showed the beauty of a small world that had never been seen before.

The beauty and personal feelings of the natural world were then expressed through marbling. Marbling is an artform based on the principle that water and oil do not mix. Filling a square-shaped container with water and some paint, and loosening the marbling paint, will create a free pattern. When you stir the paint using a stick, water and paint move and make patterns. Through the speed and direction of stirring, the process of constantly making patterns was experienced. Once the water and paint patterns looked similar to the patterns of the stones seen through the microscope, the pupils carefully placed the paper on the water and printed a beautiful pattern expressed in marbling paint. The pupils were able to visualise, recreate and make visible the micro-world, which was otherwise invisible based on their observation and interpretation. The exhibition lobby was transformed into a space for curriculum integration space.

This activity allowed the participating pupils to discover new possibilities by using art to express their observations and feelings and incorporate scientific knowledge in the process. Through this activity, we wanted to provide a model for our student teachers for how to develop pupils' imagination and intuition by combining artistic sensitivity based on their understanding of scientific concepts. In a study comparing scientists' and artists' creative ways of thinking, it was found that they have similar psychological characteristics or use a similar way of thinking. Root-Bernstein and Root-Bernstein (2001) argued that science and art are complementary, and that artistic tendencies are correlated with scientific creativity.

The theme of the 2019 exhibition was 'Making is Thinking: Exploring Materials and Storytelling'. It sought to look at art as a creative act of understanding the world and creating one's identity through the collaboration of eyes and hands. Making has a meaning beyond a skill and skill training. It needs to be recognised as a creative act of engaging in the exploration of various materials and telling stories about oneself and the world through works. The process of artists dealing with materials, seeking a creative world and gradually creating their own stories shows how creative thinking is vividly implemented.

In this exhibition, we sought integration with various specialisms. For example, Professor Lee in the department of Korean language education developed the art exhibition-related programme 'Art works and Stories Meet' within the theory of prose literature class. This work aimed at encouraging the appreciation of works of art to provide inspiration for storytelling. In this programme, pre-service teachers visited the exhibition, appreciated artworks and created various forms of writing or storytelling based on their interpretation. After listening to a docent's explanation, the student teachers selected a piece of artwork and created their own story based on personal feelings and experiences about it. Their writings were also exhibited, which became a secondary storytelling work of various forms, including poetry, novels, essays, radio broadcasting scripts and criticisms.

The following is an excerpt from Professor Lee Ji-young's commentary on the exhibition along with the results of the class:

> Art works and students' texts are closely linked to each other. Please look at the work, read the students' storytelling, and think about who's point of view and why they wrote this story. And think of another story with your experiences and thoughts. Art works tell us diverse stories like this.

A student team chose Kim, Chang-Ki's 'Daughter and I'. This work embossed the artist's and daughter's face and hands within the canvas frame. The artist asked himself questions, such as 'What do I look like to my daughter? How do I see my daughter? Is superficial appearance everything? Didn't I try to look at it as comfortable as I could?'. This artwork tried to find answers to these questions. A reason why the team chose this artwork is that the father of a student on the team was also a sculptor and the relationship between a sculptor father and a daughter in this artwork attracted her attention. She interpreted the artwork, linked with her life and created her own meaning through intertextuality between diverse texts. Art can be a powerful tool that serves as a link to life. The following poem is written by Cho, Eu-Sil. The student reflected on her relationship with her father through the artwork and expressed her love for her father in a wonderful poem:

To my father, the sculptor
father
My father …
When I cry,
You drew me crying.
At the end
You were the one who made me smile.

Childhood had gone
Spring of growth came
I've put all my energy into growing up.
The laughter was frozen.
My relationship with you became cold.

father
I envied my friends' father,
I was ashamed of
your shiny working chair.
I was ashamed of
your hard hands
made by casting materials and hammering.

In that hard shell
I didn't see the beauty
that you bloom.
I didn't realize that.

Is it because what I hold tight the pen?
Or was it because I became an adult?
I also have a small callus on my finger.
I got the firmness to tap on my father's hard shell.

I'm finally trying to knock my father's hand.
Peel the skin off in layers
I will wait for the smiling child who will walk along with you with beautiful hands.

The concept of creativity in art education in South Korea has undergone many changes. Creativity in creative self-expression in the early twentieth century considered the free expression of individuals as the basis of creativity and recognised the pure expression of children as important. Since then, the perception of art, creativity from nothing to something, or creativity by personal expression, has been challenged as it has expanded its notion of art as a cultural expression. Based on the premise that text is not a single entity but the communicative interconnections between a text and the other (Kristeva, 1980), Park (2017) emphasised intertextuality in art education. Here, intertextuality is sharing and transforming various artistic or cultural texts and associating different texts. In other words, the process of developing creative meaning is the process of experiencing and transforming various texts within one's own life and recreating one's own story. In this programme, the pre-service teachers constantly connected with their experiences and created new meanings in the process of reading and interpreting artists' texts in the art museum. Then, student teachers experienced creating new texts by combining and reorganising previous experiences and texts using diverse forms of writings. This integrative approach around the art museum provided a place where texts could transcend one another and create new meanings, which is education for creativity. Park (2017) emphasises the need to recognise art as a meaning-making tool, and for this purpose, teachers should help pupils create their own meaning by moving away from interpretation of artworks with the perspective of artists or experts. To this end, the prospective teachers' experiences with texts and their own meaning-making creations comprises the core content of creativity education for pre-service teachers.

Meaning creation: from observer to participant and producer

Due to the development of communication media and the spread of various electronic technology equipment, we now live in a hyper-connected society. This change allows the public to form a participatory culture in which they share their thoughts and experiences with others directly. Consumers have become active and participating producers. The term 'prosumer' – simultaneously both a producer and a consumer – has begun to be used (Koong and Ryu, 2016; Toffler, 1980). In the field of museums, the visitors' role has also changed. Visitors are no longer passive receivers; they are active participants.

We wanted our visitors to be active, participating visitors. To this end, we provided an exhibition space where visitors could express their thoughts and experiences. In this case, the art museum in the university provided pre-service teachers with the opportunity to experience various interpretations of artworks and recreate their meanings based on different texts. Experiences in the museum are authentic, in that visitors interpret the works of art in their own personal experience and cultural context, while being exposed to original work. University members and local residents, including pre-service teachers, created and shared various interpretations of the artworks. As such, the art museum provided a creative experience as a process of meaning-making, which is difficult to achieve in a regular lecture theatre.

In the first exhibition, 'From the Beginning', in 2018, we developed a programme called 'I am an Art Critic' (Ahn, 2019) to help visitors with meaning-making and to foster more active participation. We wanted to go beyond providing visitors with interpretations of the artwork. We invited our university students, elementary school pupils and local residents to look at an artwork and write their interpretations of the image without providing any further information about the artwork.

In Table 2.1, you can see text on two boards, which were displayed on the right next to the work. One is a commentary on the works prepared by the art museum, and on the right is an article written by a local resident who is running a restaurant. Visitors shared various interpretations of the work by reading not only the text of the art museum but also the writings of other visitors. Through this, visitors get to experience a personal meaning-making and build a perception that this act of their own interpretations is also important.

In the 2019 exhibition 'Making is Thinking: Exploring Materials and Storytelling', our participatory programme was extended to involve visitors in creating works based on their thoughts and feelings about

Text from art gallery	Text from a local resident
Artist Young-Wook Lee has for a long time recorded the appearance of the city around his studio. The author has continued to study the limitations of human records in places where context has changed as the places have changed over time. In Young-Wook Lee's photography work, the 'scenery' is not an objective, unimpressed, stopped screen, but a place where changes in time that have swept through the place are now buried, and a living space that can constantly change and appear different, depending on the viewer. Here, we stand in a desolate, vacant lot like a ruin and look at the rides over the concrete fence. The artist is reproducing the experience of feeling unfamiliar for a moment, depending on the surrounding background of familiar and welcoming objects.	Beyond the wall, amusement parks are a world full of joy, but the scenery on the other side between the walls is reflected in dizziness, sadness and anger. If you climb high and come down with a deep desire in your heart on a ride flying back to the sky, you will feel empty, empty and sad that you have not achieved your will. Living like a hamster spinning its wheel, it seems to quietly express our dizzy lives, tangled like an electric wire.

Table 2.1 Example of artwork commentary

exhibitions. In a programme called 'Imagine a House in Me', visitors reconsidered the work 'Island in Me – House 6' that they saw at the exhibition, thought about the meaning of the space of home to them, and produced and displayed their own collage works.

The artist Jung-Sook Oh, who created 'Island inside Me – House 6', has said that home itself is a life with various emotions. The artist who lived on the island, expressed the pain and solitude of the people in the house through the warm colours and soft shapes of the houses and clouds to soothe and give hope. Houses contain people's lives. We asked visitors to imagine what a house containing one's own life would look like and then to use various materials to express that house within oneself in a variety of ways. At GINUESIUM, the docent's commentary was more like a storytelling of his work. The docent shared the author's story with the audience, allowing them to connect their lives to the exhibits.

The visitors took part in this activity and built different houses. Houses made by visitors were expressed in connection with their lives and were displayed to share with other visitors. One such artwork was created by an elementary school pupil. In his work, you can see a blue, rough-textured paper with straws tied with thread at the top and several pieces of straw rolled around on paper in the right-hand corner. In the description of his artwork, the pupil explained: 'For me, home is a protective shield.

Sky: my family's mind is like heaven. Thread: sometimes it's tangled, but it's tied up. Cotton: comfortable. Rounded: cover each other.' Various objects express images of their homes through colour, shape and composition. Here, a house implies more than a building. Just as the artist's visual appearance and the meaning of the house were expressed in the work, the pupils also expressed their feelings and thoughts about their family and the relationships between the family members.

Space for collaboration and partnership

GINUESIUM became a platform for collaboration among university professors of different professional backgrounds. In 2018, a computer science professor participated in the exhibition 'Perspectives toward Environment'. We undertook a convergence project that created two media artworks in the exhibition. We co-created 'Digital-Reminiscing' and 'Walking through a Digital Cloud'. These are interactive media art pieces, and the visitors participated in the artwork by using sound such as popular or classical music. We used coding techniques to produce a digital work and installation based on the motif of an existing exhibition work. The original work of 'Digital-Reminiscing' is an image of the artist Jung, Il's work 'Reminiscing', which uniformly arranges 81 LED bulbs and connects the Arduino system to allow different patterns of LED lights to light depending on sound. In the 'Walking through a Digital Cloud', which was based on the cloud motif in the artist Park, So-Young's work 'Walking in the clouds', a cloud-shaped light was installed, and the Arduino system was connected to allow LED lights of various colours to respond to sound according to the measured volume.

For this experiential work to be produced, we had several meetings to discuss the visual effects of the work by making small models with various materials. We considered various technical problems and visual effects, accounting for the connection with the exhibition. For example, we considered which material shows light well, where the light is placed on the back of the work, what length or beat of the light's flickering will appear, and how many LED bulbs will be used. The computer science professor said he enjoyed collaborating with colleagues from different disciplines, which hardly ever happens in regular classes. We felt the pain of creativity together and had an experience of thinking and solving technical and aesthetic matters in the process of actually implementing imaginary images. As such, the collaboration between professors from different disciplines became very natural throughout the exhibition space.

This convergence project between art and computer science is important for many reasons. First, creativity education should be practised naturally in daily life rather than merely in the classroom. In this case, the gallery is the field of university daily life, and the creativity education provided here is practised in a place that is easily accessible to university members. The convergence project offered an example or a model for our pre-service teachers to try when they become teachers. Second, the media art project through collaboration between professors helped expand the professors' expertise and rethink their own identities. Universities are basically run by discrete departments or disciplinary silos. However, by working on an integration project between professors at the university gallery, we had an opportunity to collaborate, which led to synergy. These expanded experiences on the part of the professors will have a positive impact when professors interact with pre-service teachers.

The collaboration was extended to engage high school pupils in a volunteer programme. GINUESIUM provided weekend volunteer programmes for pupils in local high schools from the 2018 exhibitions onwards. In the 2019 exhibition 'Media Sensibilia' our university students taught Scratch, a programming tool to teach coding, to high school pupils who volunteered as teen educators to participate in a programme. The pupils used Scratch for elementary school pupils, and together they produced storytelling videos with images of artworks. The high school pupils had an authentic experience of using what they had learned and experienced while teaching elementary pupils. Elementary school pupils had fun interacting and making videos with high school pupils. For example, an elementary school pupil produced a video by using Jung-Mi Yoon's work, 'The Pink and Blue Project-Seunghyuk and His Blue Things'. The Scratch coding program provides characters, buildings and various objects, so that it can be easily created by combining text and images. GINUESIUM became a space for service learning as individuals volunteered to teach younger pupils in the local community utilising their knowledge and skills in programming. At the same time, GINUESIUM is an educational platform, in which various people with different purposes find their own interests and create their own experiences. The high school pupils applied what they had learned to teach elementary school pupils. We hope this programme could lead to promoting pupils' civic engagement as well as developing collaborative skills.

Critique of the creative approach presented

For this approach to be applicable to other settings, there are three key elements to be considered. First, there must be active participation from visitors. In recent years, participation has become an important approach for art galleries. A museum should be recognised as a space where visitors can create meanings, and not as a space where the museum conveys its interpretation to the viewers in a top-down manner. To this end, various exhibitions and education strategies are being developed and applied to encourage viewers to participate. To increase the participation of visitors at GINUESIUM, we used various strategies to actively engage the interpretation of the audience in the exhibition space. Therefore, ideas and methods should be developed in which interpretations based on the viewer's feelings and thoughts are unfolded and shared in the exhibition space of the art museum. Second, curriculum integrations should be made. Universities have professors and students from various disciplines. An integrative approach is essential for professors and students from these various disciplines to communicate together and have a creative experience with the exhibition at the art museum. In the case of GINUESIUM, not only the creation of works through collaboration with computer professors, but also the use of exhibition works as an inspiration motif in literature classes are meaningful examples of integration and co-operation. Therefore, professors and students from various disciplines can be inspired and think creatively through the integrative approach to art exhibitions. Third, partnerships with a local community can extend pupils' learning. Elementary, middle and high school pupils were not only able to expand what they learned in art class through exhibition experiences, but also developed their creativity by expressing their interpretations of artworks in various ways. In addition, the collaboration between student teachers, high school pupils and elementary school pupils took the form of service learning, allowing student teachers to acquire and use their knowledge and skills in authentic contexts.

To develop and improve these activities further, a more systematic approach should be taken to evaluate the educational effects of exhibitions and exhibition-related activities at GINUESIUM. Although we came up with various ideas for programme development, there has been little reflection and evaluation of each programme so far. We expected that the programmes provided at GINUESIUM would promote the development of creativity, but we had not designed formal research gathering quantitative and qualitative data to support the achievement of our goals. When developing the programmes, we also had to define the elements of key competencies that we had implicitly in mind. Research should be done to connect key competencies with the design of each programme to evaluate whether the programmes worked as we intended and to identify what should be changed to achieve the goals.

Summary of key elements and recommendations

Key element 1

GINUESIUM, located in our university, helped change the pervasive view that a gallery is a space for exhibition. The activities and programmes linked to the exhibition did not focus only on appreciating artworks and were not limited to teaching and learning about the arts. Links with science and literature were actively made around the act of interpreting and expressing. Rather than acquiring knowledge and skills of science or literature, we intended to develop pupils' and pre-service teachers' creativity through their own interpretation of artworks and the reality that was represented in artworks.

Key element 2

Participatory programmes connected to each exhibition enabled pre-service teachers, pupils from local schools and residents to create and communicate new values and meanings. They actively interpreted artists' intentions reflected in artworks and recreated in a unique way what they thought and felt. Their works also became a part of the exhibition.

Key element 3

Creativity appears in social relationships rather than in particular individual tendencies, and in this regard, collaboration has provided creative relationships that allow people to solve problems and create meaning together. Collaboration among university professors from different disciplines led to the creation of diverse forms of artwork and contributed to a discussion for an interdisciplinary course. The joint activities between pre-service teachers and local elementary, middle and high school pupils expanded learning beyond service and beyond the voluntary programme.

Recommendation 1

Since we believe that creativity comes from the process of people making, sharing and transforming meanings in their own lives, various approaches and strategies need to be developed to encourage viewers to participate and make their own meaning in a university gallery. In the case of an art gallery residing in a university, it was necessary to find connections with academic courses to increase the participation of pre-service teacher students. Participatory elements in the exhibition space should be secured to draw the attention and participation of various audiences. By expressing and sharing their own thoughts and feelings with others in the very space where exhibition was held, they became part of the art museum and created a new culture.

Recommendation 2

Since in convergence education, art plays an important role in connecting various disciplines or student life and education, art should not be approached merely for the art itself. Instead, the art should be integrated with other areas and involve people of different academic backgrounds. Kim (2014) has called this role of art education a 'chain link', because art as a thinking tool can assist creativity. Therefore, we must emphasise art-based convergence education not only in formal education but also in informal education.

Recommendation 3

It is necessary to establish a place for communication between university students and local residents through various educational programmes, including volunteer programmes, at the university art museum. In the case of GINUESIUM, university students were able to directly experience what it means to be a mentor by setting up programmes to teach local pupils. By participating in the previously emphasised art-based interdisciplinary education programme, university students had experience as mentors and recognised the important role of art in education. The process by which visitors with various levels of understanding and interest participate in, communicate within the university art museum and create their own meaning, shows that creativity education is distributed not only in classrooms but also in everyday life.

References

Ahn, K. H. 2010. 'An investigation on diverse discourses of the creativity in art education', *Journal of Art Education*, 28: 109–41.

Ahn, K. H. 2019. 'A study on exhibition connected education programs based on participation and communication', *Journal of Art Education*, 58: 245–70.

Beane, J. 1997. *Curriculum Integration: Designing the core of democratic education*. New York: Columbia University.

Kim, S. A. 2014. 'The role and characteristics of art in convergence education: Based on the teacher FGI', *Art Education Review*, 51: 93–110.

Koong, S. Y., and Ryu, S. H. 2016. 'Consumer can produce? Change of consumerism and emergence of new prosumer'. *Journal of Social Thoughts and Culture*, 19(2): 129–68.

Korean Ministry of Education. 2015. 'The Art Curriculum: Notice from the Ministry of Education 2015–74', Annex 13. Sejong-si: Ministry of Education.

Kristeva, J. 1980. *Desire in Language: A semiotic approach to literature and art*. New York: Columbia University Press.

Lee, J. Y., and Ahn, K. H. 2020. 'Exploring storytelling that works in exhibitions and education in university art museums', *Art Education Research Review*, 34(4): 85–113.

Organisation for Economic Co-operation and Development (OECD). 2019. 'PISA 2021 creative thinking framework: Third draft'. Paris: OECD.

Park, J. 2017. 'How does creativity form and how can we teach it?', *Journal of Research in Art Education*, 18(2): 57–71.

Root-Bernstein, R., and Root-Bernstein, M. 2001. *Sparks of Genius: The thirteen thinking tools of the world's most creative people*. Boston MA: Mariner Books.

Rychen, D. S., and Salganik, L. H. 2003. 'A holistic model of competence'. In *Key competencies for a successful life and a well-functioning society*, edited by D. S. Rychen and L. H. Salganik, 41–62. Cambridge MA: Hogrefe & Huber Publisher.

Toffler, A. 1980. *The Third Wave: The classic study of tomorrow*. New York: Bantam.

Yoon, J. Y., and Ohn, J. D. 2016. 'Exploration of the direction for designing competency-based curriculum in terms of the holistic nature of competency', *The Journal of Curriculum Studies*, 34(2).

A response from the perspective of Chile

Roxana Balbontín-Alvarado and
Cristian Rivas-Morales

The chapter presents a very interesting experience of creativity through curriculum integration and collaboration in South Korea, specifically from a university that trains elementary school teachers. Following the national curriculum, which focuses on nurturing creative and integrative learners and on the development of some key competencies through a cross-curricular approach, the university designed a project to foster creativity and develop these key competencies in pre-service teachers; namely, self-management skills, communication skills, creative thinking, knowledge-information processing skills, aesthetic-emotional competency and civic competency. The main idea of the project is to integrate different subjects and disciplines into a unique learning experience around art exhibitions, which take place in an art gallery called GINUESIUM, part of the university.

In recent years, the university has launched different exhibitions in which pre-service teachers can interact with primary and secondary pupils from local schools, as well as other visitors. This is a very positive learning experience for student teachers, who normally have the role of mentors for pupils, as it provides an authentic opportunity for those pre-service teachers to learn how to teach from a creative and cross-curricular perspective. In turn, this experience strengthens their pedagogical training. One exhibition organised under the theme of 'Perspectives Towards the Environment' presented a programme called 'Beautiful World in Microscope', which integrated the arts and sciences by inviting pupils from different school levels to observe plant cells and stone flakes through microscopes, and to then express their perceptions and interpretations of the observed micro-world with paper marbling techniques.

Another exhibition's theme was 'Making is Thinking: Exploring Materials and Storytelling'. The purpose of this platform was to present the creative act or the act of 'making' as something involving meaning and expression of one's own identity. Pre-service teachers visited one of the exhibition-related programmes called 'Art Works and Stories Meet', which integrated literature and arts through the appreciation of art pieces and their interpretation using storytelling or various writing forms including poetry and essays.

In our view, these previously discussed experiences presented in the chapter were very positive in many ways. First, they represent a real approach in the development of creativity in students and pupils from different educational levels through the integration of the arts with various other subjects. Students and pupils train their capacity to create, observe, perceive, express, interpret and write. They approach a phenomenon from different perspectives, making their learning experience more complete. Second, university students who are training to become elementary school teachers can experience authentic teaching and learning scenarios where they learn to teach creative ways to approach certain phenomena from different perspectives and simultaneously develop key competencies, which will be necessary as future teachers, such as communication skills, creative thinking and aesthetic-emotional competency, among others.

The project provides a platform for learning through collaboration and partnership. Teacher educators collaborate with each other in order to integrate their discipline into a unique learning experience. Student teachers collaborate with pupils by tutoring them throughout their creative journey, while secondary school pupils also collaborate with primary school pupils: the older pupils guide and engage the younger pupils in the different activities proposed in the exhibitions. It seems like a circular experience where everyone engages in collaborative learning through curriculum integration (Beane, 1997).

Finally, regarding some feasible improvement for the project, it seems necessary to measure the real educational effect of the programmes and to promote the critical reflection of the students' experiences.

In some key aspects, Chile and South Korea have a similar school system. For instance, they both have 12 years of education divided into different stages, following a centralised curriculum. However, there are some important differences in terms of what is taught in schools and how the subjects are organised. In South Korea there is more space for moral education and what are called 'creative experiential activities'. In addition, some subjects are organised as subject clusters and it seems that there is more integration between different disciplines. In contrast, in Chile the school curriculum tends to be very formal and rigid (Barraza *et al.*, 2019) with few opportunities to develop creativity and with a tendency to excessive academisation, particularly at secondary school level. In addition, unlike in South Korea, cross-curricular integration is uncommon in Chile and moral or creative education has very limited space in the curriculum.

Regarding Chilean university teaching programmes, unlike South Korea, there is an excessive focus on specific disciplines rather than on pedagogical, creative and generic competencies. This is probably because there is a strong focus on accountability in education in Chile. Universities are evaluated through national accreditation bodies, which are more focused on students' academic achievement, the quality of academic staff, the quality of the infrastructure and on student satisfaction, than on the evaluation of the curriculum, which should balance the different types of competency that future teachers require. In fact, in a national educational context, where accountability is essential, the integration of generic competencies, life skills and so-called twenty-first-century competencies, including the development of creativity, have inevitably been neglected (Bellei and Morawietz, 2016). Nonetheless, preschool and primary school teaching programmes include some, albeit limited, space for creativity, as at those levels teachers are expected to use creative teaching approaches, including play, arts and discovery through trial and error.

Given the context, the creative approach presented in the South Korean chapter could be applied in Chile, but we would expect there to be some opposition as a result of Chile's formal and rigid educational system and because academics from different fields would not easily integrate their disciplines into a joint educational experience. It would also be a challenge to change the misconception and the prejudices surrounding the idea that soft skills, life skills and generic competencies are necessary to train good professionals.

References

Barraza, P., Preiss, D., and Pardo, M. 2019. 'The development of creativity in Chilean kindergarten and school children' ('Desarrollo de la creatividad en párvulos y escolares chilenos'), *Studies in Psychology*, 40(3): 608–34. Accessed 7 July 2023. https://doi.org/10.1080/02109395.2019.1655220.

Beane, J. 1997. *Curriculum Integration: Designing the core of democratic education*. New York: Columbia University.

Bellei, C., and Morawietz, L. 2016. *Strong Content, Weak Tools, Twenty-First-Century Competencies in the Chilean Educational Reform: Teaching and learning for the twenty-first century*. Cambridge MA: Harvard Education Press.

A response from the perspective of Aotearoa New Zealand

Carolyn Julie Swanson

Each country's curriculum is a 'representation of the knowledge that a society values' (Hipkins *et al.*, 2014, foreword by Reid, 1). As different educational theories rise in popularity and society changes, curricular redevelopment occurs. One such shift occurred towards the end of the twentieth century, with governments wanting students to have the skills and capabilities to productively – and pertinent to this chapter – creatively engage with a rapidly changing society (Bull and Gilbert, 2014; So *et al.*, 2017).

Fostering creativity in South Korea has meant changes in both the curriculum and the pedagogical approaches used, which has had an impact on teacher education. The focus of pre-service education has changed from theory laden to learner-centred approaches where there is space be creative and to learn actively (So *et al.*, 2017). Ahn and Ohn have described the educational context of South Korea, from elementary to high school and the curricular focus at each year level. Of interest is that pupils in schools not only learn curricular subjects but also take part in creative experiential activities, such as clubs.

The authors describe a teaching approach used in their initial teacher education programme that supports the development of creativity and collaboration in an arts integration project. The Revised 2015 National Curriculum (Korean Ministry of Education, 2015) depicts a creative learner as one who both creates 'meaning' and 'connects ideas' across the curriculum, stating that the learner should become competent in the skills needed to function in society (Rychen and Salganik, 2003).

The authors advocate that creativity must be integrated into pre-service courses to support the development of pre-service teachers' pedagogical repertoires. In this study, creativity was fostered through interacting with art exhibits at the campus art gallery, and collaborating with pre-service educators, school pupils and artists. The creative interactions ranged from interacting with scientific exhibits through marbling their responses to the microscopic world, creating original art based on feelings imbued from viewing comments on art, and making models of their perceptions of home. They also worked collaboratively on art projects with academics and supported pupils creating videos of artworks using the coding program Scratch.

It is a shame that the research did not include designated data collection tools to ascertain whether creativity in pre-service teachers was enhanced through the art gallery interaction project. However, the researchers found positioning art galleries as active meaning-making spaces promoted participant interaction and allowed pre-service teachers to see the interconnections between different knowledge mediums. Embedding these connections within the local community enabled students to see integration in authentic contexts as well enhancing their key competencies. This collaboration allowed not only growth in the pre-service teachers' exploration of creativity but also offered space for the wider community to explore art and construct personal and collaboration relationships and meaning about art and the art-making process.

There are similarities between South Korea's 2015 revised national curriculum (So and Kang, 2014) and the New Zealand curriculum (Ministry of Education, 2007). Creativity is a common thread in the New Zealand curriculum. For example, young people should be 'creative, energetic and enterprising' (8) who demonstrate 'innovation, inquiry, and curiosity, by thinking critically, creatively, and reflectively' (Ministry of Education, 2007, 10). In the key competency 'thinking', pupils use 'creative, critical, and metacognitive processes to make sense of information, experiences, and ideas' (12). The development of creativity is supported by 'learning in, through and about the arts' (20), especially when the arts have a central rather than peripheral role (Gibson and Ewing, 2011). Learning is enhanced when pupils make 'connections across the learning areas, values and key competencies' (Ministry of Education, 2007, 39).

The New Zealand curriculum is not prescriptive, and there is freedom to be creative in the pedagogical approaches used to support learning. As long as the teaching is in accordance with the *Code of Professional Responsibility and Standards for the Teaching Profession* (Education Council New Zealand, 2017), there is scope to teach creatively. This project could therefore easily be transferred to the New Zealand initial teacher education setting. Using integrative practices and making connections with the local community are encouraged (Ministry of Education, 2007). As such, utilising community resources such as art galleries to model creative integrated approaches is a good fit. Integrating the arts and science and using STEAM are recognised teaching approaches (TKI, n.d.). Personally, I used drama to teach science and technology in my pre-service teaching.

There have been some similar projects where New Zealand initial teacher education students have interacted with art. In one such project, pre-service teachers used visual artworks to construct of the child (Craw and Grey, 2013), with the experience providing a 'space to imagine art as a place of encounter' (87). In another project, volunteer pre-service teachers and local pupils created prints with a local artist to contribute to an art exhibition honouring the life of the progressive New Zealand educator Elwyn S. Richardson (Craw and O'Sullivan, 2016). While the student teachers who volunteered worked creatively in an arts project, it was not part of routine learning and assessment.

Even though the art gallery project is feasible and provides opportunities for student teachers and pupils to be creative and connect with the community, the links to the curriculum need to be stronger. The authors needed to specify the curricular learning outcomes, the key competency focus and what areas would be examined to ascertain the project's viability. It should be mentioned that our New Zealand student teachers would be reluctant to undertake projects unless they counted towards assessment.

A final caveat must be given. While it is crucial for student teachers to be innovative, creative and curious about the world around them, incorporating the arts into teaching necessitates that pre-service educators have not only curricular content knowledge but also artistry in using the arts to teach across the curriculum (Dunn and Stinton, 2011).

References

Aitken, V. 2021. *Real in All the Ways that Matter: Weaving learning across the curriculum with mantle of the expert*. Wellington: NZCER Press.

Bull, A., and Gilbert, J. 2014. *Swimming Out of Our Depth? Leading learning in 21st century schools*. Wellington: NZCER Press.

Craw, J., and Grey, A. 2013. 'Living an art-full life: Teachers thinking in, through and with visual art'. In *Kia tipu te wairua toi: Fostering the creative spirit*, edited by B. Clark, A Grey and L. Terreni, 87–99). Auckland: Pearson.

Craw, J., and O'Sullivan, V. 2016. 'Art-at-work: Moving beyond, with the histories of education and art in Aotearoa New Zealand', *Contemporary Issues in Education*, 35(1): 46–60. Accessed 7 July 2023. https://doi.org/10.1080/00131857.2016.1158091.

Dunn, J., and Stinton, M. 2011. 'Not without the art!! The importance of teacher artistry when applying drama as pedagogy for additional language learning', *Research in Drama Education: The Journal of Applied Theatre*, 16(4): 617–33. Accessed 7 July 2023. https://doi.org/10.1080/13569783.2011.617110.

Education Council New Zealand. 2017. 'Code of professional responsibility and standards for the teaching profession'. Wellington: Education Council.

Gibson, R., and Ewing, R. 2011. *Transforming the Curriculum Through the Arts*. Sydney: Palgrave.

Hipkins, R., Bolstad, R., Boyd, S., and McDowall, S., with Reid, A. 2014. *Key Competencies For the Future*. Wellington: NZCER Press.

Korean Ministry of Education. 2015. 'The Art Curriculum: Notice from the Ministry of Education 2015–74', Annex 13. Sejong-si: Ministry of Education.

MacDonald, M. 2016. *Elwyn Richardson and the Early World of Creative Education in New Zealand*. Wellington: NZCER Press.

Ministry of Education. 2007. 'The New Zealand Curriculum'. Wellington: Learning Media.

Rychen, D., and Salganik, L. 2003. 'A holistic model of competence'. *In Key competencies for a successful life and a well-functioning society*, edited by D. Rychen and L. Salganik, 41–62). Göttingen: Hogrefe & Huber.

So, K., and Kang, J. 2014. 'Curriculum reform in Korea: Issues and challenges for twenty-first century learning', *The Asia-Pacific Education Researcher*, 23(4): 795–803.

So, K., Hu, Y-J., and Park., J. 2017. 'Making our schools more creative: Korea's efforts and challenges', *International Education Journal: Comparative Perspectives*, 16(4): 77–88. Accessed 7 July 2023. https://openjournals.library.sydney.edu.au/index.php/IEJ.

TKI Te Kete Ipurangi. n.d. *STEM/STEAM*. Accessed 7 July 2023. https://elearning.tki.org.nz/Teaching/Future-focused-learning/STEM-STEAM.

3
Bringing books alive! Working with children's librarians in Qatar

Lizbeth Bullough

The educational context of the Qatar National Library in Doha

In this chapter I engage with the wider role of creativity in education by showcasing a knowledge exchange programme co-constructed with children's librarians at the Qatar National Library in Doha. According to the Qatar National Library's webpage, its mission statement is to 'preserve the nation's and region's heritage by creating an exceptional environment for learning and discovery' (QNL, 2021). The chapter content specifically explores creativity in the context of the library's use of workshops for children and families as a means to facilitate learning and discovery through reading, play and literacy-based activities.

To understand this fully, a brief reference to Qatar and its context may be helpful. Qatar is a country in the Arabian Peninsula and Persian Gulf that shares a land border with Saudi Arabia. The official religion of the country is Islam. It has a small population, 80 per cent of which is located in the capital, Doha. Based in a new building since 2017, the Qatar National Library is a national research library with a strong emphasis on education that is overseen by the Qatar Foundation for Education, Science and Community Development. Situated within the Qatar National Library complex, the children's library caters for children up to 11 years old, offering opportunities for children to play, learn and read.

The rationale for the course in early childhood education was to enhance children's librarians' grounding in childhood development so that they could respond professionally to the needs of children at different ages and stages of development from preschool to Grade 6 (aged three to 11). The overall aim of the workshops was to enhance the skills necessary for children's librarians to subsequently plan and deliver innovative child-centred workshops to promote children's literacy skills, together with an enjoyment of reading and books. All activities were framed by creativity and creative practice. At an entry level, creative learning was defined from wider perspective, as 'being open to the acquisition of new knowledge and innovative skills, which will shape the world like no other force imaginable' (Smith, 2013, 5). Librarians are not teachers in the traditional sense. Yet, they can play a key role in teaching children how to love books, while setting up strong literacy foundations, literacy enjoyment, and establishing pre-reading skills in preparation for school (MacLean, 2008, 9). The evidence is compelling: training library staff has a positive impact on literacy behaviours, on library programmes with librarians more effectively selecting books and planning story workshops following training (MacLean, 2008). In a wider sense, while educators recognise the fundamental role of reading as a learning experience, libraries can play a unique role in opening up 'a world of books' (Merga and Roni, 2018, 675).

The role of creativity in the context of the Qatar National Library

Historically, librarians played only a marginal role in Qatari society. However, with the Qatar government's commitment to the development of a knowledge-based society together with a 'new knowledge order', the work of the Qatar National Library has begun to move centre stage together with the state-directed development of an exceptional environment with a strong emphasis on education and evidence-based practice (Nasser, 2017; Gremm *et al.*, 2018). As a non-profit organisation located within the Qatar Foundation for Education, Science and Community Development, the Qatar National Library occupies a key strategic position in these improvements that place information and knowledge, and therefore learning, at the centre of Qatar's changing economy and society:

> For a long time, librarians in Qatar did not play a significant role in the country. However, with the establishment of Qatar National Library and the will of Qatar to develop a knowledge-based society

> this is slowly changing for the better. Librarians provide access to the most important resource in this form of society, namely knowledge. The role of librarians in the state of Qatar is now to strongly support education and encourage information consumption and development. (Gremm *et al.*, 2018, 204)

This acknowledgement of the key role of librarians in Qatari society is based on the understanding that an overreliance on an economy based on natural resources such as oil, may not be a long-term option due to the depletion of those natural resources. This has been seen as an opportunity for change, not necessarily a threat, with the government support for the development of Qatar as a knowledge society seen as significant in the Qatar National Vision 2030 (Parcero, 2019). A knowledge society is not only a future information society, but also one where knowledge is available at any time or at any place (Gremm *et al.*, 2018). Therefore, the state of Qatar now sees librarians as well-placed to support this key focus on knowledge and information, and in ensuring that Qatari citizens have full access to resources necessary to achieve their full potential (Parcero, 2019).

There has been growing international evidence to suggest that education should be seen through a wider lens that connects the space 'between the public world of the services they encompass and the private world of the family' (Cameron and Miller, 2014, 163). Of critical importance here is the need to create 'new spaces for childhood', by which we mean 'physical locations and environments in which children explore and learn, are protected and claim the right to belong, inhabit and participate' (Cameron and Miller, 2014, 165). Within the sociocultural perspective that experiences of children and families are socially and culturally situated, context-dependent and context-rich, it is essential that any interpretation of creativity is underpinned by the recognition of the cultural capital that children and families bring with them (Cohen *et al.*, 2007). Therefore, an agreed prerequisite of this programme was that workshop content should build on the home and cultural context in cultivating a love of reading to prepare the child for a more structured learning situation (Daiment-Cohen, 2007).

What all of this suggests is that the Qatar National Library recognises libraries as being uniquely placed to provide a space between the public world of children's services and the private world of the family. It is a pivotal role of librarians to capture a child's interest and imagination at an early stage, to set the foundations for literacy, books and libraries as a valued part of children's lives (MacLean, 2008). This presents opportunities to draw on children's and families' lived experiences to create awareness of history, culture and tradition, as reflected in the Qatar National Library Mission statement, and serves to develop awareness of local and national identities along with a 'sense of belonging and connectedness' (Cameron and Miller, 2014, 165).

Because the librarians operate, in this context, between the child's own cognitive development and their social and historical context, they also help the child develop the various social and even soft skills related to teaching and learning (MacLean, 2008). These include listening, asking questions, taking turns and receiving instructions (MacLean, 2008). In addition, they foster creativity, fun and enjoyment for both the children and their families.

Teaching creativity in the context of the Qatar National Library

The workshops were initiated by the Head of Children and Young Adults at the Qatar National Library on the premise that it is essential for librarians to build on their professional knowledge to understand how children grow and learn in order to be sensitive to their needs. This enables the librarians to leverage their extraordinary and unique abilities to plan innovative and creative activities to support engagement with reading between children and their families. A fundamental aim of these workshops was to build on librarians' knowledge of practice and research to enhance the engagement of children and families in library workshops, establishing a fun and creative approach to books to promote a love of learning and literature within the heritage of Qatar society. This is based on the belief that librarians are well-placed to draw on evidence-based research to support parents in literacy activities, not only within the library context but also in their homes (Merga and Roni, 2018). A key feature of this programme involved modelling activities that focused on the needs of participant librarians. This was based on evidence that modelling active participation has a significant impact on attitudes towards literacy, whether with training or in workshops with children, parents and families (MacLean, 2008). The content of the course specifically explored the theory, principles and research that underpin early childhood development study and culminated in participants engaging in planning workshops. All sessions were underpinned by a language and literacy focus.

Creative strategies to personal reflection and reflexivity

Programme design commenced with reflective and reflexive tasks, where participants reflected on how their personal and professional knowledge and experiences impact on their working life (Kitto and Bullough, 2021). Activities were underpinned by the socio-constructive perspective framing this research, in acknowledging that our constructs of the world as being dynamic (Bandura, 2001). Parents and families play a fundamental role in the learning and engagement of young children, so it was essential for librarian participants to understand the connection between their own personal timelines and experiences. Therefore, recognising the culture of the children attending the workshops maximises meaningful experiences and provides a powerful vehicle to support the how, why and what of children's education, and more specifically engagement in literacy activities (Colwell *et al.*, 2021). In co-construction with librarian leaders, a key component was considering their professional attitudes through the lens of timelines, individual biographies and critical incidents, which could be extrinsic, intrinsic or personal in the reflective task below (Sikes *et al.*, 2001). As a scaffold to professional reflection on practice, in this introductory activity participants were asked to complete the following tasks:

- Think about your reasons for choosing to work with children and young people.
- Take 10 minutes to write a short paragraph that tells your story of being a children's librarian.
- Highlight the incidents in your story in a different colour for extrinsic, intrinsic or personal (Sikes *et al.*, 2001).
- Create a personal timeline of these critical incidents.

The following three questions were posed as prompts for reflection and as prompts for considering how incidents might impact on their professional life:

- What part of your engagement with children, parents, families or colleagues might you change in light of this knowledge?
- Who influenced you in your education and life choices?
- Who might you identify to talk to share your experiences? (Activity adapted from the workshop developed by Kim Insley, Associate Professor (Teaching), UCL, IOE; Lahore, 2014.)

Participants agreed that this reflective task was meaningful when employed as a tool to reflect on and to potentially amend practice as lifelong learners (Kitto and Bullough, 2021). They recognised the influence of 'a library staff's enthusiasm, educational background and materials available to them' (MacLean, 2008, 7) and the subsequent impact of this on the outcomes of the programmes and workshops that they plan and deliver. At a deeper level, this activity supported the children's librarians in their development as creative professionals in being open to designing and delivering new approaches, while reflecting on practice (Smith, 2013). Participants acknowledged the relationship between this self-reflection and staff confidence mediated through communication and constructive feedback as a vehicle to most effectively accommodate the needs of children and their families in their practices (Mills *et al.*, 2016).

Creative approaches to partnership with children, parents and families

Engaging families was at the core of course design of workshops. With the Qatar National Library seeing children as the future of society, it was a key priority of any professional development that librarians refine their practices to ensure that all children and parents are welcomed into an inclusive environment to empower them with knowledge and resources (Mahmoud, 2022). Within the understanding that sharing books is a social practice, this programme and Qatar National Library leaders also recognised the fundamental role of parents as key social agents, not only in establishing a love of reading, but also in maintaining a positive identity as a passionate reader over the course of children's and young people's futurity (Merga and Roni, 2018).

It was also fundamental to programme design that input should enhance children's librarians with understanding learning theories and developmental research to support children's librarians in fully explaining how children build up their knowledge and understanding. It was acknowledged by all stakeholders that a greater focus on creativity would most likely result in a paradigm shift regarding the theoretical perspectives framing librarians practice, particularly through the 'changed dynamics of teaching and learning' (Collard and Looney, 2014, 348). This was underpinned by the recognition of the importance of embracing a holistic model of child development to inform the planning and delivery of library activities (Rose and Wood, 2016). A café conversation activity supported this. Participants worked in groups to plan key aspects and activities you might see in a workshop underpinned by a specific theoretical approach to learning. Given the timescale, initial input provided a '*condensed history*' of key theoretical models; for example, behaviourism, constructivism and social constructivism. Engaging with the ecological systems theory of Bronfenbrenner also supported participants in recognising how everything in a child and the child's environment influences how a child grows and develops, as well as the unique role of children's librarians in building on this to extend this knowledge (Bronfenbrenner, 2005).

To connect theoretical perspectives with practice, participants worked in small groups to develop a 'thinking cloud' of potential activities that reflected a particular theoretical approach to learning. To do this, the participants, in turn, randomly selected a theorist card from a 'lucky dip' bag. They then considered the main approaches and philosophy underpinned by specific educational theories, specifically behaviourism, constructivism and social constructivism. The children's librarians then identified facilitation or pedagogical techniques and activities that might be underpinned by that specific theoretical approach (e.g. a constructivist library workshop) and implications for planning and facilitation. We then engaged in role play to model that particular approach through the 'lucky dip' activity and planned a selection of workshop activities, which might be underpinned by that particular theoretical perspective. When completed, an 'expert' remained in that group to take questions, while other participants moved to other tables to view alternative theoretical approaches. Evaluations reflected the value the participants placed on these modelling activities in supporting their understanding of the relevance of learning theory on their own planning and pedagogy as children's librarians, including the implications of this on their practice.

Building on this need for any engagement to reflect the lives and experiences of the families and community they serve, and the unique role of children's librarians in this, participants explored activities that would promote meaningful library and home engagement. The following example demonstrates how participants modelled an activity to each other in sharing objects that were significant to them. This was an activity adapted from the 'Boxing Clever' research where shoeboxes, filled with children's artefacts, supported a range of literacy-related activities in school contexts (Greenhough *et al.*, 2005). This entry-level task scaffolded participants in exploring the impact of 'creative learning' through the lens of sociocultural and creative practices based on children's constructions of their own life experiences (Smith, 2013; Barron and Powell, 2002). Objects brought in by librarians were diverse and practically illustrated the importance of drawing on and recognising the knowledge and experience children and their families bring from home in library activities, resources and workshops. One expatriate librarian who had lived in many countries brought in 'a box of teabags', explaining that this was something that she took all over the world that made her feel comfortable. Other objects ranged from family and home photos, and, unsurprisingly, a favourite children's book, to a cherished small mirror kept always to hand as it had been given to the participant by her mother.

Participants agreed that incorporating cultural experiences in their practices in this way has the potential to foster educational partnership to support literacy learning and reading at home (Merga and Roni, 2018). Concluding thoughts reflected on the potential of adapting this activity to personalise child and family engagement more widely with activities, workshops and resources (Greenhough *et al.*, 2005).

Creativity in planning library activities and workshops

An additional feature of the case study design was to draw on session content to plan a specialist library workshop for children and their parents, to be displayed as a mini-poster and delivered to fellow librarians in a five-minute presentation, including key points, on the final day of the programme. The poster presentation supported participants in conceptualising creativity from a wider perspective and was a basis for engagement with multimedia through wider collaborative arts and cultural projects (Smith, 2013). The reasoning behind this is underpinned by research that suggests that the most effective, exciting and stimulating story times and literacy workshops are intentional in planning, are interactive, and avoid a focus on performance (Mills *et al.*, 2016).

To support workshop planning we engaged with evidence-based research promoting creativity in literacy activities, particularly including storytelling, story sacks and drama, to incorporate multimodal approaches to support the development of children's communication skills. Multimodality involves engaging with the modes present to communicate meaning, which might include embodied modes such as gestures, facial expressions and movements, as well as disembodied modes; for example, words, music, pictures and sound (Cremin *et al.*, 2013). This provided participants with the opportunity to make links between multimodal methodology and sociocultural perspectives previously examined in the session on learning theories, with practical application at a 'grass roots' level (Vygotsky, 1978).

The use of 'story sacks' was explored as a multisensory tool, particularly in examining how they could be utilised in family workshops to support children and parents in making reading memorable and promoting the enjoyment of books, while additionally establishing links between the library workshops and home contexts (Weinberger and Stafford, 2004). A story sack is a large cloth bag containing a favourite children's book and supporting materials to assist children's engagement with story narratives (National Literacy Trust, 2022). Although story sacks can be purchased commercially, participants considered how they could assemble them themselves in an informal way, using cardboard boxes, cloth bags, pillowcases or shopping bags. As a workshop activity, participants selected a book from the library and chose models, props and prompts that they could use to support children in engagement, discussion and retelling of the story. Story sacks explicitly provide an opportunity for children's creativity to be developed through 'problem solving, questioning, hypothesising and creating works of art' (Noonan-Lepaon and Ridgway, 2009, 92).

Viewing workshop planning through a creative lens also included engagement with new practices to build on children's interests by including digital technology, media, music and popular culture, which in contemporary times underpin the world view of children's and young people's lives (Grieshaber *et al.*, 2021). With literacy experiences framed by the social world, any examination of what it means to 'be literate' in this technological era must also acknowledge the impact of 'new literacies', which require acquisition of expertise, knowledge and awareness of a range of skills in a variety of media (Flewitt, 2011). This approach to literacy practices can in some ways be challenging in being contradictory to the traditional view of learning through play-based activities. Yet again, they also provide an opportunity to underpin literacy learning by the cultural, linguistic and social capital that they bring from their home contexts.

Concluding thoughts

Key learning, which emerged from the programme, was demonstrated in evaluations from both facilitators and participants. In assessing the effectiveness of the workshops as a vehicle for their own learning, participants expressed that in the future they would:

- listen to the children and wait for the spark!;
- think out of the box;

- facilitate fun-filled and meaningful learning;
- incorporate more self-assessment to improve my programmes;
- increase partnership with families and diverse users;
- impactfully engage with cultural institutions; and
- move to a child-centric approach.

What was significant was that the collaboration demonstrated by librarians and their enthusiasm to engage in professional development and growth through feedback from peers and both reflective and reflexive self-reflection (Mills *et al.*, 2016).

This programme demonstrated how creative planning, training in best practice and incorporating an evidence-based approach in the context of the public library's use of workshops for children and families make a difference in instilling fun and enjoyment in books and literacy activities (MacLean, 2008). Presentations provided evidence of a clear commitment by children's librarians to a developing community of practice, with recognition of the importance of peer feedback, planning to clear success criteria and positive attitudes to professional development and growth. Librarians acknowledged the key role that public libraries can play in children's and young people's attitude and engagement with books and reading (Merga and Roni, 2018). An overarching feature was the recognition of each child as a unique individual and an acknowledgement that all library practices must take into account the social, cultural and environmental factors that shape children's and families' understanding of the world.

Critique of creative approach presented

Overall, this knowledge exchange endeavour provided an exciting opportunity to creatively develop a bespoke successful training model to underpin this programme. However, a few key challenges must be acknowledged, both regarding planning the content and the delivery. This is particularly related to addressing the professional development needs of children's librarians who were not conventional teachers. Content also needed to be specifically targeted at this group of professionals working not only within this unique institution, but also taking into account the sociocultural context of the setting.

Although librarians were committed to supporting literacy outcomes in workshops, their role was not related explicitly to improving teaching quality and the outcomes of children in the classroom (EEF, 2021). However, there were many parallels in the rationale for the training needs of both librarians and teachers; for example, to build on an understanding of the child and the child's world. As far back as the 1980s, research proposed that an essential requirement of children's librarians is that they have a clear knowledge of child development to inform their practice (Smardo, 1980). In addition, there must be an acknowledgement of the changing landscape of library activities within the digital age. Therefore, training is necessary to support librarians not only in embracing new technologies, but also in updating skills to respond knowledgeably to developments and changes within the information service context (Campbell-Meier and Goulding, 2021).

An overwhelming highlight of training outcomes was the active engagement of children's librarians. They embraced each task positively, with a dedication to professional learning in order to enhance the experiences of the children and families they worked with. It was evident that their vision of continuous professional development was consistently underpinned by their willingness to create an inclusive community of practice (Wenger, 1998). This was demonstrated by the mutual engagement of all participants, how they understood their context, their reflectivity and reflexivity in developing skills and repertoire (Kennedy, 2005; Wenger, 1998). The commitment of the librarians to transformative practice accompanied by an ability to present ideas clearly, take risks and embrace new ideas in a creative way was evidenced by the high-quality presentation delivered by librarians at the end of the training (Abels *et al.*, 2003).

Summary of key elements and recommendations

- A key role of children's librarians is establishing a positive attitude to books, reading and literacy activities.
- Any interpretation of creativity must be underpinned by the recognition of the experiences, cultural and family contexts that children and families bring with them.
- Creativity in education must be viewed through a wider lens of public and private domains.
- There is a positive impact of self-reflection, reflexive practice and evaluation on the learning outcomes of children and young people.
- Successful learning contexts embed a clear commitment to developing trust within a community of practice underpinned by positive attitudes to professional development and growth.

References

Bandura, Albert. 2001. 'Social cognitive theory: An agentic perspective', *Annual Review of Psychology*, 52: 1–26.

Barron, I., and Powell, J. 2002. 'Story sacks, children's narratives and the social construction of reality', *Citizenship, Social and Economics Education*, 5(3): 129–37.

Bronfenbrenner, U. (ed.). 2005. *Making Human Beings Human: Bioecological Perspectives on Human Development*. Thousand Oaks CA: SAGE Publications.

Campbell-Meier, J., and Goulding, A. 2021. 'Evaluating librarian continuing professional development: Merging Guskey's framework and Vygotsky Space to explore transfer of learning', *Library and Information Science Research*, 43(4): 1–12.

Cohen, L., Manion, L., and Morrison, K. 2007. *Research Methods in Education*. London and New York: Routledge.

Collard, P., and Looney, J. 2014. 'Nurturing creativity in education', *European Journal of Education*, 49(3): 348–64.

Colwell, J., Gregory, K., and Taylor, V. 2021. 'Examining preservice teachers' perceptions of planning for culturally relevant disciplinary literacy', *Journal of Teacher Education*, 72(2): 195–208.

Cremin, T., Swann, J., Flewitt, R., Faulkener, D., and Kucirkova, N. 2013. *Evaluation Report of Make Believe Arts Helicopter Technique of Storytelling and Story Acting*. Milton Keynes: Open University/MakeBelieveArts.

Daiment-Cohen B., Prendergast, T., Estrovitz, C., Banks, C., and Van der Veen. K. 2007. 'We play here! Bringing the power of play into children's libraries', *The Journal of the Association for Library Service to Children*, 10(1): 3–10.

Education Development Institute (WDI) Qatar. Accessed 7 July 2023. https://edi.qa/. Qatar National Library (QNL). Accessed 7 July 2023. https://www.qnl.qa/en.

Education Endowment Foundation (EEF). 2021. 'Guidance Report EEF, 2021'. Accessed 7 July 2023. https://educationendowmentfoundation.org.uk/education-evidence/guidance-reports/effective-professional-development.

Flewitt, R. 2011. 'Bringing ethnography to a multimodal investigation of early literacy in a digital age', *Qualitative Research*, 11(3): 293–310.

Greenhough, P., Scanlan, M., Feiler, A., Johnson, D., Yee, W., Andrews, J., Price, A., Smithson, M., and Hughes, M. 2005. 'Boxing clever: Using shoeboxes to support home-school knowledge exchange', *Literacy*, 39: 97–103.

Gremm, J., Barth, J., Fietkiewicz, K. J., and Stock, W. 2018. *Transitioning Towards Knowledge Society: Qatar as a case study*. Cham: Springer International Publishing.

Grieshaber, S., Krieg, S., McArdle, F., and Sumsion, J. 2021. 'Intentional teaching in early childhood education: A scoping review', *Review of Education*, 9(3): e3309.

Jones, R. 2003. 'Competencies for Information Professionals of the 21st Century', *Information Outlook*, 7: 11–21.

Kennedy, A. 2005. 'Models of Continuing Professional Development: A framework for analysis', *Journal of In-service Education*, 31(2): 235–50.

Kitto, E., and Bullough, L. 2021. 'Reflective practice'. In *The Early Years Foundation Stage*, edited by I. Palaiologou, 315–28. London: SAGE.

MacLean, J. 2008. *Library Pre-school Storytimes: Developing early literacy skills in children*, 1–13. State College PA: Penn Hill State University.

Mahmoud, M. 2022. 'Qatar National Library Hosts Virtual Tour of the Children's Library for Children with Special Needs', 24 January 2022. *Qatar National Library*. Accessed 7 July 2023. https://www.qnl.qa/en/about/news/qatar-national-library-hosts-virtual-tour-childrens-library-children-special-needs.

Merga, M., and Roni, S. 2018. 'Parents as social influences encouraging book reading: Research directions for librarians' literacy advocacy', *Journal of Library Administration*, 58(7): 674–97.

Miller, L., and Cameron, C. (eds). 2014. *International Perspectives in the Early Years*. London: SAGE.

Noonan-Lepaon, F., and Ridgway, A. 2009. 'Story sacks: Look what is inside!', *The OMEP Ireland Journal of Early Childhood Studies*, 3(1): 87–99.

Mills, J. E., Campana, K., Haley, G., and Hutchins, D. 2016. 'Supercharged storytimes, supercharged solutions: Enhancing storytimes with a research-based community of practice', *PNLA Quarterly*, 81(1): 18–25.

Nasser. R. 2017. 'Qatar's educational reform past and future: Challenges in teacher development', *Open Review of Educational Research*, 4(1): 1–19.

National Literacy Trust. 2022. 'Why are story sacks useful?', *NLT web resources*. Accessed 7 July 2023. https://literacytrust.org.uk/resources/how-make-and-use-story-sack/.

Parcero, O. J. 2019. 'Transitioning towards a knowledge society: Qatar as a case study', *Journal of Arabian Studies*, 9(2): 293–5.

Rose, J., and Wood, F. 2016. 'Child development'. In *A Guide to Early Years and Primary Teaching*, edited by D. Wyse and S. Rogers, 85–105. London: SAGE.

Sikes, P., Measor, L., and Woods, P. 2001. 'Critical phases and incidents'. In *Teacher Development: Exploring our own practice*, edited by J. Soler, A. Craft and H. Burgess, 104–15. Thousand Oaks CA: SAGE Publishing.

Smardo, F. A. 1980. 'Are librarians prepared to serve young children?', *Journal of Education for Librarianship*, 20(4): 274–84.

Smith, D. 2013. *Review of arts in education: Final report*. Accessed 18 July 2023. https://www.gov.wales/review-arts-education-final-report.

Soler J., Craft, A., and Burgess, H. (eds). 2000. *Teacher Development: Exploring our own practice*. Thousand Oaks CA: SAGE Publishing

Vygotsky, L. S. (1978). *Mind in Society: The development of higher psychological processes*. Cambridge MA: Harvard University Press.

Weinberger. J., and Stafford, A. 2004. 'Using storysacks to talk with parents about young children's literacy learning', *Education 3–13*, 32(1): 31–8.

Wenger, E. 1998. *Communities of Practice: Learning, meaning and identity*. Cambridge: Cambridge University Press.

A response from the perspectives of Malawi and Mauritius

Rosemary Davis

The author of the chapter has clearly had close involvement with in-service initiatives in Qatar, in addition to similar work in a number of countries. This is an interesting chapter with considerable relevance to children's creativity, literacy and overall human development.

Population demographics and information on religion and culture provide a good background for the reader. It would have been interesting to have some information on the teaching of literacy, methods and language of instruction in the public sector, as we could have seen the important work of the librarians in its cultural and educational context. However, the Qatar government's commitment to a knowledge-based society is of real importance. Its declared aims are indubitably worthwhile with real potential for sound foundations in education for children's potential. The declared emphasis on evidence-based practice is an important development. Consistent with the need to avoid Eurocentric practices and to work within a culture, the aims for the librarians do appear to have a general application.

The librarians operate between the child, the child's cognitive development and the social and historical context. It is, however, worth noting that a child's cognitive development is not non-cultural. The social and cultural context, the habitus, in which a child is born and grows, helps to shape the nature of thinking and development (Bourdieu, 1986). The cultural capital that is entailed is further enhanced through the institutions and practices. As such, the developments of the librarianship initiative have enormous potential for children's social and intellectual development.

The training of librarians for their roles in children's development is highlighted in the case study of teaching creativity in the Qatar context. It was argued, validly, that to fulfil their roles appropriately, librarians must understand how children grow and develop. This is an important point in the choice of their use of language and material. Anything that helps to bring together children's families in the educational/development process is sound practice. It was one of the fundamental principles in the now disregarded Plowden Report (CACE, 1967). The important role of home in reading development was highlighted by Merga and Roni (2018).

Overall, this chapter is convincing in its rationale and description of the approach to be taken in the training and work of the librarians and their important role in children's literacy development. The encouragement of reflective activity described in the chapter has validity for the aims of the training. The approaches presented throughout the case study would appear to have every chance of success in encouraging creative thinking.

Creativity is a human potential, but it must be nurtured in conducive conditions for it to be released. Many developments, including inventions, have begun with individuals who can 'think outside the box'. Creativity takes many forms and Qatar's innovation with the librarians is a worthwhile case in point. Direct comparison with other countries' initiatives is not possible, but a relevant example is that of the children's library part of Mzuzu University in north Malawi. Malawi was, and is, a poor country with a real need for support. Mzuzu University was newly created to train teachers to work in secondary schools with its library intended to reflect the academic role of a university library. The librarian of the time, with support from the university as a whole, wanted to reach out to the community. It was therefore made possible for local people to use the library. A real innovation was the establishment of a children's library where local children could borrow books. These were made possible by international donations and the initiative was met with pleasure locally. Books that can be shared at home were shown to contribute to children's reading development (Merga and Roni, 2018; MacLean, 2008). This is regarded as particularly important in countries such as Malawi where books, even in schools, have often been absent or in short supply.

An extension of the potential of the library could have been for university staff to provide support to parents or caregivers in Malawi. This could be done by guiding them to provide support. A creative example of how this could be achieved would be to invite parents/caregivers to the campus, perhaps providing a cup of tea or coffee, and demonstrating the adult role in fostering enjoyment of books and a love of reading. The event would provide an opportunity to communicate the rationale to parents/caregivers, while gathering the children around, reading to them and showing illustrations or texts would be a fine example of what a good role model would look like.

Knowledge and understanding of children's development is an essential aspect of work with children. A four-year consultancy, funded by the United Nations Development Programme (UNDP) and UNICEF working with the Ministry of Education enabled a set of developmental charts to be developed in Mauritius with the master teacher trainers covering cognitive development, language and communication, and physical and social-emotional development. Another programme was initiated where the master teacher trainers would make games. As their consultant, I taught them to make lotto, dominoes and other games in workshops, which provided models for the master teacher trainers to use in their own training work. Materials necessary for the project were funded by the UNDP, which I personally hand-carried from the United Kingdom.

A further innovation, particularly relevant to the work of the librarians in Qatar, was the creation of a taped story. This was adapted from the Aesop's fable 'The North Wind and the Sun' and became 'The Cyclone and the Sun'. Cyclones are common in Mauritius and the cold wind is from the south. The tape was reproduced with UNDP and UNICEF funding, together with the games. Sets of charts, games and tapes were distributed to all preschools that had registered with the Ministry of Education, Arts and Culture. Eventually, most registered preschools made good use of the materials, while others needed help to do so. Initiatives that work with a culture, such as in Qatar, have great potential to improve children's creativity and add to their cultural capital through worthwhile endeavours.

References

Bourdieu P. 1986. 'The forms of capital'. In *Handbook of Theory and Research for the Sociology of Education*, edited by J. Richardson, 201–58. Westpoint CT: Greenwood.

Central Advisory Council for Education (CACE). 1967. *Children and their Primary Schools*. London: Her Majesty's Stationery Office.

MacLean J. 2008. *Library Preschool Storytimes: Developing early literacy skills in children*. State College PA: Penn State University.

Merga M., and Roni S. M. 2018. 'Parents as social influencers encouraging book reading: Research directions for librarians' literacy advocacy'. *Journal of Library Administration*, 58(7): 674–97. Accessed 7 July 2023. https://doi.org/10.1080/01930826.2018.1514841.

Republic of Mauritius Ministry of Education, Arts and Culture. 1989. 'Strengthening of Pre-Primary Education. MAR/84/00', *End of Project Report*. Port Louis: Republic of Mauritius.

A response from the perspective of Sweden

Sally Windsor

Fantastic to hear of a programme of professional development for librarians in Qatar that has the support of education authorities in the small nation; a nation whose economy has for many decades been 'over reliant' on natural resources such as oil. It is also interesting to read that the development of the role of library educators to contribute to increasing literacy and creativity is seen as an opportunity and not a threat.

All too often education is conflated with mere schooling (Kemmis, 2014), and we do not tend to accept that teaching and learning should be cultivated everywhere, outside school contexts. Librarians and educators all over the world, as with all educators more broadly, understand the importance of out-of-school settings such as libraries, museums, zoos, science centres, forests and gardens for increasing different literacies and engaging with families in unique ways. These varied contexts are increasingly important links between families and the educational experiences that their children can have. As this chapter noted, libraries 'foster creativity, fun and enjoyment both for the children and their families'. I really enjoyed reading about the preliminary activities outlined, they each appear to be quite pedagogically engaging. It is also interesting that container metaphors were used – for example, 'box' and 'sacks' – but in terms of 'creativity' this makes sense. After all, stimulating and engaging creativity usually requires a creative 'object' to be produced, which, in turn, is evidence of learning and creativity.

Globally, there is an increasing focus on sustainability education particularly within the framework of the UN Sustainable Development Goals (United Nations, 2022). In the current socio-ecological context, educators working within Education for Sustainable Development (ESD) (UNESCO, 2022) are in a critical position to help develop the capacity for significant engagement in the key issues of our time and to promote practices such as 'anticipatory thinking, integrative thinking, dealing with complexity and ambiguity . . . and to create learning spaces for the development of qualities such as care, empathy and solidarity' (Peters and Wals, 2012, 183). As this chapter shows, libraries are, or at least can be, learning spaces that not only 'foster creativity' but also the important qualities of care, empathy and solidarity for the future.

In Sweden there has been considerable research into the value of aesthetic and creative experiences when provided to children and young people. This focus has, in particular, been centred on creative approaches to engaging with the natural world (e.g. Hagerman *et al.*, 2018; Hipkiss and Nyberg, 2022; Nyberg, 2017; Windsor and Sanders, 2022), perhaps because environmental and outdoor education have deep roots in Scandinavian countries (Hipkiss *et al.*, 2020).

The creative approach recounted in this chapter could well be applied in Sweden in a range of settings. As in many parts of the world, 'literacies' (plural), is part of the vernacular and the specific activities included in the case study could be used to enhance the professional development of a range of educators to address literacy, in a range of school and out-of-school settings. Of particular note in this chapter is the emphasis on affective or emotional aspects that enhance a love of learning, which can be better engaged in situ, in this case the library, but equally in gardens (Hipkiss *et al.*, 2020), museums (Mangione, 2016) or the local area in which children live (Roberts, 2017; Windsor and Sanders, 2020).

References

Hagerman, F., Jeppsson, F., Axell, C., Frejd, J., and Sultan, U. 2018. *Naturvetenskap och teknik genom estetiska lärprocesser i förskolan*. Stockholm: Natur och kultur.

Hipkiss, A. M., Windsor, S., and Sanders, D. 2020. 'The girl with the garden gloves: Researching the affordances of sensual materialities in the school garden', *Ethnography and Education*, 15(3): 350–62. Accessed 7 July 2023. https://doi.org/10.1080/17457823.2019.1698309.

Kemmis, S. 2014. 'Reflections on how the theory of practice architectures is being used in the Nordic context'. In *Lost in Practice: Transforming Nordic Educational Action Research*, edited by K. Rönnerman and P. Salo, 205–17. Rotterdam: Sense Publishers.

Mangione, G. 2016. 'Making sense of things: Constructing aesthetic experience in museum gardens and galleries', *Museums and Society*, 14(1): 33–51.

Nyberg, E. 2017. 'Aesthetic experiences related to living plants: A starting point in framing humans' relationship with nature?' In *Ethical Literacies and Education for Sustainable Development*, edited by O. Franck and C. Osbeck, 137–57. Cham: Springer.

Peters, M. A., and Wals, A. E. J. 2016. 'Transgressive learning in times of global systemic dysfunction: interview with Arjen Wals', *Open Review of Educational Research*, 3(1): 179–89. Accessed 7 July 2023. https://doi.org/10.1080/23265507.2016.1217166.

Roberts, M. 2017. 'Geographical education is powerful if', *Teaching Geography*, 42(1): 6–9.

UNESCO. 2022. *Education for Sustainable Development (2015–19)*. Paris: UNESCO. Accessed 7 July 2023. https://en.unesco.org/globalactionprogrammeoneducation.

United Nations. 2022. *The United Nations Sustainable Development Goals: The 17 goals*. New York: United Nations Department of Economic and Social Affairs. Accessed 7 July 2023. https://sdgs.un.org/goals.

Windsor, S., and Sanders, D. 2022. 'Being bird and sensory learning activities: Multimodal and arts-based pedagogies in the "Anthropocene"', *Educational Philosophy and Theory*, 1–17. Accessed 7 July 2023. https://doi.org/10.1080/00131857.2022.2088353.

4
The role of creativity and innovation for teaching in disruptive times: the case of Chile

Roxana Balbontín-Alvarado and Cristian Rivas-Morales

Introduction to the educational context of Chile

Chile is a South American country and one of the leading economies in Latin America. In 2010, it became the first South American country to join the Organisation for Economic Co-operation and Development (OECD). According to the Human Development Index Ranking 2020 (UNDP, 2020), Chile is 43rd out of 189 nations, the best position for a Latin American country. Unfortunately, Chile is also characterised by high economic inequality, which is also evident in the educational system.

Chile has 12 years of mandatory education, divided into eight years of primary education (ages six to 13), followed by four years of secondary education (ages 14 to 17). Until 2003, secondary education was not compulsory, but system reform, which came into effect in 2004, made 12 years of education mandatory for all pupils. Preschool education is not compulsory, but most children attend preschool before primary school for at least one year, normally at the age of five, or sometimes earlier. Higher education degrees, certificates or diplomas are provided by universities, professional institutes or technical colleges.

Initial teacher training is necessary to enter a teaching career, and since 2014 it can be provided only by universities. The following programmes are offered: preschool education teaching; primary education teaching; secondary education teaching (with different disciplinary specialisations); and special education teaching training (OECD, 2017). In Chile, initial teacher education is a five-year undergraduate degree. Students can begin their teacher education after graduating from secondary school, normally at the age of 18, although university courses are open to people of all ages. The formal requirement to enter university is an access test – the university transition test – and, depending on the students' results in this evaluation, along with consideration of their secondary school results, students can apply for different university degrees.

In 2016, the promulgation of Law 20.903 about the teaching career introduced new and more demanding requirements to enter teacher education programmes, which included higher scores in the university access test and better secondary school attainment levels. This new policy aims to attract better candidates into the teaching profession to improve education quality.

Initial teacher education programmes are structured according to the autonomy granted to higher education institutions. However, to be accredited by the National Accreditation Commission, programmes must cover four key training areas: general aspects (social and cultural issues, the education system, and ethics and responsibilities); specialised contents (disciplinary knowledge and curricular content); professional issues (learning and teaching methods, and tools for teaching); and practical concerns (practice in schools) (OECD, 2017).

After pre-service teachers finish at university, they must complete an induction process, which is mandatory in the case of state schools. This involves mentoring at the school by an experienced and effective teacher. The induction process takes place during the first or second year of professional experience and lasts for up to 10 months.

The role of creativity in Chile

The Chilean educational context is very formal and rigid (Barraza *et al.*, 2019) with few opportunities to develop creativity and with a tendency to excessive academisation, especially at secondary school level. According to Barraza *et al.* (2019), the reasons for this rigidity are market-orientation and accountability. The Chilean system is strongly market-oriented, as Cristian Bellei discusses extensively in his book *The Great Experiment*, in which he analyses the process of privatisation of the Chilean education (Bellei, 2015).

High importance is given to accountability measures through national standardised tests, which are applied in years 2, 4, 6 and 8 of primary school (corresponding to the ages seven, nine, 11 and 13) and in years 2 and 3 of secondary school (corresponding to the ages 15 and 16). This examination tradition fosters competition between schools because institutions that do better in tests are provided with more funding opportunities. As a result, due to funding cuts based on results, poorer performing schools risk becoming even poorer. It is certainly true that test results can be useful for monitoring and improvement purposes. However, a significant number of Chilean schools prepare students for examinations by dedicating a lot of time to subjects such as mathematics and the Spanish language, and through reducing time spent on the arts, applied technology or complementary extracurricular activities that focus on the development of artistic, creative, scientific and technological competencies.

Educational policymakers have received harsh criticism for encouraging Chilean schools to focus educational processes on the increase of standardised test scores, which is fostered by the need to compete at a global level, since Chilean educational results are below the median of OECD countries (Meckes and Carrasco, 2010). Naturally, the development of creativity within a rigid and formal school system is not an easy task. Despite this, creativity has some modest presence in the Chilean school curriculum, especially in preschools where teachers are expected to use creative approaches and strategies in learning, including play, arts and discovery through trial and error, among others. At primary and secondary school levels, creativity education is developed mainly through the arts curriculum and extracurricular activities and in higher education through integral education. Unfortunately, the space for this kind of training is reduced and, occasionally, it is even optional, especially in higher education. Having said that, an initiative led by the National Council of Culture and Arts in conjunction with the Ministry of Education was initiated in 2011 to bring arts and culture closer to the school system. The programme is called 'Acciona', and its main objective is the promotion of art in education (National Council of Culture and Arts, 2016). Through this programme some schools are allocated artists who act as art tutors and deliver workshops for pupils as part of the extracurricular activities. These art tutors work in collaboration with schoolteachers, who receive in-service training. Unfortunately, the coverage of the Acciona programme is still limited.

Within teacher education programme curricula, creativity and innovation have a very low presence. There is an excessive focus on specific disciplinary knowledge, rather than on creative, generic and life skills, which is a major weakness of teacher education in Chile, an issue that will be analysed in depth in the following sections.

Case study: Creativity in Chilean teacher education

We will present an introductory section with reflections on the links between creativity, innovation and education (Beghetto and Kaufman, 2007, 2014; Couros, 2015; West-Knights, 2017), followed by a discussion on the role of creativity in responding to crisis and social disruption. We highlight the importance of promoting the development of creativity in education as a strategy for individual and collective empowerment, which implies having teachers prepared for this purpose (Craft, 2002, 2005).

In the third section of this case study, we undertake an analysis of pre-service teacher education programmes curricula at the national level, to verify whether topics and skills such as creativity, innovative thinking, problem-based education and information and computer technology (ICT) skills for education are included in training itineraries (Schreiber, 2018). We then discuss critically the findings of the analysis, highlighting the importance of creativity-related areas for teacher training. We also mention examples of alternative ways in which creativity is developed through different strategies and tools that are learned and used in most of the teacher training programmes in Chile. We conclude by presenting suggestions and recommendations on how universities, teaching programmes, pre-service teachers, educational policymakers and curriculum advisers could address change, disruptive educational scenarios and school challenges, through the encouragement of policies and practices that highlight the importance of the integration of creativity-related competencies in the teacher training curriculum.

Creativity, education and innovation

Over the past 100 years, creativity has been considered a topic of major concern for many areas and disciplines, such as psychology, education, arts, sciences, humanities and technology, among others. Scholars have researched the concept and provided some key definitions. Many agree that creativity is the capacity to generate new and original ideas, products and solutions to problems (Guilford, 1967; Mumford, 2003; Sternberg, 2011). A more complex definition that considers creativity as a response to an unsolved issue has been provided by Torrance (1966):

> a process of becoming sensitive to problems, deficiencies, gaps in knowledge, missing elements, disharmonies, and so on; identifying the difficulty; searching for solutions, making guesses, or formulating hypotheses about the deficiencies: testing and retesting these hypotheses and possibly modifying and retesting them; and finally communicating the results. (6)

These prominent experts have also researched the connections between creativity and other factors, such as intelligence, personality traits and mental health. Through their findings they have acknowledged the importance of encouraging creativity through education in order to achieve long-term technological and economic development. An early creativity model was created by Wallas (1926). The initial model described four different stages involved in the creative process, comprising preparation, incubation, illumination and verification. According to Kaufmann (2003), at least until the twentieth century, this model was still a core element for understanding creativity. Kaufman and Beghetto (2009) developed four categories of creativity:

- 'Big C' – sometimes called 'high' creativity, 'Big C' creativity describes the work of an elite individual that transformed a discipline, such as the work of Einstein, Darwin, Picasso or Beethoven, among other great minds.
- 'Pro c' – 'pro c' creativity concerns the type of creativity that has involved time and effort to develop, such as might be expected from musicians or researchers, among others.
- 'Little c' – 'little c' creativity describes flexible behaviour, intelligence and novelty in everyday endeavours. This kind of creativity can be found in people who can resolve complex problems at work.
- 'Mini c' – 'mini c' creativity refers to a learner's capacity in finding several ways of approaching a maths problem. Individuals with this type of creativity make connections between their previous knowledge and new information to improve their understanding. This type of creativity can be nurtured by teachers and parents and is frequently associated with, but not limited to, children's creativity.

Although the concept of creativity encompasses innovative thinking and original solutions to problems, the construct frequently associated with these elements is innovation (Couros, 2015; West-Knights, 2017). The main distinction between creativity and innovation lies in the fact that the latter requires implementation. Creativity is the production of novel and useful ideas, and innovation is the implementation of creative ideas (Amabile and Pratt, 2016). Innovation is more than a new idea or an invention because it requires being put into use or made available for use by other parties, individuals or organisations (OECD/Eurostat, 2018). In addition, innovation implies a target and hard work to achieve that target, as highlighted by Cambridge Assessment International Education (2011):

> Innovation contains the idea of output, of actually producing or doing something differently, making something happen or implementing something new. Innovation almost always involves hard work; persistence and perseverance are necessary as many good ideas never get followed through and developed. (53)

In previous decades, creativity has been applied to different areas and one of the main focal points of developed and developing societies is fostering creativity through education and training to encourage innovators to solve global economic, social and environmental issues. Nevertheless, the stigma of educational systems that failed to promote the development of creative and innovative thinking remains present. In fact, many prominent creative minds have at once time declared that school was an unhappy experience for them (e.g. Albert Einstein and Thomas Edison), and many of the most famous innovators never finished their university education (e.g. Steve Jobs, Bill Gates and Mark Zuckerberg). Sadly, it seems that formal education systems are considered barriers to developing and releasing of creative potential (Shaheen, 2010).

Throughout the twentieth century education was associated mainly with the reproduction of traditional knowledge and the development of conformist thinkers, rather than creative and original individuals (Rogers, 1970, as cited by Shaheen, 2010). The focus of teaching and learning processes was on knowledge acquisition. Schools were sometimes called places that *kill creativity* (Kaila, 2005) and classrooms *worksheet dungeons* (Schreiber, 2018). This situation began to change by the end of the twentieth century and throughout the first two decades of twenty-first century. Creativity has since become a global and popular concern (Bloom and Dole, 2018). There have been calls for the inclusion of creativity in education as a fundamental life skill (Craft, 1999, as cited by Shaheen,

2010) that is necessary to survive and thrive in the twenty-first century (Parkhurst, 1999). Important global organisations have considered creativity an essential skill for twenty-first-century education and have recognised its importance for personal, social and economic development. Through campaigns to foster creativity and innovation, they have raised awareness; for example, using the slogan 'Imagine-Create-Innovate' (European Commission, 2008).

We have experienced a significant shift in educational policy around the world. 'Education for life' has become an important focus for many countries and international organisations that advocate for education. Considerable effort has been made to integrate knowledge and other essential skills, such as creativity. In some places, such as the United States, China, the United Kingdom and some European countries, creativity has become a focus of curriculum and pedagogy (NACCCE, 1999; Wilson, 2005) and part of the official agenda for improving schools (Burnard, 2006). This is not necessarily the case in Latin American countries, where there are good intentions to integrate creativity into the school curriculum, but the focus remains on equality and educational justice, as well as the basic skills that children are expected to develop, such as Spanish literacy and maths. It seems that Latin American education systems do not apply enough creativity in their schools because they are more focused on other foundational educational concerns (Educational Revolution in a Century, n.d.).

In Chile, the main focus of educational policy is on accountability. The government provides accreditation bodies that evaluate school and university systems to ensure that pupils and students are learning the key skills necessary. For example, in the school system, these essential skills are to do with specific disciplines, such as maths and the Spanish language, while at the higher education level, these key skills are related to the disciplinary standards that the graduate profiles require. The integration of generic competencies, life skills or so-called twenty-first-century competencies (learning skills, literacy skills and life skills) is declared but not evident in the schools and universities curricula. Education policymakers, whose focus is on accountability, believe that basic skills and essential disciplinary content must be developed first and the promotion of the twenty-first-century competencies should come later or can also be incorporated into accountability mechanisms. Unfortunately, in a national educational context, where accountability is pivotal, the twenty-first-century competencies, including the development of creativity and innovation, have inevitably been neglected (Bellei and Morawietz, 2016).

The role of education and creativity in times of disruption

Disruption scenarios are very frequent nowadays and require specific competencies to tackle new challenges. UNESCO has reported that in previous decades, large-scale outbreaks of pandemic diseases, natural disasters or serious air pollution incidents have taken place at a global scale. This situation has not only affected population health, but also the education sector. For instance, at the end of 2002, SARS affected several countries around the world, including China, and consequently face-to-face teaching was banned in several regions to tackle the virus (Huang *et al.*, 2020). A similar situation took place in 2009, when the H1N1 influenza (swine flu) affected people from around the world, causing school closures in many countries, such as Bulgaria, China, France, Italy, Japan, New Zealand, Serbia, South Africa, Thailand, the United Kingdom and the United States (Cauchemez *et al.*, 2014).

More recently, at the end of 2019, we witnessed the outbreak of the worst pandemic in modern times: Covid-19. This disease has affected education systems worldwide, including tertiary education, and emergency remote teaching (Hodges *et al.*, 2020) as a response to crisis has been implemented all around the world (IAU, 2020; Marinoni *et al.*, 2020; Reimers and Schleicher, 2020; UN, 2020). The closing of educational institutions brought many challenges for higher education and teachers worldwide. The quick transition did not allow enough time for organisation or pedagogical planning for the new educational format, which generated disruption for the educational systems and institutions and a lot of stress for educational stakeholders.

In the case of Chile, in the past decade, higher education has faced a series of challenges that have interrupted its normal functioning. In 2010, higher education institutions opened their doors two months after the usual initial period, due to the 8.8 grade earthquake that struck Chile and affected the infrastructure and services of many universities nationwide. Along with this, in 2011 student marches, protests and university occupations took place and lasted for months. The demonstrators demanded an end to the for-profit Chilean higher education system calling for free and high-quality education. During the subsequent years, those student demonstrations continued, but for shorter periods. However, these frequent interruptions had a significant impact on the usual functioning of higher education. Further, in October 2019, Chile faced unprecedented social unrest, probably the most complex social crisis in recent decades. It was triggered by the evident and deep-rooted social injustices that have always characterised the country, but that have become more evident and less tolerable for a young and less conformist Chilean population. According to the OECD (2021), Chile is one of the most unequal developing societies. This shocking reality led thousands of Chilean people to demonstrate against a neoliberal market model. They demanded a more central role of the state as guarantor of fundamental rights for the population. The country has advanced in its development rates in recent decades and part of the poorest population now have more opportunities to access state benefits (UNDP, 2020). Nevertheless, lower middle classes cannot access such benefits and continue to become indebted; and this in a country where it is increasingly expensive to live and where social inequalities are profound (OECD, 2021).

A last disruptive and unexpected scenario was the health crisis resulting from Covid-19, which significantly impacted on the Chilean education system. By March 2020, higher education institutions closed their doors and moved to online teaching. This rapid change did not necessarily allow for any coherent and intentional planning for online teaching. Rather, face-to-face courses turned abruptly into virtual courses, in what can be termed emergency remote education (Hodges *et al.*, 2020). Considering these scenarios, it is worth asking ourselves, what happens when the educational paradigm that we are used to is broken, and traditional classrooms must close, having to open spaces to new forms of interaction? Well, the answer is probably to be prepared to respond to crisis and disruption and provide creative solutions to new challenges.

According to Shaheen (2010), the fostering of creativity in the field of education has intended to respond to many different challenges and concerns, such as a fast-changing society, future uncertainties and the role of the economy to encourage higher economic achievement. Nations require a specialised and creative workforce to respond to economic needs (Craft, 2005).

Today, graduate profiles should include development of essential life skills or twenty-first-century competencies. The labour market is demanding professionals who can communicate assertively, work collaboratively, solve problems, make strategic decisions, create, innovate and be resilient, among other qualities, to face stressful situations and disruptive scenarios. In sum, we need professionals who are capable of adding value to what they do and contributing to society. It seems that our societies are less focused on knowledge, moving competencies forward and encouraging the abilities required to apply knowledge in practical situations (Vetter and Helldén, 2020). An education that integrates the acquisition of knowledge, as well as the development of essential life skills would be the answer to these demands. More than two decades ago Jacques Delors proposed the four pillars of education: learning how to learn; learning how to do; learning how to work together; and learning how to be (Delors, 2000). These four pillars highlight the role of education in contributing to the development of the whole person. Referring to developing countries where creativity remains neglected and where education that encourages creativity and productivity is essential, Shaheen (2010) suggested reformulating the four pillars of education as follows: learning how to learn critically; learning how to do creatively; learning how to work constructively; and learning how to be wise.

It seems that in a fast-changing society where the future is uncertain, a new education for self and collective empowerment that is characterised by the promotion of creativity, innovation, critical thinking, problem-solving skills, peace, citizenship and resilience is essential for a promising world future.

Teacher education in Chile: Are we preparing creative teachers?

In the previous sections, we discussed the importance of preparing creative teachers (Beghetto and Kaufman, 2007, 2014) to overcome challenging educational scenarios derived from a fast-changing society and from unpredictable events, such as natural disasters, pandemic diseases and global conflicts. However, it is important to bear in mind what we mean by 'creative teachers'. To respond to this, we return to the conceptualisation of different types of creativity as developed by Kaufman and Beghetto (2009). In our view, one sort of creativity that should characterise teachers is defined as 'little c' creativity. This kind of creativity describes intelligence, innovative thinking, flexible behaviour and competencies to solve complex problems. This does not mean that teachers cannot be characterised by other kinds of creativities or creative behaviours. However, we argue that those personal traits and professional competencies might favour a good professional performance in challenging education circumstances.

In the following section, we present an analysis of pre-service teacher education programme curricula at the national level, to show whether topics and skills such as creativity, innovative thinking, problem-based education and information technologies are included in training itineraries. To this end, four samples of universities were analysed, including institutions that offer the teacher training programmes explored. All the universities included in the samples belong to a selective group of traditional and prestigious higher education institutions known as the 'Chilean Universities Rectors' Council'. The specific programmes that were analysed are:

- the preschool education teaching programme;
- the primary education teaching programme;
- the Spanish language teaching programme; and
- the science teaching programme.

The categories of analysis considered the following:

- creativity subjects, including such topics as creative writing, play, drama, arts, creative didactics and technology education, among others;
- innovation subjects, including topics related to innovative thinking and innovation projects;
- problem-based educational subjects, including topics that relate to project design, problem-solving strategies, decision-making and critical thinking; and
- ICT subjects, considering topics that include digital education and information technologies.

This latter type of course, concerning digital competences, was considered pivotal for today's discussions about innovation if the field of education and e-learning.

Table 4.1 presents an analysis of preschool education teaching programmes in 23 Chilean universities. In these institutions, a total of 51 courses are associated with the topics under analysis; an average of 2.2 per university. This number is quite low if we consider that, on average, a university teaching programme in Chile has approximately 60 courses. This result evidences the low importance given to this type of training. Regarding the distribution of subjects, 43 per cent are ICT courses; 29 per cent are subjects related to creativity; 22 per cent are problem-based educational courses; and 6 per cent are courses related to innovation. Overall, findings evidence insignificant curricular weight for the kinds of subject explored, especially in the case of innovation subjects. We would have expected to find more courses associated with the topics explored, especially within the preschool teaching curricula. Surprisingly, ICT training seems to be the area of major concern for these university programmes, although some universities provide no training in these areas.

Universities	Preschool education teaching programme				
	Creativity subjects	Innovation subjects	Problem-based educational subjects	ICT	Total
Universidad de Chile	2	0	1	0	3
Universidad de Valparaíso	1	0	1	1	3
Universidad de Antofagasta	1	0	1	0	2
Universidad de la Serena	0	0	1	0	1
Universidad Magallanes	1	1	1	1	4
Universidad de Talca	0	0	0	2	2
Universidad de Atacama	0	0	0	2	2
Universidad de Tarapacá	0	0	1	1	2
Universidad Arturo Prat	1	0	0	1	2
Universidad Mt. Cs. de Educación	1	0	0	1	2
Universidad de Playa Ancha	0	0	0	2	2
Universidad del Bío Bío	0	0	0	2	2
Universidad de los Lagos	0	0	0	2	2
Universidad de O´Higgins	0	0	1	1	2
Pont. Universidad Cat. de Chile	0	0	0	0	0
Universidad de Concepción	0	0	0	1	1
Pont. Universidad Cat. de Valpo.	2	1	0	1	4
Universidad Austral de Chile	2	1	1	2	6
Universidad Diego Portales	0	0	0	0	0
Universidad Cat. del Maule	1	0	1	1	3
Universidad Cat. de la St. Concepción	0	0	1	0	1
Universidad Cat. de Temuco	1	0	1	1	3
Universidad Alberto Hurtado	2	0	0	0	2
Total	15	3	11	22	51

Table 4.1 Preschool education teaching programmes analysis

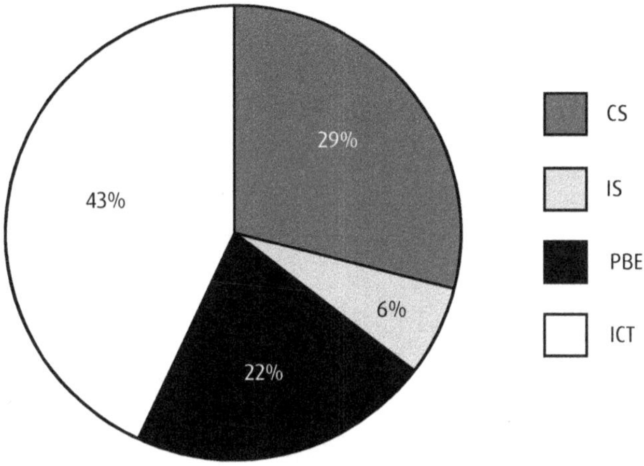

Figure 4.1 Subject distribution across universities (preschool education teaching programmes)

Table 4.2 shows the analysis of primary education teaching programmes in 23 Chilean universities. A total of 49 courses are related to the topics explored, an average of 2.1 per university, which is undoubtedly low. These findings suggest that little attention is given to this type of the training in the case of primary education teaching programmes. In regard to the distribution of subjects, 41 per cent are ICT courses; 43 per cent are creativity subjects; 12 per cent are problem-based educational courses; and 4 per cent are innovation subjects. In sum, findings show the insignificant curricular weight for the subjects under exploration, especially in the case of innovation subjects. Creativity subjects and ICT training seem to be areas of higher concern for these university programmes, although their presence is quite low and some institutions have no training in these areas.

Universities	Primary education teaching programme				
	Creativity subjects	Innovation subjects	Problem-based educational subjects	ICT	Total
Universidad de Chile	1	0	0	0	1
Universidad de Santiago de Chile	1	1	1	0	3
Universidad de Antofagasta	1	0	0	0	1
Universidad de la Serena	0	0	1	0	1
Universidad Magallanes	2	1	1	1	5
Universidad de Talca	0	0	0	2	2
Universidad de Atacama	0	0	0	2	2
Universidad de Tarapacá	1	0	0	1	2
Universidad Arturo Prat	4	0	0	1	5
Universidad Mt. Cs. de Educación	0	0	0	1	1
Universidad de Playa Ancha	1	0	1	2	4
Universidad del Bío Bío	2	0	0	1	3
Universidad de los Lagos	2	0	0	0	2
Universidad de O´Higgins	0	0	1	1	2
Pont. Universidad Cat. de Chile	0	0	0	0	0
Universidad de Concepción	0	0	0	1	1
Pont. Universidad Cat. de Valpo.	1	0	0	1	2
Universidad Austral de Chile	1	0	1	1	3
Universidad Diego Portales	0	0	0	0	0
Universidad Cat. del Maule	2	0	0	1	3
Universidad Cat. de la St. Concep.	1	0	0	2	3
Universidad Cat. de Temuco	1	0	0	1	2
Universidad Alberto Hurtado	0	0	0	1	1
Total	21	2	6	20	49

Table 4.2 Primary education teaching programmes analysis

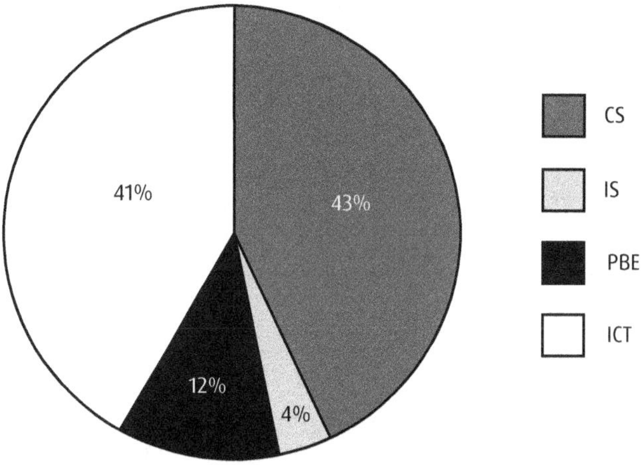

Figure 4.2 Subject distribution across universities (primary education teaching programmes)

Table 4.3 presents the analysis of Spanish language teaching programmes in 20 Chilean universities. The data show a total of 26 courses related to the topics explored, an average of 1.3 per university. These findings demonstrate the little emphasis given to this sort of training. Regarding the distribution of subjects, 62 per cent are ICT courses; 15 per cent are creativity subjects; 15 per cent are problem-based educational courses; and 8 per cent are innovation subjects. Concluding, results show insignificant curricular weight for the subjects under analysis, especially in the case of innovation subjects. ICT training seems to be the area of higher emphasis for these university programmes, although this kind of training is not present in all the institutions analysed.

Universities	Spanish language teaching programme				
	Creativity subjects	Innovation subjects	Problem-based educational subjects	ICT	Total
Universidad de Santiago de Chile	0	1	0	0	1
Universidad de Antofagasta	0	0	0	0	0
Universidad de la Serena	0	0	1	0	1
Universidad de la Frontera	0	0	0	2	2
Universidad Magallanes	0	0	1	1	2
Universidad de Tarapacá	0	0	0	0	0
Universidad Arturo Prat	0	0	0	1	1
Universidad Mt. Cs. de Educación	0	0	0	0	0
Universidad de Playa Ancha	1	0	0	2	3
Universidad del Bío Bío	0	0	0	2	2
Universidad de los Lagos	0	0	1	1	2
Pont. Universidad Cat. de Chile	0	0	0	0	0
Universidad de Concepción	0	0	0	1	1
Pont. Universidad Cat. de Valpo.	0	0	0	1	1
Universidad Austral de Chile	1	1	1	1	4
Universidad Diego Portales	0	0	0	0	0
Universidad Cat. del Maule	1	0	0	1	2
Universidad Cat. de la St. Concep.	1	0	0	1	2
Universidad Cat. de Temuco	0	0	0	1	1
Universidad Alberto Hurtado	0	0	0	1	1
Total	4	2	4	16	26

Table 4.3 Spanish language teaching programmes analysis

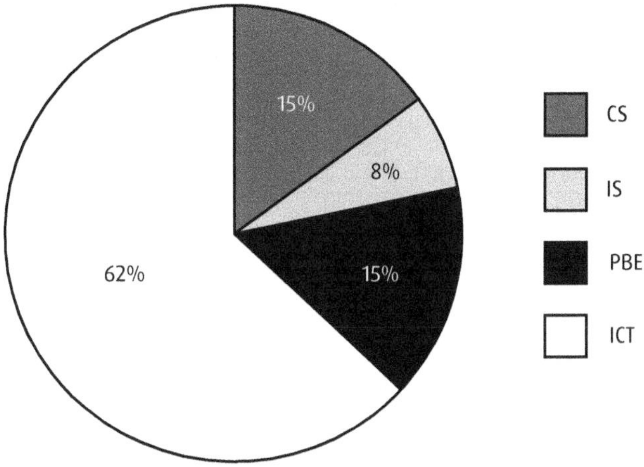

Figure 4.3 Subject distribution across universities (Spanish language teaching programmes)

Table 4.4 shows the analysis of science teaching programmes in 16 Chilean universities. Based on the data, it is possible to observe a total of 14 courses associated to the topics under analysis, an average of 1.1 per university. These findings evidence the low importance given to this type of training. In regard to the distribution of subjects, 72 per cent are ICT courses; 7 per cent are creativity subjects; 21 per cent are problem-based educational courses; and 0 per cent innovation subjects. Overall, results show insignificant curricular weight for the subjects explored. In the case of innovation subjects, none of the institutions analysed offer training in this area. ICT training is an area of higher concern for these universities, although many of them do not provide this type of training.

Universities	**Science teaching programme**				
	Creativity subjects	Innovation subjects	Problem-based educational subjects	ICT	Total
Universidad de Chile	0	0	0	0	0
Universidad de Santiago de Chile	0	0	0	1	1
Universidad de Antofagasta	0	0	0	0	0
Universidad de la Serena	0	0	1	0	1
Universidad de la Frontera	0	0	0	1	1
Universidad de Talca	0	0	0	1	1
Universidad de Tarapacá	0	0	0	1	1
Universidad Mt. Cs. de Educación	0	0	0	0	0
Universidad de Playa Ancha	1	0	0	2	3
Universidad del Bío Bío	0	0	0	1	1
Pont. Universidad Cat. de Chile	0	0	0	0	0
Universidad de Concepción	0	0	1	1	2
Pont. Universidad Cat. de Valpo.	0	0	0	0	0
Universidad Cat. de la St. Concep.	0	0	1	1	2
Universidad Cat. de Temuco	0	0	0	1	1
Universidad Alberto Hurtado	0	0	0	0	0
Total	1	0	3	10	14

Table 4.4 Science teaching programmes analysis

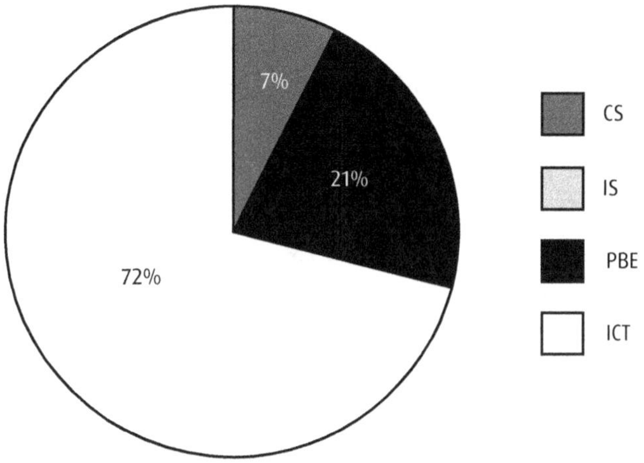

Figure 4.4 Subject distribution across universities (science teaching programmes)

Critical discussion of the case

In the previous section we presented an analysis of four Chilean teaching programmes, which aimed to verify whether specific areas such as creativity, innovation, problem-based education and ICT education are included in formal curricula. The findings clearly establish that these areas are not considered pivotal for teacher training in Chile. Results show a very low presence of these areas in training itineraries in all the universities analysed. These findings demonstrate a major weakness of teacher education in Chile, especially considering that the programmes analysed were expected to include more topics in creativity-related areas. Two of the programmes explored (the preschool teaching programme and the primary education teaching programme) prepare student teachers to educate children at young ages, specifically at the stage where research has shown the importance of nurturing creativity through play, brainstorming, discovering through trial and error, and problem-solving strategies, among others. Nevertheless, on average, these programmes offer very limited preparation in creativity-related areas. In the case of the other two programmes (Spanish and science teaching programmes), the occurrence of subjects related to these areas is even lower. This is equally disappointing, as the processes associated with the teaching and learning of languages and sciences should include the development of some creativity-related processes.

It seems clear that in Chile, university teacher training programmes are not connected with the needs of society. Perhaps the problem lies in the fact that teacher training programmes focus on the disciplines over pedagogical, professional and life competencies. Of course, a teacher must be well prepared in his or her specific discipline, but essentially, a teacher should be prepared to 'teach' that discipline.

Today, our fast-changing and unpredictable world prepares 'teachers to teach disciplines in different circumstances'. Teacher training programmes should foresee possible future scenarios and prepare students to face disruption, uncertainty and crises, through solid training that incorporates life skills. Teacher education must respond to societal needs and adapt to a changing and challenging world. It is essential that such subjects as creativity in education, innovation, resilience in education, education and diversity, and education for social justice have a presence.

Current educational models propose the integration of different competencies (disciplinary, pedagogical and generic, including life skills), which should be visible in courses with less traditional approaches; for example, teaching mathematics for diversity, innovation in the sciences classroom, teaching English in vulnerable contexts, creative literature and education for challenging scenarios, among other possible courses. A training model that includes these types of competencies and topics would ensure a better preparation for future teachers.

In addition, teacher training programmes should consider the development of resilience as a fundamental issue for initial training. Preparing student teachers to better face the challenges of an increasingly complex education system requires the development of resilience, as Gu and Day emphasise:

> Efforts should be made to help pedagogy students to be more aware of the potential experiences they could have as future teachers. Rather than considering teacher resilience as a personality characteristic associated with inheritance, teacher educators need to reflect with their students about internal and external factors that could strengthen teachers' resilience and thus better prepare them for reality of teaching. (2013, 40)

The need for changes in the teacher education curriculum due to the lack of courses regarding creative thinking and innovation is evident. Nevertheless, in Chilean teacher training universities, as part of pedagogical subjects or in the context of practical immersion experiences, the use of some strategies, methods and resources that might possibly contribute to a better adaptation and preparation for the real educational context is common. These strategies include case studies, action research, critical reflection on practice and school projects involving creative approaches.

In most of the universities analysed, case studies are frequently used to teach certain strategies and tools to approach the analysis of schools at different levels: school level, classroom level or pupil level. For example, during the practicum, student teachers must undertake case studies to better understand the real dynamics taking place in schools, such as discussing issues around the school climate, classroom management strategies or learner motivation. The findings of these cases might provide an opportunity to find creative solutions and strategies to tackle problems, from a problem-based education perspective. Student teachers who are doing their practicum can even undertake case studies within an action research approach that will provide immediate solutions for the problems observed. Action research is a very effective approach to learning because pre-service teachers can reflect critically on their own pedagogical practices for learning and improvement purposes. In addition, they can become agents of change through concrete actions within their educational contexts.

In terms of school projects, as part of the final practicum, student teachers must create a school improvement project often related to the disciplines that they teach. In doing so, student teachers get the guidance of their university tutors, who challenge them to find solutions for real school problems. Through the application of knowledge, practice and collaborative reflection, student teachers are expected to develop skills to solve the problems and initiate innovative strategies to approach them. For example, a pre-service science teacher might observe that a school lacks innovative ways to manage different types of trash or rubbish and has no recycling plan, so they develop a project, find support and funding, involve pupils and present the project.

Preparing pre-service teachers to face future challenges and provide solutions to real-life problems is an effective approach to creativity, as it requires the capacity to think outside the box and find innovative ways to provide solutions. Transitioning from pre-service teacher to teaching professional can be a shocking experience for early careers teachers, thus universities must prepare their teaching students to become resilient, creative professionals, with problem-solving skills who can adapt to the new challenges imposed by the society. However, this preparation needs to be part of the formal teacher training curriculum and not only an aspect of a course. It needs to be guaranteed for all pre-service teachers and included in the National Standards for Teaching Training.

Summary of key elements and recommendations

- Current times require us to educate people who will be able to solve future problems and deal with uncertainties and world crises.
    - Recommendation: governments, policymakers and universities should promote teaching programmes that respond to the real needs of society foreseeing possible future scenarios and preparing future teachers to face disruption, uncertainty and crises through solid training that integrates life skills.
- A fast-changing and unpredictable society requires creative teachers who can find solutions and innovate in times of disruption.
    - Recommendation: governments, policymakers and universities should foster an education through the inclusion of creativity, innovation, problem-solving strategies, technology and life skills within the standards expected for teacher education.
    - Recommendation: teacher training programmes should include the development of creativity, innovation, problem-solving strategies, technology and life skills in their curricula.
- Today, the fast-changing and unpredictable world requires us to prepare 'teachers to teach disciplines in different circumstances'.
    - Recommendation: teacher education programmes must advance the integration of different competencies (disciplinary, pedagogical and generic, including life skills), which should be visible in courses with less traditional approaches, such as teaching mathematics for diversity, innovation in the science classroom and teaching English in vulnerable contexts, among others.

References

Amabile, T. M., and Pratt, M. G. 2016. 'The dynamic componential model of creativity and innovation in organizations: Making progress, making meaning', *Research in Organizational Behavior*, 36: 157–83. Accessed 7 July 2023. https://doi.org/10.1016/j.riob.2016.10.001.

Barraza, P., Preiss, D., and Pardo, M. 2019. 'The development of creativity in Chilean kindergarten and school children' ('Desarrollo de la creatividad en párvulos y escolares chilenos'), *Studies in Psychology*, 40(3): 608–34. Accessed 7 July 2023. https://doi.org/10.1080/02109395.2019.1655220.

Beghetto, R. A., and Kaufman, J. C. 2007. 'Toward a broader conception of creativity: A case for mini-c creativity', *Psychology of Aesthetics, Creativity and the Arts*, 1: 73–9.
Beghetto, R. A., and Kaufman, J. C. 2014. 'Classroom contexts for creativity'. *High Ability Studies*, 53–69.
Bellei, C. 2015. *El gran experimento: Mercado y privatización de la educación chilena*. Santiago de Chile: Lom ediciones.
Bellei, C., and Morawietz, L. 2016. *Strong Content, Weak Tools, Twenty-First-Century Competencies in the Chilean Educational Reform: Teaching and Learning for the Twenty-First Century*. Cambridge MA: Harvard Education Press.
Bloom, L., and Dole, S. 2018. 'Creativity in education: A global concern', *Global Education Review*, 5(1): 1–4.
Burnard, P. 2006. 'Reflecting on the creativity agenda in education', *Cambridge Journal of Education*, 36: 313–18. Accessed 7 July 2023. https://doi.org/10.1080/03057640600865801.
Cambridge Assessment International Education. 2011. 'Innovation and creativity'. In Developing the Cambridge Learner Attributes. Accessed 7 July 2023. https://www.cambridgeinternational.org/support-and-training-for-schools/teaching-cambridge-at-your-school/cambridge-learner-attributes/.
Cauchemez, S., Van Kerkhove, M. D., Archer, B. N., Cetron, M., Cowling, B. J., Grove, P., Hunt, D., Kojouharova, M., Kon, P., Ungchusak, K., Oshitani, H., Pugliese, A., Rizzo, C., Saour, G., Sunagawa, T., Uzicanin, A., Wachtel, C., Weisfuse, I., Yu H., and Nicoll, A. 2014. 'School closures during the 2009 influenza pandemic: national and local experiences', *BMC Infectious Diseases*, 14(207). Accessed 7 July 2023. https://doi.org/10.1186/1471-2334-14-207.
Craft, A. 2001. *An Analysis of Research and Literature on Creativity in Education*. Carrickfergus: Qualifications and Curriculum Authority.
Craft, A. 2002. *Creativity and Early Years Education: A lifewide foundation*. Continuum Studies in Lifelong Learning. London: Continuum.
Craft, A. 2005. *Creativity in Schools: Tensions and dilemmas*. London: Routledge.
Couros, G. 2015. *The Innovator's Mindset: Empower learning, unleash talent, and lead a culture of creativity*. San Diego CA: Dave Burgess Consulting.
Delors, J. (2000). 'The four pillars of education', *Education Horizons*, 6(3): 14–18.
Educational Revolution in a Century. n.d. Accessed 7 July 2023. https://failover.www.gob.mx/mantenimiento.html.
European Commission. 2008. 'Media launch of the European year of creativity and innovation 2009'. Press release data base. Accessed 7 July 2023. http://europa.eu/rapid/press-release_IP-08-1893_en.htm.
Feldman, D. H., and Benjamin, A. C. 2006. 'Creativity and education: An American retrospective', *Cambridge Journal of Education*, 36(3): 319–36. Accessed 7 July 2023. https://doi.org/10.1080/03057640600865819.
Gu, Q., and Day, C. 2013. 'Challenges to teacher resilience: Conditions count', *British Educational Research Journal*, 39(1): 22–44.
Guilford, J. P. 1950. 'Creativity', *American* Psychologist, 5: 445–54.
Guilford, J. P. 1967. 'Creativity: Yesterday, today, and tomorrow', *The Journal of Creative Behavior*, 1(1): 3–14. Accessed 7 July 2023. https://doi.org/10.1002/j.2162-6057.1967.tb00002.x.
Hodges, C.H., Moore, S., Lockee B., Trust T., and Bond A. 2020. 'The difference between emergency remote teaching and online learning', *Educause Review*. Accessed 7 July 2023. https://er.educause.edu/articles/2020/3/the-difference-between-emergency-remote-teaching-and-online-learning.
Huang, R. H., Liu, D. J., Tlili, A., Yang, J. F., Wang, H. H., *et al.* 2020. *Handbook on Facilitating Flexible Learning During Educational Disruption: The Chinese Experience in Maintaining Undisrupted Learning in COVID-19 Outbreak*. Beijing: Smart Learning Institute of Beijing Normal University.
International Association of Universities (IAU). 2020. *Covid-19: Higher education challenges and responses*. Paris: International Association of Universities. Accessed 7 July 2023. https://www.iau-aiu.net/COVID-19-Higher-Education-challenges-and-responses.
Kaila, H. 2005. 'Democratizing schools across the world to stop killing creativity in children: An Indian perspective', *Counseling Psychology Quarterly*, 18: 1–6. Accessed 7 July 2023. https://doi.org/10.1080/09515070500099728.

Kaufmann, G. 2003. 'What to measure? A new look at the concept of creativity', *Scandinavian Journal of Educational Research*, 47(3): 235–51. Accessed 7 July 2023. https://doi.org/10.1080/00313830308604.

Kaufman, J. C., and Beghetto, R. A. 2009. 'Beyond big and little: The four C model of creativity', *Review of General Psychology*, 13(1): 1–12. Accessed 7 July 2023. https://doi.org/10.1037/a0013688.

Marinoni, G., van't Land, H., and Jensen, T. 2020. *The Impact of COVID-19 on Higher Education Around the World*. Paris: International Association of Universities. Accessed 7 July 2023. https://www.iau-aiu.net/IMG/pdf/iau_covid19_and_he_survey_report_final_may_2020.pdf.

Meckes, L., and Carrasco, R. 2010. 'Two decades of SIMCE: An overview of the National assessment system in Chile', *Assessment in Education: Principles, Policy & Practice*, 17: 233–48.

Mumford, M. D. 2003. 'Where have we been, where are we going? Taking stock in creativity research', *Creativity Research Journal*, 15(2–3): 107–20.

National Advisory Committee on Creative and Cultural Education (NACCCE). 1999. *All Our Futures: Creativity, culture and education*. London: DfES.

National Council of Culture and Arts. 2016. *Acciona: Programme of Art Promotion in Education*. Chile: National Council of Culture and Arts.

OECD. 2021. *Income inequality (indicator)*. Paris: OECD. Accessed 7 July 2023. https://data.oecd.org/inequality/income-inequality.htm.

OECD/Eurostat. 2018. *Oslo Manual 2018: Guidelines for collecting, reporting and using data on innovation* (4th edn). Paris/Luxembourg: OECD/Eurostat.

OECD. 2017. 'The teacher workforce in Chile', *OECD Reviews of School Resources: Chile 2017*. Pairs: OECD. Accessed 7 July 2023. https://doi.org/10.1787/9789264285637-en.

Parkhurst, H. 1999. 'Confusion, lack of consensus and the definition of creativity as a construct', *Journal of Creative Behavior*, 33: 1–21.

Reimers, F., and Schleicher, A. 2020. *A Framework to Guide an Education Response to the COVID-19 Pandemic of 2020*. OECD. Accessed 7 July 2023. http://www.oecd.org/education/.

Schreiber, J. B. 2018. 'Creativity and pre-service teacher education: What you see is what you get', *Global Education Review*, 5(1): 5–19.

Shaheen, R. 2010. 'Creativity and education', *Creative Education*, 1(3): 166–9. Accessed 7 July 2023. https://doi.org/10.4236/ce.2010.13026.

Sternberg, R. J. 2011. 'Creativity'. In *Cognitive Psychology* (6th edn). Belmont CA: Cengage Learning.

Torrance, E. P. 1966. *The Torrance Tests of Creative Thinking – Norms – Technical Manual Research Edition – Verbal Tests, Forms A and B – Figural Tests, Forms A and B*. Princeton NJ: Personnel Press.

United Nations (UN). 2020. *Policy Brief: Education during Covid-19 and beyond*. New York: UN. Accessed 7 July 2023. https://www.un.org/development/desa/dspd/wp-content/uploads/sites/22/2020/08/sg_policy_brief_covid-19_and_education_august_2020.pdf.

United Nations Development Programme (UNDP). 2020. *Human Development Report 2020. The Next Frontier: Human development and the Anthropocene*. New York: UNDP. Accessed 7 July 2023. http://hdr.undp.org/en/content/human-development-report-2020.

Vetter, R., and Helldén, E. 2020. 'Shifting policy and the need for coordination'. In *Digital Education in the EU: Going from knowledge to competence*, European Liberal Forum, edited by E. Helldén. Accessed 7 July 2023. https://liberalforum.eu/publication/digital-education-in-the-eu-going-from-knowledge-to-competence/.

Wallas, G. 1926. *The Art of Thought*. New York: Harcourt Brace.

West-Knights, I. 2017. 'Why are schools in China looking west for lessons in creativity?', *Financial Times*. Accessed 7 July 2023. https://www.ft.com/content/b215c486-e231-11e6-8405-9e5580d6e5fb.

Wilson, A. 2005. *Creativity in Primary Education: Theory and practice (achieving QTS cross-curricular strand)*. Exeter: Learning Matters Ltd.

A response from the perspective of Hong Kong

Denise Wu

I found the contribution from Chile to be interesting and thought-provoking. Several arguments in the chapter resonate with me and my previous experience as a primary school teacher, a university lecturer and now as a doctoral student in Hong Kong.

Like the Chilean educational context, Hong Kong's education system can also be rigid and structured. This is particularly true for local schools in Hong Kong. In my experience, even in primary schools, emphasis is placed on examinations, and there are few opportunities to foster creativity. Moreover, Hong Kong has a reputation for rote learning and excessive drilling, and I found that my experience of teaching at the primary level reflected this. As classes were taught by individual subject teachers, there was little time to stray from the prescribed syllabus. Since there was a limited amount of time, we would see the pupils only on the days that we had lessons with them. Furthermore, to avoid complaints from parents, all the teachers teaching in the same grade needed to teach and use the same materials to ensure fairness and standardisation. Because there was an emphasis on standardisation to avoid complaints from parents, I felt pressured not to deviate from the set materials based on the syllabus and lesson plans. Evidently, there was little room for creativity on my part and pupils were only able to exercise their creativity in minimal ways, such as through their writing, although the topics were again prescribed there.

Furthermore, the chapter also discusses the Chilean standardised tests at the primary and secondary level resulting in more class time dedicated to examinable subjects. In Hong Kong, too, there are high-stakes examinations at the primary level (Territory-wide System Assessment and Internal Assessments) and secondary level (the Hong

Kong Diploma of Secondary Education Examination). While art and STEM classes are offered, preparation for examinations generally dominate class time, meaning that there are fewer opportunities for pupils to foster their creativity and other interests. Especially at the senior secondary level, pupils spend most of their time completing past papers and checking the answers with their teachers. Overall, there is more emphasis on knowledge acquisition for the purpose of academic achievement than there is on fostering creativity. Based on the reading, I feel that there are many aspects of the Chilean context that mirror the situation in Hong Kong.

The chapter proposes several creative approaches in teacher training to prepare pre-service teachers with abilities to incorporate and foster creativity. The chapter mentions creativity subjects, innovation subjects, problem-based educational subjects and ICT subjects. Case studies are frequently used in Chilean universities for student teachers to build their abilities to think from a problem-based education perspective through identifying and developing creative remedies at the school of their practicum. Student teachers are encouraged to investigate and find solutions to issues related to classroom management, learner motivation or the school climate. It would be easy to implement case studies as part of pre-service teacher training for practicums in Hong Kong. In some bachelor of education programmes in Hong Kong, field experience practicums are conducted throughout the five-year programme (Education University of Hong Kong, 2021). In those practicums, student teachers are expected to build an e-portfolio through collecting learning for reflection. The addition of case studies for student teachers to complete a case study within action research would be beneficial for them to incorporate more critically reflective elements to their learning and to apply creative solutions. This would allow for the pre-service teachers to further the reflective process and build on the current practice. This would also be a feasible addition for student teachers since they are already engaged in teaching practicums in their third and fifth year of study.

Moreover, in their final year of study, Hong Kong student teachers continue to develop their e-portfolio by recording their reflections and development under the guidance of their instructors (Education University of Hong Kong, 2021). The school improvement projects that pre-service teachers in Chile need to complete in their final year could be an interesting requirement for Hong Kong schools to adopt. Rather than just acquiring experience in teaching, student teachers would be able to develop and strengthen skills related to innovation strategies that could resolve problems at the schools. However, as the teaching practicum are only for eight weeks, additional time may be necessary for student teachers to complete such a project. Still, this would allow for student teachers to exercise their creative and innovative strategies that would be beneficial for their teaching later. A possible hurdle in the implementation of this project may be the co-operation of the teaching practicum schools, as most schools may be reluctant to adopt real changes based on the student teachers' ideas. The overall projects introduced by the Chilean chapter seem reasonably applicable in the Hong Kong context despite the modifications necessary for programmes and co-operation from the schools.

References

Education University of Hong Kong. 2021. *Bachelor of Education (Honours) (Primary) – General Studies/Mathematics*. Accessed 7 July 2023. https://www.apply.eduhk.hk/ug/programmes/bedpri.

A response from the perspectives of Botswana and Namibia

Rosemary Davis

This is a very interesting chapter concerning Chile and its education context, in particular the issue of creativity. The chapter describes in some detail the economic status of the country and its education system. It is clear that Chile has had a difficult time following the major 8.8 earthquake. I know first-hand what devastation can be caused, as I was in the Philippines in 1991 when it was struck by a 7.6 earthquake – 3,500 people died and, while we were safe, our apartment was badly damaged. Chile has also suffered because of the Covid-19 pandemic and has had its share of social unrest with its population wanting better social justice. Paradoxically, Chile is the victim of its own educational improvement developments. The more educated the population, the better able Chileans are to examine their own conditions for living and to rebel against the shortcomings.

In terms of its education system and the opportunities, or lack of them, for creativity in teacher education, I would suggest that a mind shift is needed. Suggestions for this are in the following section with examples of some possibilities. The case study is a good strategy and has the potential to bring life to the issue of fostering creativity. The conclusions and recommendations are useful and cast light on the overall issue of how to foster creativity.

I suspect that the typical teaching style in schools and universities is almost certainly didactic, with little opportunity for questions and discussion. These would provide opportunities for discussion and potential problem-solving. Chile's teachers and teacher educators are probably repeating their own experiences. They will need help to break the cycle: 'Many ideas which seem to have some importance in the city often lose their relevance when carried on the long and difficult journey to the more remote parts of the country'. This was published in the UNICEF Situation Analysis of Children and Women in Nepal (UNCEF, 1997) and quoted by Davis (1997). It applies to many attempts to assist developing countries such as Botswana and Namibia. These, potentially, provide examples for creative approaches to teaching and learning in schools or universities. Chile has clearly recognised the importance of creativity and has incorporated its principles into teacher education. This is relevant to Botswana, which became independent from the United Kingdom in 1964. Much of the University of Botswana's work was directed towards training secondary school teachers. Like other developing countries, the teaching style was didactic with frequent multiple choice course assessments. To help promote creative thinking, problems were posed for discussion; no easy task with a large group of 150 student teachers. A session drew on Torrance's (1966) tests of creativity, using verbal and non-verbal tasks to assess children's creativity. In one session, learners were asked to write down how many uses they could think of for a paperclip – one suggestion was to clear wax from ears; not a safe idea but, nevertheless, a 'creative' one within Torrance's category of unusual uses.

Chile has also drawn on Torrance (1966) for developing creativity and has incorporated the general principle into its teacher education programmes. The issue is how best to enable creative thinking and problem-solving in teacher education, for which Chile has created the subject area of problem-based education. In Botswana, creative content was provided by using in-service bachelor of education students to collect and analyse data during a research project on comprehension of the English language. These education students were trained to collect, score and analyse data, then record their results. This approach meant that they understood the statistical data (Davis, 1988a). During field work, they encountered a number of issues and their attempts at finding solutions provided content: a practical manifestation of Chile's problem-based education and of Torrance's (1966) understanding of creativity.

A creative technique to help teachers in schools was to offer to teach a game to the pupils. Classrooms often lacked books, so 'reading' was taught by chanting. Simple games such as 'Constantinople' or 'Big Boggle' helped to bring a creative approach to literacy at primary and secondary levels, encouraging understanding and retention. Following workshops with teachers, a teachers' handbook of games and suggestions was produced and distributed to all schools (Davis, 1988b).

This participatory approach was also used in Namibia. Namibia's context was different, having just become independent from South Africa and having experienced the end to apartheid in Namibia. A new constitution was introduced that aimed at democratising the country through its education system. The 10 different education ethnic administrations were replaced with one. The approach was to be learner-centred, participatory and deemed to foster independent thinking, thus providing potential for creativity. The workforce needed to be trained accordingly, which included headteachers, inspectors and chief education officers. In addition to workshops with problem-solving agendas, a manual for headteachers was developed with members from each of the then five regions. This was achieved through a series of workshops where regional representatives brainstormed and developed their drafts. This was a novel experience for the participants who had grown up to be passive and obedient, and who had not known that they had a voice to be heard. On each occasion, I was present but remained in the background for comment if needed. I edited the final drafts, which were collated and produced by the Ministry of Education and Culture with funding from Florida State University where I was contracted to provide training for all primary headteachers in the country. UNICEF also provided funding. The completed manual to support school management was distributed to all schools in the country (Ministry of Education and Culture, 1995).

The technique of participation and involvement in decision-making and tasks is considered transferable to many other situations and is suggested as a useful way forward: a practical demonstration of Chile's problem-based education.

References

Davis, R. 1988a. 'Needs Assessment of English Language Proficiency Project Vol. I and II'. Gaborone: Botswana Ministry of Education.

Davis, R. 1988b. 'Reading with Understanding. Guidelines for Teachers'. Gaborone: University of Botswana.

Davis, R. 1991. 'Reading English with Understanding', Working Paper 58, National Institute of Development Research and Documentation. Gaborone: University of Botswana.

Davis, R. 1997. 'Educating teachers practice and problems for developing countries', Occasional papers. Oxford: Oxford Brookes University School of Education.

Ministry of Education and Culture, Republic of Namibia. 1995. 'Manual for Primary School Principals, with support from UNICEF'. Windhoek: Ministry of Education and Culture.

Torrance, E. P. 1966. *The Torrance Tests of Creative Thinking-Norms-Technical Manual Research Edition-Verbal Tests, Forms A and B- Figural Tests, Forms A and B*. Princeton NJ: Personnel Press.

UNICEF. 1997. *A Situation Analysis of Children and Women in Nepal*, 37. New York: UNICEF.

5

Creativity and critical thinking in online learning: addressing social justice, equity and inclusion in a graduate course in the United States

Karen Ramlackhan

Introduction to the educational context of the United States

The US Department of Education creates policy, implements education laws passed by Congress and oversees and co-ordinates federal assistance to education. Its mission is focused on achievement and on preparing learners for global competitiveness through excellence in education and equal access (US Department of Education, 2018). However, the federal role in education has limitations. The Constitution of the United States is the governing document comprising of basic rights and fundamental laws. Education is not mentioned in the Constitution. Under the 10th Amendment, education is mainly the responsibility of states and local regions that establish schools and universities, develop curricula and determine enrolment and graduation requirements (US Department of Education, 2021). Funding for the elementary and secondary level to serve approximately 18,200 school districts with more than 50 million pupils comes from non-federal sources such as public and private organisations. The Elementary and Secondary Act 1965 includes a federal aid programme providing financial assistance to local education agencies and schools with high percentages of children from low-income families to help children meet state standards. The Higher Education Act 1965 provides assistance for post-secondary education and for college students in need. Both acts have seen numerous reauthorisations to adapt to contemporary times.

One important reauthorisation of the Elementary and Secondary Act occurred in 2001 with the No Child Left Behind Act. The goal was to raise academic achievement through high-stakes standardised testing with particular emphasis on improvements for pupils of colour, pupils from low-income households, English learners and pupils with disabilities. The increased testing and accountability strategies had detrimental consequences, as it narrowed the curriculum, increased test preparation for reading and mathematics, limited non-tested subject areas such as the arts and history (Cook-Harvey *et al.*, 2016), and restricted teacher instructional and pedagogical autonomy. The passage of the Every Student Succeeds Act in 2015 maintained the annual state level high-stakes accountability testing but included equity provisions to ensure that pupils have resources and supports to succeed. Specifically, the Every Student Succeeds Act advances equity for 'America's disadvantaged and high-need students' and 'Requires – for the first time – that all students in America be taught to high academic standards that will prepare them to succeed in college and careers' (US Department of Education, 2017, 1).

The most recent reauthorisation of the Higher Education Act in 2008 included many changes regarding educator preparation. For example, grants are provided to improve teacher education programmes, to increase teacher recruitment and educator diversity, and to train general educators to teach learners with disabilities and those who are English learners (AACTE, 2021). Funding can also be used for leadership development to prepare individuals for professions as superintendents, principals or administrators, to prepare graduate teacher candidates for digital-age learners, and to ensure technology-rich teaching and learning environments (Smole *et al.*, 2008). The US government has no national authority over higher education institutions. Consequently, there is variability in how controlled or independently institutions operate in states. Accreditation, then, becomes important for quality determinations.

Each state creates its own standards and the associated standardised test for learners to be assessed on. The development, implementation and evaluation of tests are state-based leading to great variability among each of the 50 states. Policies, practices and expectations are influenced by political ideologies (Bolotin Joseph, 2011). States have much authority in the responsibility of providing a free public education for all learners, including for learners who are non-English speakers (*Lau v Nichols*,

1974), for learners with disabilities (mandated by federal legislation, the Individuals with Disabilities Education Act) and for learners who are undocumented (as per the court findings of *Plyler v Doe*, 1982). Undocumented learners are persons who reside in a country without legal documentation.

The role of creativity in the United States

In the United States, the educational context of the state-school pupils including the federal, state and local dynamics, impact primary, secondary and post-secondary schooling practices. The Every Student Succeeds Act advances equity in education for all pupils through multiple measures to assess school performance and progress through resource equity, evidence-based and equity-enhancing interventions for school improvement, thereby reflecting twenty-first-century learning that state standards and assessments should measure higher-order thinking skills (Cook-Harvey *et al.*, 2016). The Every Student Succeeds Act allows for states to have more control over academic standards and encourages innovation in state education to move past memorisation and standardisation. Most importantly, it offers opportunity to create accountability strategies that consider differences in learning and assessment. The act's expansion of opportunities for all subject areas opens instructional spaces to include problem-based learning, project-based learning and interdisciplinary learning, which deeply engages learners and provides opportunities for creativity to flourish.

Yet, continual monitoring of academic performance is still a requirement, and it is emphasised for populations such as low-income pupils, English language learners and pupils with disabilities. This process reinforces punitive aspects, as harsh measures and school closures are enforced in the lowest-performing schools, which disproportionally impacts on traditionally marginalised pupils. Currently, there are no widespread national policies or procedures focused specifically on creativity in education, and there is not a requirement to use creativity in teacher education or leadership programme, nor within programme development and implementation. However, best practices for the twenty-first-century learner foster innovative thinking through creativity.

Due to different factors that affect institutions of higher education programmes, teacher and leadership preparation programmes may vary. Some programmes may emphasise creativity in coursework in colleges of education or within other colleges in universities; others may offer spaces to engage creatively in innovative classrooms or technology labs. Often in compulsory education from kindergarten to 12th grade (K-12, ages five to 18), creativity can be found in research, policies and practices for the gifted and talented population (Dai *et al.*, 2011), along with an emphasis on critical thinking and problem-solving. However, this is limiting, as only one grouping of pupils are provided with this type of educational experience. Further, gifted education research has a long-standing issue of underrepresentation of culturally diverse pupils, specifically Black and Hispanic pupils (Ford, 2010), which compounds the issue of who gets access to a curriculum that emphasises critical thinking, problem-solving and creativity. Examples of creativity in K-12 through local district policies are evident and growing, along with efforts to address the issue of underrepresentation.

In pursuit of equitable outcomes

Educational inequity is a growing global challenge recognised by the United Nations and UNESCO. Educational policies must relate directly to the economic and social policies that reduce societal inequality (Sahlberg and Cobbold, 2021). Research indicates that ethnic and class discrimination happen through the same structural arrangements created for the advantaged and affluent (Parsons, 2019), and can result in low educational achievement. The growing global challenge of educational inequity must be addressed alongside economic and social policies to reduce inequality in nation states. To do so, the curriculum, pedagogical tools and assessment designs should be reflective of cultures of minoritised learners and their communities (Sahlberg and Cobbold, 2021) and allow for open-ended ways to represent learning for all pupils.

According to the National Center for Education Statistics, the current trajectory of the pupil population in the US state school system is increasing in relation to race/ethnicity (e.g. Hispanic, Asian or two or more races categorisations), while the teaching workforce is homogenous. Specifically, teachers are 79 per cent white and school principals are 78 per cent white (US Department of Education, NCES, 2020). By contrast, the pupil population is currently 47 per cent white 27 per cent Hispanic; 15 per cent Black; 5 per cent Asian; 4 per cent two or more races; and 1 per cent or less Pacific Islander and American Indian/Alaska native (US Department of Education, NCES, 2020).

Researchers have indicated the effects of the cultural differences between teachers and pupils and suggest ways to address this issue

(Brown-Jeffy and Cooper, 2011; Gay, 2010; Ladson-Billings, 2014). Importantly, there is a critical need to prepare in-service and pre-service educators as well as school leaders to meet the needs of their culturally and linguistically diverse learners (Coady, Harper and DeJong, 2015; Cochran-Smith and Villegas, 2015; Gay, 2010; Gullo and Beachum, 2020; Sleeter and Owuor, 2011). Further, there is a need for educators and leaders to prepare the diverse populations of learners for the complex matters of the global economy. The skills required for these learners and educators involve critical thinking and problem-solving, collaboration and leadership, agility and adaptability, initiative and entrepreneurialism, effective communication, assessing and analysing information, as well as curiosity and imagination (Wagner, 2008). Creativity in education is imperative for students, student teachers, educators and educational leaders to be ready to address the demands of the twenty-first century.

As demonstrated since Stein's 1953 definition and the differing conceptions developed subsequently, creativity is an abstract and multilayered concept (Kleiman, 2008). Creativity has focused on intellectual and individual skills, such as the application of divergent thinking or perceiving a unique problem instead of configuring original solutions (Csikszentmihalyi, 1988). Creativity can also be a reaction to problems and social challenges (Runco, 2004), and creativity can be a collective process (Hargadon and Bechky, 2006). Tanggaard (2013) emphasises creativity in social practice indicating that it is an everyday phenomenon, a constant process of making the world. The relationship between humans and material tools is close in the creativity process and already existent materials, tools, institutions and normative practices are beginning points for new creations. Glăveanu (2013) expressly justified a thorough, systemic contextual and dynamic approach of understanding creativity via the 5A's framework: actor; action; artefact; audience; and affordances. Further along these lines, Glăveanu *et al.* (2019) explored creativity as a sociocultural phenomenon that weaves together dimensions previously studied separately.

For this chapter the following of Glăveanu *et al.*'s (2019) points are significant: that creativity is culturally mediated action; that creative action is, at all times, relational; that creativity is meaningful; that creativity is fundamental for society; that creativity is dynamic in meaning and practice; and that creativity researchers have a social responsibility. The dynamic view of creativity as explained by Walia (2019) below also informs this chapter:

> Creativity is an act arising out of a perception of the environment that acknowledges a certain disequilibrium, resulting in productive activity that challenges patterned thought processes and norms, and gives rise to something new in the form of a physical object or even a mental or an emotional construct. (242)

The current education system in the United States is focused on individualisation, competition in merit and achievement through assessments underpinned by neoliberal ideologies (Ramlackhan, 2019). As a result, high-stakes testing functions to standardise curriculum and teaching, how knowledge is taught, as well as the structure of curricular content knowledge that can disempower and deskill educators (Au, 2011). This has detrimental effects on minoritised pupils. Too often low-income children of colour and ethnic minorities attend schools with the least resources resulting in lower scores, which compounds pressures to perform on these high-stakes tests that focus on test preparation through drills and rote memorisation (Bolotin Joseph, 2011). High-stakes accountability concentrates on specific tested subjects while side-lining others and does not allow for or promote collaborative, creative and critical thinking. Interestingly, though, countries that are the highest achieving in global achievement tests centre their curriculum on critical thinking and problem-solving (Cook-Harvey *et al.*, 2016; Bolotin Joseph, 2011).

The enaction of the Every Student Succeeds Act brings change. Specifically, four areas can be used by educators, researchers and advocates for equitable schooling: higher order skills for all learners; multiple measures to assess school performance and progress; resource equity for underserved learners; and the use of equity strategies and evidence-based interventions (Cook-Harvey *et al.*, 2016). To advance excellence and equitable schooling change it can be helpful to provide opportunities for formal and informal educational leaders to learn with and from each other to solve problems, take on collective leadership responsibility to increase learning outcomes through create collaborative structures with teachers, administrators and other school personnel. For example, teacher leaders' knowledge, skills and capacities may provide perspectives and experiences to improve school reform regarding curriculum, teaching, pedagogy, assessment, overall school culture and organisation. Shared and distributed leadership empowers, builds trust and contributes to learning gains system-wide (Boylan, 2013) and can lead to addressing rigour for the twenty-first-century learner (Wagner, 2008) in innovative and creative ways.

Pedagogy for social justice praxis

As neoliberalism is the orthodoxy in education from elementary schools to higher education, social justice and inclusion can be problematic in educational systems that are dominated by competition, high-stakes standardised accountability measures and market-driven reforms (Bhopal and Shain, 2016). Teacher and school accountability and compliance are connected to pupil performance on state-determined high-stakes assessments that are aligned with state-specific standards. For transformative change and feasible possibilities of improvement for equity and justice to take place, interconnecting the dynamics of creativity, critical thinking and problem-solving is necessary to combat this neoliberal orthodoxy that is the driving force of education policy and practices. More recently, the educational, legislative and political contexts have shifted further. The onset of the global pandemic, along with the killing of George Floyd, which echoed occurrences of previous killings of Black individuals and the racial injustices experienced over the years, compounded the challenges of remote learning, educating culturally and linguistically diverse learners, and maintaining meaningful relationships with families and communities. Locally, the politicisation of Covid-19 precautionary procedures by state officials also created divisions among communities.

Since creativity is an important skill for the twenty-first century and within higher education, Jahnke *et al.* (2015) studied how university teachers conceptualise student creativity. The findings provide a six-facet model whereby higher education teachers see student creativity demonstrated through students' self-reflections, independent decision-making, curiosity, motivation, through the process of producing something, in multi-perspectives, and the students' development of original ideas. This model supports how creativity is seen in this graduate course and specifically in the students' demonstration in their final projects. Creativity is necessary in higher education courses for the development of content knowledge, to hone skills of investigation, co-operation, connection, integration and synthesis, and to use problem-solving as a pedagogy of practice (Livingston, 2010).

To ensure opportunities to make connections between curriculum, pedagogy and culture, I use an autoethnographic approach to explore the ways in which online learning can be employed for graduate students to engage creatively with social justice issues and challenges regarding culturally diverse populations in US schools.

Autoethnography (Ellis *et al.*, 2011) is an interpretive framework to research and writing that examines personal experiences to understand cultural phenomena within the broader social and political context. I connect cultural approaches (Gay, 2010; Ladson-Billings, 2014; Paris, 2012) in combination with Freire's problem-posing approach (2000) to construct the learning and teaching experiences in an online course. I also draw on Freire's (2000) concept of praxis, the reflection and action specific to transforming oppressive structures that impede learning for marginalised and culturally or linguistically diverse learners. Praxis is the active engagement of reflection and action for transformation. Both are constitutive of each other and illustrative that there is no dichotomy between theory and practice (Freire, 2000). In the following, I introspectively explore how my teaching methodology steers the development of culturally affirming learning spaces in the virtual classroom, so that graduate students demonstrate knowledge garnered creatively in a nuanced, critical and reflective manner. Specifically, I share examples of the final project, which is a creative representation assignment that encourages students to demonstrate culminative learning in original ways.

I am a former Pre-K-12 educator (ages four to 18) in one of the 10 largest school districts in the United States (the school district has more than 200,000 pupils). I was a special education teacher in elementary school and a high school algebra teacher in inclusive classrooms. Currently, I teach in a large urban research-intensive university. I am a cis-gender assistant professor of educational leadership and policy studies, and I previously taught on special education undergraduate and graduate programmes. I recognise the shifting nature of identity. As an immigrant woman from the West Indies, I have experienced being othered due to intersectional, socially constructed characterisations related to race/ethnicity, socio-economic status, gender, ability, religion and citizenship. The subjectivity and identities of teacher educators are important because 'who we are in relationship with and how we are seen and heard shapes what we do, and being critically reflexive of this, needs to be at the core of teaching' (Daniels and Varghese, 2020, 61). I would further add that professional identities are influenced by marginalised experiences and identities (Field, 2012) that are shaped by sociopolitical, economic, cultural and historical factors. Therefore, 'identities are forged from overlapping intersecting subjectivities connected to social constructs' (Caraballo, 2019, 1284) and cultural dimensions. I share this information to provide a subjective contextual understanding of my dynamic identity framing that informs my work as a researcher and a teacher in higher education.

Students on this graduate course are twenty-first-century learners who are in educator and leadership preparation programmes to develop and enhance K-12 pupils' learning and educational experiences. Given the demographic makeup and its continued shift, interlacing creativity in problem-solving with a culturally responsive pedagogy and culturally relevant teaching and leading is necessitated (Gay, 2010; Ladson-Billings, 2014). I promote students' critical thinking, I foster deep engagement with theories, extant literature and critical self-reflection as presented in the modules, and I encourage interconnections with their own experiences, histories, cultures, perspectives and values. This enables students' agency in learning and the development of creative possibilities of addressing equity and inclusion issues in their own schools and districts.

Application and representation of creativity for social justice, equity and inclusion

Context of the course

I have taught courses on a teacher education programme for special education and on an educational leadership programme. The specific course of emphasis for this chapter is housed within the educational leadership programme, although students from other educational graduate programmes, such as elementary education, teacher leadership, exceptional student education, curriculum and instruction, and specific subject area focus such as secondary maths and science, can also enrol. The content is focused on the foundations of curriculum development, its implementation and analysis, along with the utility of this knowledge to address the educational needs of diverse populations of children in primary and secondary schools. This course is offered completely online and brings attention to social justice, equity and inclusion for culturally responsive schooling in relation to theories of curriculum construction and application, the dynamic roles and responsibilities of leaders/educators, and the historical and contemporary curricula policies, processes and practices. This course encompasses graduate students from varying cultural and linguistic backgrounds with valuable personal and professional experiences and knowledges to offer.

My teaching methodology consists of using both critical pedagogical and traditional instructional approaches to build and maintain culturally affirming learning spaces. For example, critical pedagogical instructional approaches engage students with challenging curriculum issues in the

US educational system: marginalisation, inclusion and equity. The types of assignment that they complete may include critical analysis of papers, article critiques, online discussion posts that require deeper thinking and application of course content, creative representation assignments that encourage students to demonstrate learning in original ways, and reflexive writing assignments for students to conscientiously focus on leading, teaching and learning theories/practices (i.e. praxis) that impact on diverse learners such as those with disabilities, pupils who are English learners, pupils from low-income communities, pupils of colour and immigrants.

Students learn about culturally sustaining pedagogy and curriculum to become critically conscious social justice-oriented leaders/educators (i.e. administrators, teacher leaders, educators and other school personnel). Further, they garner information about how social justice praxis can be used to create classroom environments that are welcoming and inclusive of all learners, and to embrace culturally relevant techniques and strategies to meet the needs of diverse learner populations (i.e. race/ethnicity, socio-economic status, gender, dis/ability, sexuality, religion, immigrant status and other markers of marginalising differences). They also garner resources that can be used within their own contexts to support leading and teaching for equity and inclusion through culturally responsive pedagogy and culturally relevant methods (Gay, 2010; Ladson-Billings, 2014). To engage in creative means of problem-solving, my students participate in online dialogue regarding the viability of enacting this work. They identify existing barriers or facilitators. And they suggest shifts to be made in their contexts regarding curriculum issues that are tied to high-stakes accountability measures, federal, state and local politics and policies, and funding mechanisms affecting learners from marginalised communities. Thus, students' learning experiences involve critical thinking about complex educational issues and challenges, engagement with multiple perspectives in course readings and content material, and opportunities to critically engage with each other via discussion posts, undertake critical self-reflections through reflective assignments and demonstrate creativity and originality through a final work product.

Approach and application

Using constructivist approaches to learning and understanding about curriculum cultures in schools and educational systems (Bolotin Joseph, 2011) furthers the appreciation that students bring with them multiple perspectives, varied experiences and conditioned values and dispositions, which, in turn, interplay with their construction, understanding and subsequent action.

Mills *et al.*'s (2019) research on social justice dispositions of principals and teachers advances current conceptions of activism. It also considers how individuals' dispositions influence schooling practices with the aim of developing socially just outcomes in advantaged and disadvantaged Australian schools. The researchers suggest that curriculum justice or a counter-hegemonic curriculum is needed, as is an epistemological justice that values the knowledges and experiences of marginalised groups as knowledges of importance and legitimation. Although this study is focused on another country, the findings are relevant and appropriate for the context that I have described earlier. Also, the findings substantiate the learnings and outcomes on my course; specifically, that all students bring their experiential and cultural assets with them to schools. I provide the following examples below as descriptions of demonstrations of creative representations of learning as a final assessment outcome where these students focused on equity, social justice and inclusion. Each student provided permission for use of their assignment as exemplars.

Board game focused on school leadership

One student created a board game with the explanation that:

> it is a fun way to learn about curriculum theories and concepts. Players experience the challenges of being a school leader attempting to effect meaningful transformation through curriculum mapping, identifying challenges, mastery of standards and assessment as players move their student pieces towards graduation.

There is a starting deck of cards that contain traditional, transactional explicit, implicit and null curriculum cards. Then there are levelled cards that are used as the player progresses or moves forward in the game. Each level of cards focuses on different but interrelated aspects to consider when transforming schools to be more equitable. Players are engaged in deliberations and decision-making based on the cards selected and the information provided on the cards. This determines whether players move forward.

The first level includes foundational theories of the US educational system: experientialism; constructivism; behaviourism; and the structure of the disciplines. The next level relates to the underlying concepts of the foundational theories: social constructivism; student-centredness; cognitive complexity; and standards-based instruction. Alternative assessment cards, enrichment cards (enriching curricula for creative endeavours) and innovation cards (challenge and sparks curiosity) are also included. Another level of cards (data analysis, quality instruction, cultural responsiveness and equity) represents the accountability of standardised assessments established through federal regulations. And yet another level includes reflection and enquiry, disrupting assumptions, reconceptualising the curriculum and community involvement to effect meaningful school reform and to critically examine the history of curriculum studies. For example, there is an absence of communities of colour in foundations of curriculum studies so including historical contributions of African Americans, Mexican Americans and other marginalised groups can lead to a reconceptualisation of the school curriculum. Examining biases cards, shared norms and values, shared leadership and trust cards are further ways that may transform cultures of schools. The most powerful cards in the game are the transformational leadership cards focused on empowering teachers to be leaders and the building cultures of trust and empowerment cards.

The directions indicate that cards are drawn and decision-making occurs based on the information on the cards. There are challenge cards, assessment rolls and specialist and standards cards that also adds to the complexity of this game. This game is comprehensive. Once a player has reached graduation, which is the 12th grade, the game ends; the points are added to determine the winner.

Podcast focused on social justice

Another student developed a podcast series consisting of seven episodes. Each episode builds on the previous one and incorporates theoretical information, research literature and practitioner experiences. The episode titles are 'What is Curriculum?', 'Curriculum Theorists and Educational Theories', 'Hidden Curriculum Theorists', 'Standardised Curriculum and Assessment', 'Rethinking Structures and Methods of Instruction', 'Professional Development' and 'Teaching about Racism and Social Justice'. The podcast includes administrators' and teachers' voices. Critical thinking, synthesis and problem-solving are clearly demonstrated. This is a thoughtfully presented and well-organised podcast series by a student who learned about the podcast platform specifically for this assignment. A final comment shared was, 'It was fun! I can't wait to show my students how to create podcasts of their own and I'm already thinking of some additional series ideas!'.

Newspaper focused on civics curriculum for equity and inclusion

Another student created a newspaper with different sections focused on events, general interest and opinion pieces. The issue included articles on the breadth of curriculum, 'what's the point?' and satirical opinion pieces: 'The Need for More White Representation, Technical Article: Traditional and Behaviourist', 'The Impact of High Stakes Testing on the Curriculum', and 'When Should Students Learn Civics, Letter to the Editor: Recommendations for Improving the Curriculum'. In addition, graphics, photographs, highlighted quotes and a comic strip are also included. The student shared this comment:

> I enjoyed having the opportunity to turn this assignment into a newspaper instead of a traditional paper. The format allowed for a more free [*sic*] look at the limitations of the current curriculum, while still integrating research from the course readings and other supplemental research.

For students to determine and develop their creative representations for this final assignment, there were activities, tasks and assignments used throughout the course. Students engaged in critical thinking activities focused on curriculum issues in education and used problem-solving skills to determine challenges and possible solutions. Course modules included readings, videos, online discussions and analysis assignments to think about ways to address curriculum issues in creative ways. Critical reflective assignments allowed students to be deeply self-reflective about their assumptions, experiences and biases (i.e. Freire's notion of critical consciousness). Students used online discussions via their posts and responses to each other to discuss difficult and controversial education topics impacting on their teaching and learning schooling environments. Students were able to build trust in this online community as they appreciated and valued each other's perspectives (even though they may be different from their own) to discuss culturally responsive ways to approach equity and inclusion in schools. Creativity and open-ended thinking were highly encouraged when problem-solving curriculum-related issues. Examples were provided and students were encouraged to bring their unique strengths and abilities in representing their learning throughout this course through a creative representation that they selected based on their own. Much autonomy is provided to students to 'think outside the box' when making the determination about how they will creatively represent the information for this final assignment.

Ultimately, these examples provide instantiations of students' constructions of equity, social justice and inclusion in relation to issues of curriculum within their contexts as practitioners in local schools. The assignment is a critical analysis of curriculum where students shared from their own perspectives, garnered learning from course content and provided an explanation of what curriculum is and how it is understood, explained, constructed, implemented and assessed. They interrogated curriculum through their localised contexts and experiences and provided explanations through insightful synthesis of course content and the extant literature using critical thinking and problem-solving to provide practical solutions. In addition, in this final assignment, the critical analysis was done via creative representations.

Students' assignments fostered critical thinking and problem-solving about curriculum challenges, deeper reflexivity about their assumptions, their actions and dispositions as they engaged with research literature, readings and course content 'to understand how educational inequalities are perpetuated in advanced market-driven democracies' (Mills *et al.*, 2019, 615) in relation to the historical and contemporary US context. Neoliberal approaches to education are a perpetuation of hierarchies and competitive mechanisms where teachers and administrators are entangled in performative pressures that impact on schooling, teaching as a profession of knowledge/skill and autonomy. As Ball (2003) explains about performativity, 'It requires individual practitioners to organize themselves as a response to targets, indicators, and evaluations. To set aside personal beliefs and commitments and live an existence of calculation' (215). As a result of the pressures of policies and practices associated with high-stakes standardised testing, educators may be compelled to teach to the test, which has become common practice under the adage that 'teaching to the test substitutes for deeper intellectual inquiry' (Sleeter, 2008, 148). High-stakes testing narrows the instructional curriculum, increases the amount of instructional time dedicated to tested subjects and promotes the use of pre-packaged scripted curricula that limits teachers' use of their full range of expertise and knowledge (Au, 2011), in development, implementation and assessment of learning activities. Consequently, power and control are diminished from the classroom level and concentrated within hierarchical structures, such as within schools, districts and agencies from administrators and policymakers.

Students on this course contribute by sharing their experiences in these high-stakes accountability schooling environments. They are often educators who grapple with curriculum issues that are interconnected with social issues, such as the quick and unexpected move to remote learning at the onset of the pandemic, and the concurrent social racial unrest happening. Current polarising politics and subsequent development of educational policies (e.g. from the effects of racialised conflicts) create issues related to curriculum content, theories and practices, which lead to restrictions, regulations or bans in schools, districts and states (e.g. aspects of slavery, critical race theory). These measures will have long-lasting impacts on what to teach and how to teach topics and subject matters in state schools. Race issues in education are important to discuss as they shape many of our pupils' and students' lives, as well as the communities they live in. They also shape our own personal lives and practices as educators and leaders. Schools and our broader society are interconnected, so the social issues that are experienced are relevant to educational contexts and complex matters of curriculum. There is a need for culturally responsive pedagogy and culturally relevant practices for leading, teaching and learning in education systems. Culturally sustaining pedagogy is an imperative as it promotes linguistic, literate and cultural pluralism through democratic schooling and as a response to demographic and contemporary social changes (Paris and Alim, 2017).

Critique of the creative approach presented

The approach to creativity (Glăveanu *et al.*, 2019) focused on social justice or equity inclusion work may be challenging. Using creativity towards social justice aims may be very nuanced and particular to the US context, as previously described. The approach has its limitations in research and practice. Depending on views of marginalisation and oppression of particular populations within different communities in other countries, the emphasis on social justice, equity and inclusion on this course may not be important in those other contexts. Some may not agree with approaches to learning with a social justice focus, especially in the current contentious state of politics and subsequent policy generation in the United States that have polarised matters related to culturally responsive practices and culturally relevant teaching in school systems. Within different states there may be limitations that impact what teachers teach. These limitations also affect professors in higher education. Moreover, not everyone is willing or ready to engage with social justice praxis in teacher and leadership preparation programmes as it is tied deeply to broader social inequities and involves self-introspection about own's biases, perspectives, attitudes and how they shape professional actions. However, equity, inclusion and justice can be applicable outside the United States as minoritised populations are part of societies in other countries. It may be beneficial to address issues with their schooling within educational systems in their localities, including performance outcomes, using creativity in critical thinking and problem-solving.

Summary of key elements and recommendations

Aspects shared are grounded in social justice praxis for creativity in higher education teaching contexts. Elements include the following:

- Engage in deep introspection for critical consciousness about oneself (e.g. bias, assumptions) that shape pedagogical choices, instructional approaches, curricula and assessment.
- Use culturally responsive teaching and assessment approaches that allow for meaningful connections to build trust and a respectful classroom community for open discussion about difficult/controversial topics and creativity in approaching issues and solutions in schools.
- Highlight the importance of creativity in critical thinking and problem-solving to improve and transform education for all students (e.g. those who are marginalised by factors such as race/ethnicity, class, gender, dis/ability, sexual orientation, religion, immigrant status, language and other identity markers). Build professional networks and leadership capacity.

In consideration of future directions, the following provides ways to move forward social justice praxis for leading, teaching and learning in educational contexts through creativity. As researchers and educators in higher education, it is important to be self-reflective with regard to what they know, how they come to know what they know, and their critical racial and cultural consciousness (including their perspectives and biases) (Milner, 2007). In preparation of educators and leaders in higher education programmes, the following recommendations may be helpful to incorporate in course curricula, pedagogy and instruction:

- Cultural responsiveness and creativity: Glăveanu *et al.* (2019) explained that creativity is a sociocultural phenomenon. A focus on culturally responsive education where curriculum can be a tool of power to disrupt marginalisation (Gay, 2010) in pedagogy, instruction and content can be embedded and focused within educational leadership and teacher education programmes in university as well as in K-12 school systems. Culturally responsive practices may include building a welcoming classroom community that respects all learners contributions and cultural capital, using various instructional formats such as co-operative learning in small group activities, pedagogical strategies that can allow for open dialogue about different topics, and using students perspectives and interests to meaningfully engage with curriculum content as well as in selecting their method of assessment as a demonstration of their learning. Woodley *et al.* (2017) explain best practices of culturally responsive online teaching that includes validating students' pre-existing knowledge with relevant activities, providing comprehensive and multidimensional learning opportunities, transforming student learning with synchronous online meetings, and empowering students through liberatory leadership opportunities.

- Inclusive processes for achievement: To restructure for equity and inclusive systems, Ladson-Billings (2014) shared three primary focused domains: academic success; cultural competence or the ability to help students appreciate and celebrate their cultures of origin while gaining knowledge of and fluency in at least one other culture; and sociopolitical consciousness. Create professional learning opportunities for leadership and teacher preparation for creativity in problem-solving for equity and inclusive education. School-based collaborations such as with administrators and teacher leaders to influence system change and broaden leadership network and capacity (Boylan, 2013).
- Justice-oriented problem-solving: Creative problem-solving using critical thinking and creativity in theory, research and practice are essential to addressing long-standing issues in education grounded in oppressive structures, policies and institutions (Kleiman, 2008; Walia, 2019). Use professional development and school-wide approaches to develop critical thinking via creativity in problem-solving such as using technology and innovative means to address challenges (Wagner, 2008).

References

American Association of Colleges for Teacher Education (AACTE). 2021. *Higher Education Act*. Accessed 8 July 2023. https://aacte.org/federal-policy-and-legislation/higher-education-act/.

Anzaldúa, G. 1990. *Haciendo Caras/Making Face, Making Soul: Creative and critical perspectives by women of color.* San Francisco CA: Aunt Lute Press.

Au, W. 2011. 'Teaching under the new Taylorism: High-stakes testing and standardization of the 21st century curriculum', *Journal of Curriculum Studies*, 43(1): 25–45.

Ball, S. J. 2003. 'The teacher's soul and the terrors of performativity', *Journal of Educational Policy*, 18(2): 215–28.

Bhopal, K., and Shain, F. 2016. *Neoliberalism and Education: Rearticulating social justice and inclusion*. London: Routledge.

Bolotin Joseph, P. (ed.). 2011. *Cultures of Curriculum*. New York: Routledge.

Boylan, M. 2013. 'Deepening system leadership: Teachers leading from below', *Educational Management Administration & Leadership*, 44(1): 57–72.

Brown-Jeffy, S., and Cooper, J. E. 2011. 'Toward a conceptual framework of culturally responsive pedagogy: An overview of the conceptual and theoretical literature', *Teacher Education Quarterly*, 38(1): 65–84.

Caraballo, L. 2019. 'Being "loud": Identities-in-practice in a figured world of achievement', *American Educational Research Journal*, 56(4): 1281–317.

Clarke, M. 2009. 'The Ethico-politics of teacher identity', *Educational Philosophy and Theory*, 42(2): 185–200.

Coady, M., Harper, C., and De Jong, E. 2015. 'Aiming for equity: Preparing mainstream teachers for inclusion or inclusive classrooms', *TESOL Quarterly*, 50(2): 129.

Cochran-Smith, M., and Villegas, M. A. 2015. 'Framing teacher preparation research: An overview on the field, part 1', *Journal of Teacher Education*, 66(1): 7–20.

Cook-Harvey, C. M., Darling-Hammond, L., Lam, L., Mercer, C., and Roc, M. 2016. *Equity And ESSA: Leveraging educational opportunity through the Every Student Succeeds Act.* Palo Alto CA: Learning Policy Institute.

Csikszentmihalyi, M. 1988. 'Society, culture, and person: A systems view of creativity'. In *The Nature of Creativity: Contemporary psychological perspectives*, edited by R. Sternberg, 325–39. Cambridge: Cambridge University Press.

Dai, D. Y., Swanson, J. A., and Cheng, H. 2011. 'State of research on giftedness and gifted education: A survey of empirical studies published during 1998–2010', *Gifted Child Quarterly*, 55(2): 126–38.

Daniels, J. R., and Varghese, M. 2020. 'Troubling practice: Exploring the relationship between whiteness and practice-based teacher education in considering a raciolinguicized teacher subjectivity', *Educational Researcher*, 49(1): 56–63.

Ellis, C., Adams, T. E., and Bochner, A. P. 2011. 'Autoethnography: An overview', *Forum: Qualitative Social Research*, 12(1): 345–57.

Field, S. 2012. 'The trials of transition, and the impact upon the pedagogy of new teacher educators', *Professional Development in Education*, 38(5): 811–26.

Ford, D. Y. 2010. 'Underrepresentation of culturally different students in gifted education: Reflections about current problems and recommendations for the future', *Multicultural Issues*, 33(3): 31–5.

Freire, P. 2000. *Pedagogy of the Oppressed*. New York: Bloomsbury.

Gay, G. 2010. 'Acting on beliefs in teacher education for cultural diversity', *Journal of Teacher Education*, 61(1–2): 142–52.

Glăveanu, V. P. 2013. 'Rewriting the language of creativity: The Five A's framework', *Review of General Psychology*, 17: 69–81.

Glăveanu, V. P., Hanchett Hanson, M., Baer, J., Barbot, B., Clapp, E. P., Corazza, G. E., Hennessey, B., Kaufman, J. C., Lebuda, I., Lubart, T., Montuori, A., Ness, I. J., Plucker, J., Reiter-Palmon, R., Sierra, Z., Simonton, D. K., Neves-Pereira, M. S., and Sternberg, R. J. 2019. 'Advancing creativity theory and research: A socio-cultural manifesto', *Journal of Creative Behavior*, 54(3): 741–5. Accessed 18 July 2023. https://doi.org/10.1002/jocb.395.

Gullo, G., and Beachum, F. 2020. 'Does implicit bias matter at the administrative level? A study of principal implicit bias and the racial discipline severity gap', *Teachers College Record*, 122(3): 1–28.

Hargadon, A. B., and Bechky, B. A. 2006. 'When collections of creatives become creative collectives: A field study of problem solving at work', *Organization Science*, 17(4): 484–500.

Hempel-Jorgensen, A. 2015. 'Learner agency and social justice: What can creative pedagogy contribute to socially just pedagogies', *Pedagogy, Culture & Society*, 23(4): 531–54.

Izadinia, M. 2014. 'Teacher educators' identity: A review of literature', *European Journal of Teacher Education*, 37(4): 426–41.

Jahnke, I., Haertel, T., and Wildt, J. 2015. 'Teachers' conceptions of student creativity in higher education', *Innovations in Education and Teaching International*, 54(1): 87–95. Accessed 8 July 2023. https://doi.org/10.1080/14703297.2015.1088396.

Kleiman, P. 2008. 'Towards transformation: Conceptions of creativity in higher education', *Innovations in Education and Teaching International*, 45(3): 209–17.

Ladson-Billings, G. 2021. 'Three decades of culturally relevant, responsive, & sustaining pedagogy: What lies ahead?', *The Educational Forum*, 85(4): 351–4.

Livingston, L. 2010. 'Teaching Creativity in Higher Education', *Arts Education Policy Review*, 111(2): 59–62. Accessed 8 July 2023. https://doi.org/10.1080/10632910903455884.

Mills, C., Gale, T., Parker, S., Smith, S., and Cross, R. 2019. 'Activist dispositions for social justice in advantaged and disadvantaged contexts of schooling', *British Journal of Sociology of Education*, 40(5), 614–30. Accessed 8 July 2023. https://doi.org/10.1080/01425692.2019.1582322.

Milner, H. R. 2007. 'Race, culture, and researcher positionality: Working through dangers seen, unseen, and unforeseen', *Educational Researcher*, 36(7): 388–400.

Paris, D. 2012. 'Culturally sustaining pedagogy: A needed change in stance, terminology, and practice', *Educational Researcher*, 41(3): 93–7.

Paris, D., and Alim, H. S. 2017. *Culturally Sustaining Pedagogies: Teaching and learning for justice in a changing world*. New York: Teachers College Press.

Parsons, C. 2019. 'Social justice, race and class in education in England: Competing perspectives', *Cambridge Journal of Education*, 49(3): 309–27. Accessed 8 July 2023. https://doi.org/10.1080/0305764X.2018.1524848.

Peterson, E. R., Rubie-Davis, C., Osborne, D., and Sibley, C. 2016. 'Teachers' explicit expectations and implicit prejudiced attitudes to educational achievement: Relations with student achievement and the ethnic achievement gap', *Learning and Instruction*, 42: 123–40.

Ramlackhan, K. 2019. 'Restricting social justice practices in public education: The neoliberal stronghold'. In *Handbook on Promoting Social Justice in Education*, edited by R. Papa. Cham: Springer.

Runco, M. A. 2004. 'Creativity', *Annual Review of Psychology*, 55: 657–87. Accessed 18 July 2023. https://doi.org/10.1146/annurev.psych.55.090902.141502.

Sahlberg, P., and Cobbold, T. 2021. 'Leadership for equity and adequacy in education', *School Leadership & Management*, 41(9): 1–23. Accessed 8 July 2023. https://doi.org/10.1080/13632434.2021.1926963.

Sleeter, C. 2008. 'Teaching for democracy in an age of corporatocracy', *Teachers College Record*, 110(1): 139–59.

Smole, D. P., Naughton, B. A., Kuenzi, J. J., and Skinner, R. R. 2008. *The Higher Education Opportunity Act: Reauthorization of the Higher Education Act*. CRS Report to Congress. Accessed 8 July 2023. https://crsreports.congress.gov/product/pdf/RL/RL34654/12.

Tanggaard, L. 2013. 'The socio-materiality of creativity', *Culture and Psychology*, 19: 20–32.

US Department of Education. 2017. *Every Student Succeeds Act (ESSA)*. Accessed 8 July 2023. https://www.ed.gov/essa?src=rn.

US Department of Education. 2018. *An Overview of the U.S. Department of Education*. Accessed 8 July 2023. https://www2.ed.gov/about/overview/focus/what.html#whatis.

US Department of Education. 2021. *The Federal Role in Education*. Accessed 8 July 2023. https://www2.ed.gov/about/overview/fed/role.html.

Wagner, T. 2008. 'Rigor redefined', *Educational Leadership*, 66(2): 20–5.

Walia, C. 2019. 'A dynamic definition of creativity', *Creativity Research Journal*, 31(3): 237–47.

Woodley, X., Hernandez, C., Parra, J., and Negash, B. 2017. 'Celebrating difference: Best practices in culturally responsive teaching online', *Tech Trends*, 61: 470–8.

A response from the perspective of the United Kingdom

Áine McAllister

This chapter offers a nuanced overview of the educational context in the United States and the implications of educational policy developments. It offers valuable insights into the tension between policy-driven high-stakes standardised testing and performance measures intended to improve outcomes for minoritised, disadvantaged students and their actual impacts: a narrowing curriculum, widening achievement gaps, increased focus on test preparation, reduced teacher autonomy. Poignantly, the chapter points out that despite policy developments that ought to facilitate creativity to flourish, this is not widely the case in policy, procedure or programme implementation. And where it is the case (in gifted and talented provision), there is an underrepresentation of racially marginalised students. More optimistically though, the chapter also notes moves to address this.

This is an important chapter for any educator concerned with addressing structural inequality, whether through leadership, curriculum, pedagogy or assessment, particularly for those of us concerned with the implications of the phenomenal failure of education when it does not recognise the cultural and linguistic repertoires of racially and culturally minoritised students as valid. Creativity as a culturally mediated and dynamic practice is rightly foregrounded, as is its relationship with critical thinking. Creativity is a critical act in itself (Li Wei, 2011), not just the midwife to critical thinking. This is a notion that I would like to see explored further in culturally responsive and relevant pedagogy. To this end, the field needs to embed intercultural creativity as critical practice. Intercultural creativity recognises ways of knowing beyond those championed by dominant Western culture to offer powerful opportunities for learning, for knowledge production and decolonisation, and to transcend the tyranny of neoliberalism that this chapter correctly calls out as a perpetuator of inequity.

The chapter exemplifies how culturally responsive/relevant and critical pedagogical approaches along with praxis facilitate students to develop understandings and demonstrate learning creatively. Culturally responsive pedagogy is a 'pedagogy which celebrates difference as an asset' (Davis, 2021, 6), and that fosters conditions in which students' identities are valorised and in which injustices are challenged. In culturally responsive pedagogical spaces the teacher, or teacher educator, and the learner, the pre-service and in-service teachers, develop their critical consciousness. Significantly, the chapter emphasises how important it is for the teacher educator, and in turn the teacher, to critically reflect on their own positionality and identity as part of the process. In this way we not only raise our consciousness of our own biases, but we also develop the necessary empathy. This awareness is the foundation for the underpinning ethos of the course set out in this chapter: that the knowledge and experience of minoritised students are assets and that schools and classrooms should affirm this. These assets should be legitimised at policy and leadership level, through curriculum design and in pedagogy, and this chapter offers an illuminating exemplification of how this can be achieved through cultural responsiveness.

Policies and practices associated with testing and punitive performance measures are also relevant to any discussion about educational leadership, curriculum, pedagogy and assessment in the United Kingdom. We also experience policy-driven and neoliberal-ideology-influenced narrowing of the curriculum, teaching to the test and attempts to de-intellectualise the teacher and 'flat pack' pedagogy. All these trends contribute to a significant failure to recognise the funds of knowledge that minoritised and disadvantaged students bring to the classroom.

Culture and language exist as parts of an integral whole (Shaules, 2016). Culture is in language, and language is loaded with culture (Agar, 1994). Given the pervasiveness of standard and racialised language ideologies in the education system in the United Kingdom, or at least in England, it is urgent that teacher education programmes are alive to the importance of culturally responsive/relevant pedagogies such as discussed in this chapter. These ideologies influence pedagogy, curriculum and policy design at school level. They are evident in widespread language policing in schools, where all aspects of students' talk are controlled. This impacts on minoritised learners' sense of identity, delegitimising them in the context of their own education (Cushing, 2021) and it perpetuates the racial and class hierarchies that are the ongoing legacies of British colonialism (Cushing and Snell, 2022). In England, the Department for Education's recent subject content review for modern foreign languages proposes three pillars: phonics, vocabulary and grammar. A case has been made by languages educators (Zhu *et al.*, 2022) in the United Kingdom about the potential value of including culture as a fourth pillar and about the role different forms of creativity play. They discuss considerations pertinent to acknowledging the diverse linguistic and cultural repertoires of learners in the design of curriculum content and languages pedagogy, which is culturally relevant/responsive.

Challenges presented by the neoliberal, recolonial forces shaping pedagogy, curriculum and educational policy design at school level mean that it is incumbent on teacher educators across curriculum areas to offer student teachers a model for creating critical, constructivist and culturally relevant pedagogic spaces. I agree with John Yandell (2014) when he writes that part of the respect that teachers owe to learners is to attend to their lives and cultures beyond the school gates. I would like to suggest that central to culturally responsive/relevant pedagogical approach is dialogue. That dialogue should be informed by the Freirean ideals of care, dignity and consciousness raising (Davis, 2021), espoused in this chapter. It should also be informed by translanguaging principles, which emphasise the importance of cultivating spaces of creativity and of critical exchange (Li Wei, 2018). Translanguaging principles also require that in such spaces, learners full cultural and linguistic repertoires for meaning-making are drawn on and diverse ways of knowing are considered to be legitimate.

References

Agar, M. 1994. *Language Shock: Understanding the culture of conversation*. New York: Perennial.

Cushing, I. 2021. 'Language, discipline and "teaching like a champion"', *British Educational Research Journal*, 47: 23–41. Accessed 8 July 2023. https://doi.org/10.1002/berj.3696.

Cushing, I., and Snell, J. 2022. 'The (white) ears of Ofsted: A raciolinguistic perspective on the listening practices of the schools inspectorate', *Language in Society*, 52(3), 363–86. Accessed 8 July 2023. https://doi.org/10.1017/S0047404522000094.

Davis, C. 2021. 'Sampling poetry, pedagogy, and protest to build methodology: Critical poetic inquiry as culturally relevant method', *Qualitative Inquiry*, 27(1): 114–24. Accessed 8 July 2023. https://doi.org/10.1177/1077800419884978.

Department for Education. 2013. *Languages Programmes of Study: Key Stage 3 National Curriculum in England*. Accessed 8 July 2023. https://assets.publishing.service.gov.uk/government/uploads/system/uploads/attachment_data/file/239083/SECONDARY_national_curriculum_-_Languages.pdf.

Li, Wei. 2011. 'Moment analysis and translanguaging space: Discursive construction of identities by multilingual Chinese youth in Britain', *Journal of Pragmatics*, 43(5): 1222–35.

Li, Wei. 2018. 'Translanguaging as a practical theory of language', *Applied Linguistics*, 39(1): 9–30. Accessed 8 July 2023. https://doi.org/10.1093/applin/amx039.

Shaules, J. 2016. 'The developmental model of linguaculture learning: An integrated approach to language and culture pedagogy', *Juntendo Journal of Global Studies*, 1: 2–17.

Yandell, J. 2014. *The Social Construction of Meaning. Reading Literature in Urban English Classrooms*. London: Routledge.

Zhu, H., Conlon, C., Smith, C., Diamantidaki, F. and McAllister, A. 2022. 'Language teaching and learning beyond vocabulary and grammar, our success stories', *IOE Blog*, 15 March 2022. Accessed 8 July 2023. https://blogs.ucl.ac.uk/ioe/2022/03/15/language-teaching-and-learning-beyond-vocabulary-and-grammar-our-success-stories/.

A response from the perspective of Finland

Anne-Mari Souto, Sirpa Lappalainen and Anna-Maija Niemi

The chapter authored by Karen Ramlackhan addresses creativity and critical thinking in the context of online learning in academia, which during the times of (post)-Covid-19 has turned out to be one of the most burning issues in university pedagogy. As educators in academia, we all struggle with questions of how to sustain our students' enthusiasm and engagement, and how to deal with the power relations in both on-site and online interaction. Moreover, challenging taken-as-granted notions on society can be a cognitively and emotionally charged experience for both teachers and students. These are challenges that become emphasised in online learning where our pedagogical practices as well as students' participation are mediated by digital technology. Therefore, we must seek sensitive ways to facilitate learning of critical thinking.

After reading the chapter, we would like to direct attention and elaborate further on a question of atmosphere within teaching situations and among heterogeneous student groups. In various approaches of critical pedagogy, such as in this particular Freire-inspired chapter, a safe atmosphere is highly emphasised. However, the safe atmosphere is somehow assumed to be created spontaneously. A relatively typical feature of critical pedagogy, including Freire's approach, is that little consideration, perhaps to the point of being ignored, is given to examining the relevance of group dynamics: how social differences and power relations are related to interaction and relations between students. Social differences and power relations related to gender, race, ethnicity, social class and dis/ability are present among university students and student groups, and they have a bearing on how and when each student can and will express their opinions or share their life experiences within the student group. Taking these social differences and relations into account as a basis of the creation of the safe atmosphere is, in our view, also essential in distance learning. This is a perspective that could have been considered more in the chapter. How can we take into account the differences between students in a way that encourages these students to take part equally in interaction and group work, and also to bring out their differences and similarities and discuss these within the pedagogical practices of teacher education?

In Finland and other Nordic countries, the national self-image as a forerunner to equality and democracy obscures the view to social and cultural mechanisms of inclusion and exclusion, including the existence of social differences such as race, ethnicity, gender, social class and disability. Social differences in education have so far been examined critically mainly from a gender perspective, and generations of feminist researchers have, for example, troubled the hegemonic 'worry discourse' on underachievement of boys compared with girls, even though, internationally, Finnish boys have succeeded relatively well at school (e.g. Lahelma, 2014; Pietilä *et al.*, 2021). In addition to other social categories and variation within categories, voices of critical scholars have rarely been heard in teacher education contexts. In the recent critical study of Finnish multicultural education (Hummelstedt, 2022) it has been concluded that Finnish teachers need awareness and critical reflection on norms, power relations and privileges in order to discuss these issues with their pupils at schools. However, not all the teacher education institutions in Finland have included in their curricula even a single obligatory course concerning the topics such as social justice, power relations and culturally responsive pedagogical practices. We claim that this tendency has even been reinforced by a shift in neoliberal, individual-centred education policies to reduce social disparities. Therefore, the US way of discussing and drawing attention to various categories of differences and their connection to vulnerable social position of children and young people in teacher education contexts is exciting. For example, the Black Lives Matter movement raised the issue about the presence of structural racism in Finnish institutions, including education, but the challenges of persons belonging to ethnic or racial minorities are still widely discussed in terms of language learning rather than by looking at social class, poverty or race.

Finland invests in phenomenon-based learning, meaning a holistic pedagogical approach that breaks the subject-based approach, where, for example, STEM-related concepts are studied in STEM lessons only. Instead, arts and crafts can be harnessed for the learning of mathematical concepts. It seems to us that this phenomenon-based learning has many similarities to the pedagogical approach presented in the chapter. The way that the article discusses creativity as one of the key pedagogical and conceptual starting points could strengthen the Finnish discussion as well. Presently, the examination of creativity often falls under other themes, and, for example, the role of art-based methods is actually seen as quite instrumental as a tool for learning something that is considered more relevant, such as concepts related to the 'hard sciences'. Paying attention to the creativity perspective in a way that has been done in the article would certainly reinforce the debate on phenomenon-based learning.

References

Hummelstedt, I. 2022. 'Acknowledging diversity but reproducing the Other: A critical analysis of Finnish multicultural education', *Helsinki Studies in Education*, 138.

Lahelma, E. 2014. 'Troubling discourses on gender and education', *Educational Research*, 56(2): 171–83.

Pietilä, P., Tainio, L., Lappalainen, S., and Lahelma, E. 2021. 'Swearing as a method of antipedagogy in workshops of rap lyrics for "failing boys" in vocational education', *Gender and Education*, 33(4): 420–34.

6

Teaching creativity to future kindergarten teachers in higher education in China

Mengxuan Gao, Jinying Zhou and Ying Zhang

Context: early years education in China

In China, early years education is an important part of foundational education and it is the foundation stage of school education. Early years education has not yet been included in the compulsory education stage but the government is focusing on improving the kindergarten enrolment rate. Kindergarten in China is an institution that provides care and education for children aged three to six years old. Classes are divided into groups by age: three to four years, four to five years and five to six years. Children usually spend three years in the early years settings, and after the age of six they move to primary school.

Throughout history, early years education has had different definitions in China and the educational concept has undergone a transformation from focusing on results to emphasising process (Zhu, 2008). In the 1950s, early childhood education was based on the Soviet Union model and was managed centrally. Kindergarten education paid substantial attention to the acquisition of children's knowledge and skills, as well as to the realisation of the pre-set goals of the curriculum. Typically, this would be children sitting neatly in rows of desks and chairs listening to their teachers. In the early 1980s, with the country's transition from planned economy to market economy, more attention was paid to children's experiences and to the value of a curriculum. The Chinese educator Chen Heqin stressed that kindergartens should give children a full experience and should organise courses focusing on children's natural and social environment (Gang Su, Yunxu Zhuang, 2008). Play-based curricula such as Anji Play became popular (Coffino and Bailey, 2019). With the shift to children learning from play, play is now highly valued in early years education (Meng and He, 2021).

In China, all early years education institutions are required to follow the Learning and Development Guide for children aged three to six. This guide is a practical manual for kindergarten teachers. The manual aims to lay a good quality foundation for children's subsequent learning and lifelong development, and to promote the co-ordinated development of children's physical, intellectual, moral and aesthetic learning as the core. This guidance helps teachers and parents to establish reasonable expectations for the development of young children, to implement scientific care and education, and to let children have a happy and meaningful childhood. The guide describes young children's learning and development in five areas: health, language, society, science and art (Bullough and Palaiologou, 2019).

Teacher education in China

The professional development of kindergarten teachers in China can be divided into pre-service training and in-service training. Most of the student teachers who take the pre-service training in traditional colleges for four years are high school graduates. According to the goal of popularising preschool education, the starting point of pre-service training has been moved forward to junior high school graduates (MoE, 2018). Those who graduate from junior high school must undertake a five-year college education focusing on preschool education before they can work in kindergartens. The Ministry of Education (2018) has stressed the importance of enhancing the quality of the preschool education in teacher colleges. To achieve this goal, teacher colleges are encouraged to innovate the training system and optimise the training curriculum. This chapter focuses on one such creative initiative.

Educational standards regulate training for early years educators. The Professional Standards of Kindergarten Teachers outline the standards of early years educators into three parts (Ministry of Education, 2012). The three dimensions include professional beliefs and ethics, professional knowledge and professional skills, which have been critical for kindergartens to evaluate the quality of teachers. As for the developmental progression of kindergarten teachers, the Shanghai Curriculum and Teaching Material Committee (2008) has announced the guideline Development Manual of Kindergarten Teachers. In this document, kindergarten teachers are categorised into three levels: novice, experienced and expert. The expectations of teachers at different stages vary. For instance, the requirements of novice teachers focus mostly on professional skills such as adapting to the working environment, ensuring children's safety and organising playful activities. By contrast, experienced teachers and expert teachers are expected to display more academic abilities and to incorporate reflective thinking in their daily practice (Shanghai Curriculum and Teaching Material Committee, 2008). These requirements reflect the work on expertise in Western educational contexts (e.g. Eaude, 2012, 2018) as well as the debates about teacher professionalism.

The role of creativity in China

In recent years, there has been a significant shift in focus to competitive scientific and technological progress and innovation. Since the international financial crisis in 2008, countries have adjusted their innovation strategies, continuously improved the policy environment for innovation and increased investment in innovation infrastructure. Thus, creativity education has become an important part of basic education and a general concern for many countries (Wang *et al.*, 2016). As training innovative talents needs to start from preschool age, the national kindergarten education guidelines (Wang *et al.*, 2016) emphasises that preschool education should pay full attention to preschool children's creative activities, so that the children develop a creative spirit from early childhood and may keep it for life. In the guidelines, four important aspects for early years education are stated: a focus on the integrity of children's learning and development; respect for individual differences in children's development; an understanding of young children's learning style and characteristics; and care for children's learning disposition, such as being willing to imagine and create (MoE, 2012). Creativity education is embedded in children's development of five areas – health, language, society, science and art – using play pedagogies (MoE, 2012). Some kindergartens in China have conducted creativity education and made some progress, but on the whole the speed of advancement is still not ideal and children's creativity has not been effectively developed (Wang *et al.*, 2016).

Currently, preschool teachers struggle to cultivate children's creativity for two main reasons: first, teachers attempt to focus more on training children's creative thinking and creative skills and ignore the promotion of children's interests and curiosity; and second, teachers do not know about practical skills and actions to participate in children's creative activities, so when it comes to evaluating children's creativity, teachers tend to pay more attention to results instead of the process (Huilan, Yue, 2003).

In Professional Standards for Kindergarten Teachers (Trial) (2012), one of the professional capabilities is to support and guide children's play activities. Teachers need to encourage children to independently choose play content, partners and materials, and support children to carry out play activities actively and creatively, so that they experience the joy and satisfaction of play. At present, in the university training system for pre-service kindergarten teachers, there is no curriculum aimed specifically at teaching and learning creativity. It is more integrated into the course Kindergarten Curriculum to guide student teachers on how to design curriculum activities. Although not explicitly stated, the purpose of the kindergarten course is to help student teachers to understand the importance of creativity and the role that it plays in the processes of learning and teaching. From the perspective of professional skills, student teachers are required to understand the relationship between creativity and play to become creative teachers in the future, as well as to promote the creative development of children. From the perspective of the position of creativity in the teaching process, student teachers need to learn and understand the concept of creativity to form their own creative thinking.

Teaching creativity in China

'Creativity' is a difficult term to define. Stenhouse (1975) believes that the ultimate goal of education is to promote freedom and creativity. For early years children, play is their primary form of activity, and they need to explore themselves and construct experiences in creative play (Russ, 2003). Kindergarten activities are an evolving continuum from play to teacher-led lessons, in which every educational activity can find its place. Depending on the teacher's own educational value, such an activity may involve more play or more teacher-led content (Helm, 2016). If a teacher wants high-level control over the implementation of the curriculum, the teacher's potential educational tasks and the acquisition of academic knowledge and skills, the curriculum is usually highly structured (Sparkes, 1990). In this teacher-initiated curriculum, teaching goals are specific and depend on children's observable behaviours. The curriculum content is the teaching material, which is regarded as the transmission of knowledge to children. By contrast, low-structured activities focus on process and practice, the natural development of children, and the holistic acquisition of children's general abilities (Helm, 2016). With child-initiated activities goals are generated to reflect the internal requirements of children's growth, the process, as well as the results of problem-solving. Child-led projects can lead to rich learning experiences that build on children's own interests (Woods, 2017). These types of play emphasise the importance of children's personal development and creativity. In low-structured activities, the curriculum content comes from children's learning activities and experiences, and knowledge is learned or acquired by children rather than taught or transmitted by teachers. Children's creativity requires space and support from teachers. However, there are challenges for teacher educators. For example, for both teachers and learners, creativity is a state of mind that is difficult to define and can be reflected in daily classes in various ways (Padget, 2012). Creativity is a kind of ability rather than a specific subject. Creativity must be acquired constantly, learners do not acquire it immediately. Teachers need to provide support for the development of creative abilities. This includes support to foster a creative teaching environment within the teaching process. Within the teacher education process, creativity is applied to the design of teaching activities through independent or group work, which is understood as an application process from theory to practice.

The case study

In China, a 'normal' school is a school created to train high school graduates to be teachers. Its purpose is to establish teaching standards or norms, hence its name. Future teachers must understand the definition of the kindergarten curriculum, distinguish between the high and low structured curricula, and master the principles of activity design. It is on this basis that creative activities can be designed and implemented to support children's development. The specific case in this chapter under the Chinese context is the Kindergarten Curriculum course of Shanghai Normal University Tianhua College.

Kindergarten Curriculum is a compulsory course for student teachers enrolled on the early years education programme. The course closely combines theory and practice, and its teaching aims are as follows:

- Understand the concept, ideas and characteristics and the theoretical basis of kindergarten curriculum.

- Know the general principles, methods and matters needing attention of kindergarten curriculum design and implementation.
- Master popular and influential curriculum plans or models around the world and understand the theoretical basis or guiding ideology behind them.
- Develop the awareness of curriculum research and the ability to analyse and solve problems.

Although these aims do not explicitly refer to the promotion of creativity, the implementation of the course provides for an opportunity to be innovative and to trial a more creative approach. A variety of teaching methods are used in this course. As the most important form, lecture is derived from Kindergarten Curriculum 2nd (Jiaxiong Zhu, 2011). Seminars, case studies, group presentations and self-help learning are all auxiliary teaching methods. Through the study of basic theoretical knowledge student teachers master the general principles and methods of kindergarten curriculum design and implementation to improve their ability to teach. Through the practical operation of kindergarten activity design, the student teachers are expected to improve their abilities in care and education, and to a certain extent enhance their class management and comprehensive education. Part of the course content is designed into project modules and student teachers carry out co-operative learning on projects in groups. Thus, student teachers learn through collaboration in projects and introspection, which cultivates their abilities to communicate and co-operate.

According to the teaching objectives and tasks, teaching contents are divided into five interrelated and progressive processes covering all aspects of the kindergarten curriculum from value to implementation, from theory to practice.

There are 48 credit hours to this course, and it confers three credits. The recommended core text is by Jiaxiong Zhu, published in 2011 by 2nd East China Normal University Press, titled 'Children, Kindergarten Curriculum'. The course follows previous credited modules on early years education, developmental psychology of preschool children, children's play and guidance. A total of three classes, each with 30 student teachers are recruited, resulting in a total of 90 participants who focus on early years education. Data was collected in the form of coursework from the newly introduced participatory activities that were planned to accompany each of the five stages of the programme. In addition, student teachers were interviewed at the end of the programme using a semi-structured interview format. Table 6.1 provides an overview of the data collection and analysis for the study.

Programme part	Aim/purpose	Creative activity	Indicative example	Analysis
Part 1: Form the value of education	To realise that their educational outlook and children's view is the basis of the beginning of the course, value is an important concept and is the premise of all activities.	Students are asked to give five key words of their concepts about children. They interview people in different ages and occupations to discover what they think about the kindergarten curriculum.	Post-it notes Interview responses	Frequency of words/ types of word Thematic after Braun and Clarke (2019)
Part 2: The relationship between play and teaching	How to balance the learning, games and teaching in the kindergarten curriculum after the values are formally entered.	Students look back on the most influential games from their childhood and summarise the characteristics of play.		
Part 3: Kindergarten activities with different levels of structure	Students need to understand the characteristics of kindergarten courses with different levels of structure.	Students design a thematic network map.		

Programme part	Aim/purpose	Creative activity	Indicative example	Analysis
Part 4: Reputable Early Childhood Education programme	To understand influential early years programmes, including Montessori, Bank street, High/Scope, Direct Instruction, Project Approach, Reggio Approach, Heqing Chen educational concept, Xuemen Zhang educational concept, and Anji Play.			
Part 5: Design a creative activity for children	Summarise the semester knowledge, design a kindergarten course under the theme of Chinese traditional culture, and have a sense of creativity.	Lesson plans		
Post-programme: Semi-structured interviews	To assess students' understanding of creativity.	Three compulsory questions are required: What do you think of creativity? How important is creativity to children? How can creativity be reflected in kindergarten activities?		Thematic analysis

Table 6.1 Overview of data collection and analysis

In this case study, each of the five parts of the course were reviewed for opportunities to introduce a more creative and student-centred approach. A range of practical activities were introduced either in place of or alongside existing expectations to shift the course pedagogy from a didactic to a more collaborative and participatory design.

Views on early childhood education

To help student teachers build awareness of the diversity of educational philosophies, they were asked about their views on early childhood education. Their thoughts were captured via Post-it notes.

Throughout teaching practice, the importance of keeping an open mind and refreshing personal views on education was constantly emphasised. As such, the possibility of changing beliefs on education throughout one's career was highlighted (Zhang *et al.*, 2016). In addition to the Post-it note activity, student teachers were also required to conduct interviews to gauge public opinion on what should be included in a kindergarten curriculum. Student teachers were divided into several groups and required to conduct interviews with participants from different working fields. Groups shared their interview transcripts on an online platform so that everyone could read and leave public comments. The interview questions focused mainly on how the kindergarten curriculum is understood. During the process, student teachers were deliberately exposed to diverse perspectives to help broaden their understanding of early years education. This activity created a learning community where everyone could share interview results, express their ideas and learn from each other regarding early childhood education and care. Three main interview questions were posed:

- What do you think kindergarten curriculum is?
- Is taking care of children a part of kindergarten curriculum?
- Should literacy and numeracy be a part of kindergarten curriculum?

Although interviewees come from disciplines other than education, they provide interesting perspectives regarding what kindergarten curriculum should be like from a layperson's perspective. Most of the interviewees connect early years education with daily life experiences.

These two activities enabled student teachers to explore their own interests and insights in a constructive and student-centred manner, rather than the traditional lecture-centred approach that supports the development of a creative learning environment (Darling-Hammond *et al.*, 2005). These were indicative of the more creative approaches to the module coursework that this study introduced, which contrasts with the previous more traditional lecture and exam approach. The next section discusses the findings from the changes to the module in relation to the development of creativity and is organised by programme part.

The analysis of the Post-it activity (Table 6.1) found that the most frequent words included 'health', 'kindness', 'respect', 'creativity', 'curiosity' and 'integrity'. Most of the students valued 'health', which demonstrates that ensuring children's safety and supporting their health development was regarded as the most fundamental goal for early childhood education. This aligns with Maslow's hierarchy of needs (McLeod, 2018) and the basic health and safety requirements one would expect within an early years setting. Moral qualities and social emotional goals such as 'kindness', 'respect' and 'integrity' were also emphasised. This resonates with the Chinese focus on values and moral education (Bullough and Palaiologou, 2019). While importance was attached to learning dispositions such as 'creativity' and 'curiosity', it was to a lesser degree. More unusual contributions included 'romantic', 'resilience' and 'comprehensive'. So, while the initial analysis suggested limited importance attached to creativity, follow-up interviews with student teachers who wrote these words highlighted a greater awareness of aspects of creativity and its wider role in children's development. For example, 'romantic' referred to the ability to perceive beauty in daily life actively and live a sentimental life, which could be understood as aesthetic ability. 'Resilience' was seen as an indispensable quality for children to endure failure, which requires high levels of self-adjustment. And 'comprehensive' showed that educators should help children develop all-around competence, such as literacy, art and social emotion.

In response to the interview questions the extracts below highlight the importance given to children's social-emotional development:

> The core of kindergarten curriculum is to cultivate children's interests and hobbies, as well as develop positive daily habits. (office worker, 50 years old)

> Kindergarten curriculum should teach children love, safety and happiness. (company manager, 46 years old)

> I think kindergarten curriculum is a series of well-organised activities, and these activities should be aligned with characteristics of children's physical and mental development and the social-cultural background. Kindergarten curriculum is strongly connected to children' s day-by-day life and lays a foundation for their development in the future. (student from the Environmental Design Department, 18 years old)

Interview responses also highlight a tension between care and education. Some responses maintain that taking care of children is an important part of kindergarten curriculum, while others refute that and claim it should not be the responsibility of kindergarten teachers:

> Childcare is one of the responsibilities of kindergarten teachers, but it does not belong to kindergarten curriculum. (student from the Landscape Department, 19 years old)

> There is value of life education within childcare. Developing positive attitudes in daily life through childcare will cause long-run effects on children, and this training process can be helpful to increase children's independence and self-confidence. (kindergarten teacher with five years' working experience, 33 years old)

> Childcare should be by responsible nurses rather than kindergarten teachers. Otherwise, it would be a waste of human resources. (doctor, 47 years old)

The activity highlighted how the backgrounds of interviewees may have contributed to their responses with key differences on the positions of those who might be considered as informed and/or experienced in this area.

Finally, the interviews also picked up on a current debate within the Chinese education system and China's recent policy changes to reduce the academic workload on young children through its 'double reduction policy' (July 2021). Most interviewees hold negative attitudes towards this question suggesting that it is not developmentally appropriate considering the undeveloped situation of children's physical and cognitive ability. Yet, there are some maintaining that it is necessary to prepare children in terms of literacy and numeracy for a better performance in primary school education:

> Kindergarten teachers should enlighten children to learn and stimulate children's interests in diverse areas. So, children can be exposed to basic literacy and numeracy. (student from the Computer Science Department, 19 years old)

> Early years education should put more emphasis on cultivating children's creativity and imagination rather than knowledge, so I do not approve teaching literacy or numeracy in kindergarten curriculum. (student from the Biological Sciences Department, 18 years old)

> Definitely no. Literacy and numeracy should not be taught until primary school, because the core goal for children in kindergartens is to master life skills rather than learn theoretical knowledge. (office worker, 26 years old)

Children's games and play

The initial focus on how kindergarten curriculum might be perceived by both student teachers and members of the public provides a helpful baseline and background for introducing more innovative and creative activities. As a result, children's games were introduced alongside the existing lectures. This made links between the student teachers' own personal experiences as children and their role as teachers in learning how to integrate play into teaching through playful games that they had played previously as young children. Student teachers presented games such as 'musical chairs' and 'wolf, wolf, what time is it?'. Musical chairs aims to build children's muscles, cultivate their sense of musical rhythm and improve their responsiveness. Wolf, wolf, what time is it?, by contrast, aims to improve children's responsiveness, physical strength and numeracy skills. Student teachers then identified three words to represent the core characteristics of games:

- 'Meaningful': children can relate the game with real-world experience.
- 'Rule-based': there are always rules when playing games with other children.
- 'Joyful': children can feel joy when playing games, even when they hold serious attitudes towards them.

Such activities help stimulate student teachers' awareness of creativity education and educational philosophy. Creativity normally happens based on previous knowledge rather than appearing from nowhere (Piaget, 1970). Our subsequent data collection highlighted learners' satisfaction and their success in recalling their previous understanding of creativity in education with student teachers scoring above 90 on the content in the final evaluation. This game-based approach contrasted with the theoretical lecture, although the content of the lecture was designed to align the definition of play and the relationship between child-centred play and adult-centred instruction. The lecture presented adult-centred instruction as normally consisting of purposeful and well-planned activities during which teachers exert their educational and cultural influence on children, whereas child-centred play gives autonomy to children and respects the intrinsic potential of children. The two early childhood pedagogies are complementary to each other, and educators should integrate the two patterns in daily classroom practice (Wood, 2010). As argued by Padget (2012), when teachers plan for learning that encourages critical thinking and creativity, teachers themselves are the ones who must think creatively. Harrington (1990) puts forward a 'creative ecosystem' containing several elements which need to be integrated in a creative classroom for teacher education. One of these elements refers to the opportunity for play and exploration. Therefore, play is an essential part of teaching and learning of creativity. The playful activities and lectures in this course aim to inspire student teachers to understand the playful pedagogies in kindergarten classrooms, which are at the core of creativity education. The playful activities lead student teachers to experience what play can bring about and thus gain a deeper understanding of the significance of play in children's development. At the same time, equipping student teachers with theoretical knowledge about play is beneficial to deepen their understanding of play and consolidate their educational beliefs (Hawley and Valli, 1999).

Kindergarten activities with different levels of structure

For student teachers to understand different pedagogical theories with various objectives and content, and to learn basic principles of designing educational activities for children in kindergarten, we introduced three learning stages. First, student teachers were required to read articles relating to teacher-led instructions, guided play and free play. Through this reading, student teachers gained a basic understanding of the roles teachers and children play in different pedagogical outlooks. Then, student teachers attended a lecture to learn to identify characteristics, aims, contents and the organisation of activities with different levels of structure, from low to high (Jiaxiong Zhu, 2011).

After the lecture, student teachers created a thematic network map with ideas of activities for children in groups. Student teachers chose a topic and then generated many sub-themes of activities based on their own knowledge and ideas. After they finished the map, they submitted it on the school online platform to receive feedback from peers. Through this activity, student teachers were able to experience how a thematic activity was conducted and were entitled to their own opinions and thoughts. The peer feedback helped expand thoughts. This echoes a common approach used for thematic planning across education contexts and is linked to original work by Dewey (1974).

There is a tension between teacher control and children's freedom in a child-centred classroom, particularly in the context of traditional Chinese education (Tzuo, 2007). He claims that instead of considering teacher-controlled practice and children's free activities as opposites of each other, they could both exist with high values in the whole process of teaching and learning in the early years. Play, which allows children to have the autonomy and freedom to decide what to do and how to do it, is a crucial aspect to promote children's creative thinking actions (Cheung, 2018). This echoes the notion that creativity is best encouraged in a playful context (Craft 2007; Cremin *et al.*, 2006), where children have opportunities to build their creative thinking, to discover possibilities and to make decisions independently (Siraj-Blatchford *et al.*, 2002). However, it is important to recognise that discourses of creativity are always culture specific. We therefore need to ask ourselves whether our creativity practices are suitable in a specific cultural context (Lau *et al.*, 2004; Lin 2014). This is especially significant in the Chinese context (Weiping, 2004). Free exploration is not always equated with high levels of creative thinking behaviours in the Chinese preschool settings. Instead, higher levels of children's creative thinking behaviours were displayed during teacher-guided methods (Cheung, 2018), which has implications on how methods might be evaluated.

Understanding early childhood education programmes

To help student teachers gain knowledge of global practices in early years education, they were given a list of references for initial independent self-study, which then led to collaborative group class presentations linked to a range of selected pedagogies. The approaches introduced included: High-scope, Montessori, Bank Street, Project Approach, Direct Instruction, Reggio Emilia approach and the Early Years Foundation Stage framework, as well as the Chinese approaches, including Five-Finger Activities by Heqin Chen (Gang Su, Yunxu Zhuang (2008)), Behaviour Curriculum by Xuemen Zhang, and Anji Play. Chen, the prominent Chinese educator, advocated children's activities should be based on five areas: health, society, art, literacy and science, just like the five fingers of a hand that are connected and working together to promote children's growth and development (Su Chun, 2018). In their group presentations student teachers addressed three questions:

- What is the project approach?
- How can the project approach be conducted?
- Why adopt this approach?

Student teachers analysed the limitations of their chosen approach, highlighted the requirement for teachers to have a deep understanding of children's needs and development, and thus identified the high qualifications teachers need to be effective. This approach attempts to encourage student teachers to think creatively and independently, which can enthuse them to explore new things for themselves, to be more open to alternatives and to become more willing to co-operate with others to explore ideas and work beyond lesson time when pursuing an idea or a vision (Padget, 2012). Analysis showed that the student teachers' learning pace, levels of achievement and self-esteem all increased (NACCCE, 1999).

Final project

The final project is also organised into stages. Stage 1 is the independent study of literature, which aims to support student teachers' understanding of creativity, to help connect creativity with the curriculum, to address how creativity is reflected in kindergarten curriculum, and to lay a foundation for student teachers to design their own kindergarten activities. Three reading materials are provided: Vygotsky's (1992) 'Innovation and Creativity'; a systematic review of the literature on creating learning environments in the context of education (Davies, 2013); and a specific case study, 'Creativity in a Hong Kong classroom' (Hui, 2015). This literature informed the development of creative kindergarten activities that are aligned with the traditional Chinese culture, such as the Spring Equinox, Grain Rain, shadow puppet play, brush calligraphy, intangible cultural heritage and traditional Chinese festivals. Working in groups, student teachers are encouraged to critically map the activity along the continuum of high and low structure with a focus on creativity. This process helps foster a collective atmosphere among teacher learners, encouraging them to openly respect others' perspectives of creativity as well as reflect on their own (Johnson and Altland, 2004). The following table provides an example of lesson plans for an activity based on the Chinese New Year.

The following is a students' design on 'Twelve Chinese Zodiac' (Table 6.2).

Theme	Twelve Chinese Zodiac
Age	4–5 years old
Brief introduction to the Chinese zodiac	The Chinese zodiac signs are 12 animals that match the year of birth in China and the 12 territories, including the rat, ox, tiger, rabbit, dragon, snake, horse, sheep, monkey, chicken, dog and pig. As a long-standing folk cultural symbol, there has been left a large number of poems, spring couplets, paintings, calligraphy and folk crafts depicting the image and symbolic meaning of the zodiac. In the folk activities of the Spring Festival, the artistic image of the Chinese zodiac has a unique cultural significance.
Learning objectives	1) Understand the order of the 12 animals in the Chinese zodiac. 2) Understanding the 12 Chinese zodiac is a cycle of 12 years. 3) Be familiar with the Chinese zodiac legend and rouse interest in the zodiac. 4) Get to know parents' and friends' zodiac and enhance the relationship with them. 5) Be aware of Chinese traditional culture and enhance national pride.
Activity plan	

Table 6.2 Lesson plan for Chinese New Year activity

From an overview, detailed five-day activity plans are produced. These focus on language, art, social, science and drama/play. In each day's plan, the learning objectives, preparation and activity process are stated. Various forms of activity and material are used, such as stories, puppet show of the Zodiac, videos, crafts, the 12 zodiac lantern riddles, and so on. Parents are also invited to be involved in some activities, as illustrated in the example in Table 6.3.

Friday drama activity: shadow puppets	
Activity objective	1) Know that shadow puppets are a kind of traditional folk art, simply understand the characteristics and the production process of shadow puppets. 2) Inspire the children's interest in performing shadow puppets. 3) Improve children's understanding of the 12th Chinese zodiac through shadow play. 4) Improve children's hands-on ability, imagination ability, language ability and the development of small muscles.
Activity preparation	Shadow Shadow Turtle and Crane Materials required for making shadow puppets, such as paper, pen, scissors, coloured pens, etc. Teachers need to prepare a shadow puppet in advance Shadow Shadow Process Video Knowledge content of Chinese Zodiac and Shadow Shadow
Activity process	A) Understanding the shadow puppets. Enjoy the shadow puppet play 'The Turtle and the Crane' film. Know shadow puppets, understand the way shadow puppets perform. 1) Show shadow puppets, know shadow puppets and know that the performances with these shadow puppets are called shadow puppets. 2) Learn about the props needed to perform shadow puppets. Observe the shadow puppets, and simply understand the characteristics and the production process of the shadow puppets. Understand the characteristics of shadow puppets: shadow puppets are different, moveable, side expression techniques. B) Understand the production process of shadow puppets. 1) Watch Shadow Shadow Process. 2) Make hands-on shadow puppets.

Activity process (continued)	(1) The teacher provides materials to be placed on the desktop and then helps children group in groups. Teachers simply revisit the process of making shadow puppets. The teacher introduces various kinds of material, determined the theme '12 zodiac', and each group completes two animal shadow puppets. (2) Complete the shadow puppets step by step according to the production method group. Follow painting, colouring, pasting, cutting, etc. Teachers help guide children to complete tasks, slight modification. Each group shows their completed animal shadow puppets and takes photos with their own. C) Performing shadow puppets. 1) Teachers help young children understand various animal habits, living habits and behavioural characteristics. 2) Young children in groups perform their own animal shadow puppets. 3) Teacher sums up reviewing the content of the Chinese zodiac and shadow puppets.
Activity extension	Back at home, perform using the shadow puppets made today with the family. Try to make shadow puppets about the family. Introduce the family to the Chinese zodiac and shadow puppets that you learned today.

Table 6.3 Breakdown of a topic lesson plan into one lesson

To evaluate the introduction of a more creative approach to the teacher training, data was collected through interviews, student evaluations, feedback from teaching staff and a learner mind map activity relating to the student teachers' understanding of creativity.

The final project showed an observable change in student teachers' creativity for the output of the whole course. Student teachers' enhanced understanding of creativity and their willingness to adopt that knowledge in practice was reflected in the interview data. Creativity determines a child's behaviour pattern. It reflects the highest level of the child's comprehensive ability. The resulting works reflect children's thoughts and perspectives. So, it is important to children. This was supported by reflections from the mind map exercise and increased key word associations. For example, student teachers believe that creativity is related to imagination, that there is a positive interaction between creativity and imagination, and that creativity needs to be shown through hands-on skills. The role of the adult was also recognised in a variety of ways. Before children can be creative, teachers must improve the rich material preparation:

> I think a low structured curriculum would be better. If the process and objectives of the curriculum are very specific, then the curriculum does not give children room for creativity. For example, we can prepare a month or two weeks, and during this time, we can start a series of lessons focusing on developing the child's creativity.

Student teachers also considered differences between adults and children suggesting children have no limitations to creativity, so that children's work may reveal more possibilities:

> Adults will add something they already have such as their experience and children will add more of their own thinking. Adults have a fixed way of thinking.

> Children's creativity is a process. Children experience emotional changes during the creative process. For adults, creativity requires adults to produce positive, evolutionary outcomes. Children's experience process; adults have a purpose.

Findings, implications and recommendations

With the original course design the student teachers were required to take internship and apply their learning through the course in kindergartens. However, these internships were cancelled due to the Covid-19 pandemic. This made it more challenging to evaluate effectiveness, as the new approach lacked observation and practice opportunities for student teachers in kindergarten placements. Also, the change in assessment from standard scores to a more creative project-based approach raised the potential issue of confusion with the evaluation of a student teacher's character (Lucas, 2013). The shift to enabling student teachers to design a series of activities as the output of creativity, allowed us to evaluate their creativity ability. Instead of scores creating a recognition of student teachers' creative development, the process assessment meant that learners could show their creative tendencies in a variety of activities.

This seemed to be successful as student teachers received better feedback on their homework after receiving the course and showed improved creativity in the activities they designed for young children.

In this case, different methods are employed, such as individual reading, the final project, group work on learning, the presentations in the Reputable Early Childhood Education Programme, and lectures to the whole class. During different activities, the interactions among peers or between teachers and student teachers draw on both online platforms and the offline classroom. These changes align with growing evidence of the importance of dialogic and synergistic interactivity for enhancing learning during whole-class, group work and individual activity (Kennewell *et al.*, 2008; Laurillard, 2002; Mercer and Littleton, 2007; Wegerif, 2004).

Our own colleagues thought that it was an innovative teaching design and described creativity as an element that could be integrated with any curriculum to help train future teachers. One teacher described creativity this way: 'Creativity is like seasoning in cooking. It can be used in any class and make the class better.' While another teacher said: 'If teachers' creativity awareness is an important factor, once they have such an idea, they will design it into their teaching objectives.' Beyond the data from this case study, colleagues independently reviewed the new syllabus and observed classes. As a result, the creative kindergarten curriculum was recognised and in the new semester, the teachers of the course continue to use this approach. The course is also supported by gatekeepers and the syllabus has been approved by the department.

There are, however, challenges and limitations. One limitation is that the teacher is also the researcher planning the course activities and attempting to provide a rich, creative learning experience for student teachers while addressing the importance of creativity education in lectures. Furthermore, this creative approach is embedded in the learning of kindergarten curriculum and forms of classroom activities. Currently, there is no systematic curriculum guidance on how to develop future teachers' creativity and corresponding methods of assessment. Ultimately, teachers need tools specifically designed to track learners' progress and to determine the process of learners' creative development in an assessment method. The problem is that there is no consensus on what creativity is. In describing this approach, we explicitly identify with the existentialist curriculum. Teachers should consider the needs of learners, not the subject matter. Creativity can be stimulated only when learners choose activities that they really enjoy. According to the existentialist curriculum, the goal of a curriculum is the uniqueness of individual students emphasising individual preferences and choices. The existentialist curriculum emphasises creativity, the creation of personal meaning and self-expression (Null, 2017). Finally, the approach highly relies on teachers' awareness of creativity education and conduction of the course and will be a development point for future work.

In conclusion, this case study documents the shift in practice on a teacher education programme from a traditional didactic pedagogy to a more collaborative and participatory approach underpinned by a focus on creativity as a vehicle for student teachers' learning. These initial results are positive with universal satisfaction from student teachers, tutors and colleagues, and an adoption of the more creative approaches for further cohorts, across the faculty and team. However, a small-scale case study is not generalisable, and further research as well as a more independent review would provide valuable data for addressing some of the concerns, challenges and limitations from this study.

References

Anji Play. *The Principles of Anji Play*. n.d. Accessed 8 July 2023. https://www.anjiplay.com.

Braun, V., and Clarke, V. 2019. 'Reflecting on reflexive thematic analysis', *Qualitative Research in Sport, Exercise and Health*, 11(4): 589–97.

Bullough, L., and Palaiologou, I. 2020. 'Early childhood education in People's Republic of China: A literature review of the publications written in English'. London: UCL IOE, 2020. Accessed 8 July 2023. https://discovery.ucl.ac.uk/id/eprint/10094639/13/Bullough_%20Early%20Childhood%20Education%20in%20People%27s%20Republic%20of%20China_VoR.pdf.

Cheung, R. H. P. 2018. 'Play-based creativity-fostering practices: the effects of different pedagogical approaches on the development of children's creative thinking behaviours in a Chinese preschool classroom', *Pedagogy, Culture & Society*, 26(4): 511–27.

Coffino, J. R., and Bailey, C. 2019. 'The Anji Play ecology of early learning', *Childhood Education*, 95(1): 3–9.

Craft, A. 2007. 'Possibility thinking in the early years and primary classrooms'. In *Creativity: A handbook for teachers*, edited by A. G. Tan, 231–49. Singapore: World Scientific.

Cremin, T., Burnard, P., and Craft, A. 2006. 'Pedagogy and possibility thinking in the early years', *Thinking Skills and Creativity*, 1(2): 108–19.

Darling-Hammond, L., Hammerness, K., Grossman, P., Rust, F., and Shulman, L. 2005. 'The design of teacher education programs'. In *Preparing Teachers for a Changing World: What teachers should learn and be able to do*, edited by L. Darling-Hammond and J. Bransford, 390–441. San Francisco: Jossey.

Davies, D., Jindal-Snape, D., Collier, C., Digby, R., Hay, P., and Howe, A. 2013. 'Creative learning environments in education: A systematic literature review', *Thinking Skills and Creativity*, 8: 80–91.

Dewey, J. 1974. *John Dewey On Education: Selected writings*, edited by R. D. Archambault. Chicago IL: University of Chicago Press.

Eaude, Tony. 2012. *How Do Expert Primary Classteachers Really Work? A critical guide for teachers, headteachers and teacher educators*. St Albans: Critical Publishing.

Eaude, Tony. 2018. *Developing the Expertise of Primary and Elementary Classroom Teachers: Professional learning for a changing world*. London: Bloomsbury.

Gang Su, Yunxu Zhuang. 2008. 'Chen Heqin's educational theory and its modern value', *Modern Education Science (General Education Research)*, 6: 98–100.
Harrington, D. M. 1990. 'The ecology of human creativity: A psychological perspective'. In *Theories of Creativity*, edited by M. A. Runco and R. S. Albert. London: SAGE.
Hawley, W. D., and Valli, L. 1999. 'The essentials of effective professional development'. In *Teaching as the Learning Profession*, edited by L. Darling-Hammond and G. Sykes, 127–50. San Francisco CA: Jossey-Bass.
Helm, J. H., and Katz, L. G. 2016. *Young Investigators: The project approach in the early years*. New York: Teachers College Press.
Hui, A. N., Chow, B. W., Chan, A. Y., Chui, B. H., and Sam, C. T. 2015. 'Creativity in Hong Kong classrooms: Transition from a seriously formal pedagogy to informally playful learning', *Education 3–13*, 43(4): 393–403.
Huilan, Yue. 2003. 'Investigation on the cognition and cultivation of children's creativity – investigation on kindergarten teachers'. Doctoral dissertation, Southwest Normal University, China.
Jiaxiong, Zhu. 2011. *Kindergarten Curriculum 2nd*. Shanghai: East China Normal University Press.
John, P. D. 1991. 'A qualitative study of British student teachers' lesson planning perspectives', *Journal of Education for Teaching*, 71(3): 310–20.
Johnson, C. D., and Altland, V. 2004. 'No teacher left behind: The development of a professional collaboration', *Literacy Teaching and Learning*, 8(2): 63–82.
Kennewell, S., Tanner, H., Jones, S., and Beauchamp, G. 2008. 'Analysing the use of interactive technology to implement interactive teaching', *Journal of Computer Assisted Learning*, 24(1): 61–73.
Lau, S., Hui, A., and Ng, G. 2004. *Creativity: When East meets West*. Singapore: World Scientific.
Laurillard, D. 2002. *Rethinking University Education: A conversational framework for the effective use of learning technologies*. London: Routledge Falmer.
Lin, Y. S. 2014. 'A third space for dialogues on creative pedagogy: Where hybridity becomes possible', *Thinking Skills and Creativity*, 13(1): 43–56.
Lucas, B., Claxton, G., and Spencer, E. 2013. 'Progression in student creativity in school: First steps towards new forms of formative assessments', *OECD Education Working Papers*, 86. Paris: OECD.
McLeod, S. A. 2018. 'Maslow's hierarchy of needs', *Simply Psychology*. Accessed 8 July 2023. https://www.simplypsychology.org/maslow.html.
Meng, W., He, M. 2021. 'Utilisation and design of kindergarten outdoor space and the outdoor activities: A case study of kindergartens in Bergen, Norway and Anji in China'. In *Outdoor Learning and Play. International Perspectives on Early Childhood Education and Development*, vol. 34, edited by L. T. Grindheim, H. V. Sørensen and A. Rekers. Cham: Springer. Accessed 8 July 2023. https://doi.org/10.1007/978-3-030-72595-2_6.
Mercer, N., and Littleton, K. 2007. *Dialogue and The Development of Children's Thinking: A sociocultural approach*. London: Routledge.
Ministry of Education (MoE). 2010. 'Notification on the implementation of the National Primary and Secondary School Teacher Training Program'. Accessed 8 July 2023. http://www.moe.gov.cn/s78/A10/tongzhi/202003/t20200330_436306.html.
Ministry of Education (MoE). 2012. '2019 annual report on pre-school education in China'. Accessed 8 July 2023. http://www.moe.gov.cn/jyb_xwfb/s5147/202002/t20200203_417501.html.
Ministry of Education (MoE). 2012. '3–6 Years Old Children's Learning and Development Guidelines'. Accessed 8 July 2023. http://www.moe.gov.cn/srcsite/A06/s3327/201210/t20121009_143254.html.
Ministry of Education (MoE). 2012. 'Professional standards for kindergarten teachers (trial)'. Accessed 8 July 2023. http://www.moe.gov.cn/srcsite/A10/s6991/201209/t20120913_145603.html.
Ministry of Education (MoE). 2021. *Opinions on Further Reducing the Burden of Homework and Off-Campus Training for Compulsory Education Students*.
National Advisory Committee on Creative and Cultural Education (NACCCE). 1999. *All Our Futures: Creativity, culture and education (The Robinson Report)*. London: HMSO.
Null, W. 2017. *Curriculum from Theory to Practice* (2nd edn). Lanham MD: Rowman & Littlefield.
Padget, Steve. 2012. *Creativity and Critical Thinking*. Abingdon: Routledge.

Piaget, J. 1970. *Science of Education and the Psychology of the Child*. Trans. by D. Coltman. London: Orion.

Russ, S. W. 2003. 'Play and creativity: Developmental issues', *Scandinavian Journal of Educational Research*, 47(3): 291–303.

Siraj-Blatchford, I., Sylva, K., Muttock, S., Gilden, R., and Bell, D. 2002. 'Researching effective pedagogy in the early year', Research Report 356. London: Department of Education and Skills.

Sparkes, A. C. 1990. 'Power, domination and resistance in the process of teacher-initiated innovation', *Research Papers in Education*, 5(2): 153–78.

Stenhouse, L. 1975. *An Introduction to Curriculum Research and Development*. London: Heinemann Educational Publishers.

Su, Chun. 2018. 'Creation of ecological environment in kindergartens in China', *Higher Education of Social Science*, 15–18.

Tzuo, P. W. 2007. 'The tension between teacher control and children's freedom in a child-centred classroom: resolving the practical dilemma through a closer look at the related theories', *Early Childhood Education Journal*, 35(1): 33–9.

Vygotsky, L. 1992. 'Chapter 4: Innovation and creativity', *Developing the Cambridge Learner Attributes*, 11: 53–74.

Wang, Canming, *et al.* 2016. *Pre-school Children's Creativity Development and Education*. Nanjing: Nanjing University Press.

Wegerif, R. 2004. 'The role of educational software as a support for teaching and learning conversations', *Computers & Education*, 43(1–2): 179–91.

Weiping, Hu. 2016. 'Report on creativity research in China, vol. 1'. Xi'an: Shaanxi Normal University Press.

Wood, E. 2010. 'Developing integrated pedagogical approaches to play and learning'. In *Play and Learning in the Early Years from Research to Practice*, edited by P. Broadhead, J. Howard and E. Wood, 19–34. London: SAGE Publications.

Woods, A. (ed.). 2017. *Child-Initiated Play and Learning: Planning for possibilities in the early years*. London: Taylor & Francis.

Zhang, Yan, Hawk, Skyler T., Zhang, Xiaohui, and Zhao, Hongyu. 2016. 'Chinese preservice teachers' professional identity links with education program performance: The roles of task value. Belief and learning motivations', *Frontiers in Psychology*, 7. Accessed 8 July 2023. https://www.frontiersin.org/articles/10.3389/fpsyg.2016.00573.

Zhu, J., and Zhang, J. 2008. 'Contemporary trends and developments in early childhood education in China', *Early Years*, 28(2): 173–82.

A response from the perspective of Finland

Anne-Mari Souto, Sirpa Lappalainen and Anna-Maija Niemi

The chapter authored by our Chinese colleagues introduced a case study examining how creativity is taught to future kindergarten teachers in the study unit titled Kindergarten Curriculum. The chapter provides a comprehensive overview of the recent developments in Chinese state-centred early childhood education and training. For us, the chapter highlighted how global trends and country specific features are blended in national education institutions to form a particular kind of compound, which is in line with political atmosphere and value base of the state.

The authors point out the problem in defining creativity. After reading this chapter it seems to us that creativity is a relational concept by its origin, and it gets its content and meaning in a local context. It would be interesting to know more about how creativity is understood in this country-specific context, and what is seen as creative in this specific pedagogical approach that was introduced in the chapter. Creativity in China seems to be associated with aesthetic or art education, but also with so-called child-centred pedagogy, which is strongly emphasised in many parts of the world, from the Nordic countries to Australia, and with a participatory approach, in which pupils' or students' agency is considered in all earnest.

In the chapter's conclusion, the authors point out that the case study documents the shift in practice on a teacher education programme from a traditional didactic pedagogy to a more collaborative and participatory approach. But what is the 'traditional didactic pedagogy'? For example, in the Nordic context the concept of 'didactics' does not necessarily include authoritative connotations, which we assume to be included in the definition of 'traditional didactic pedagogy'.

After reading the chapter, we started discussing the difference and connections between the concepts of belonging/participation and creativity. We assume that in Finnish educational contexts, creativity in learning is often discussed in terms of belonging and participation; and engaging children in learning processes. The importance of play in itself is also strongly emphasised in Finnish early childhood education contexts.

The authors raised the question of whether it is the learning results or the learning processes that should receive the greatest attention and be valued more as an educational goal. In Finland, the practices of self-assessment are already embedded in the national curriculum and in teachers' pedagogical practices. Although these practices emphasise the importance of learning processes, from the critical perspective, the objective of teaching self-assessment to children can be seen as an objective of shaping children to become self-evaluative, continuously self-developing, lifelong learning individuals, thus active and productive contributors to the future's labour market.

A response from the perspective of the United States

Maria Gross

When I first began reading this chapter, I immediately thought of our Asian 'daughter' (i.e. youth exchange student). She arrived in the United States as a top student in her school, had studied English since elementary school, and yet she did not speak English. She could read English at a college level and wrote English better than her US high school peers. When asked why, she responded, 'no practice' and 'not perfect'. As we encouraged her through dinner conversations, she began to practise creating her verbal sentences and then full dialogues. Ultimately, she explained more fully that she was taught by repeating after the teacher. Students did not create their own dialogue in her English classes. She was not encouraged or required to be creative in her education.

Our three-year-old son was asked to leave preschool after his first day because he would not sit quietly and recite the colours. When I spoke to the preschool teacher about how play was included in her instruction strategies, she replied, 'we do not play, we learn'. I was shocked and decided that I could teach the colours using play and weekly colour themes (e.g. yellow = bananas, sun, lemons) and we would have fun learning. Our son, now a data engineer, and our Japanese 'daughter', now a physician, both benefited from creativity integrated in their life and education.

This chapter explores the importance and application of creative play in early years education in China. The critical statement, 'creativity . . . could be integrated with any curriculum to help train future teachers', resonated with me. The activities demonstrate how lesson planning could be creative and fun for all teacher candidates. In our introductory lesson planning course for future elementary, secondary and educational specialist teachers, I often hear that lesson planning is tedious. Our teacher candidates fill out a lesson plan template, starting with the standards and objectives. The creativity lives in the activities. However, teacher candidates are not taught how to be creative. We ask them to explore what others have done, consider how they were taught and discuss ideas with peers. We do not purposely instruct how to incorporate play and creativity into the lessons. The thematic network mapping process described in this chapter would guide teacher candidates to collaboratively explore various activities related to the standard and objective. I plan to move from the linear template completion model to this more creative mapping activity. Teacher candidates will be encouraged to think outside the traditional activities and explore more creative and fun activities to better engage their learners.

In 2010, the United States began implementing the Common Core State Standards (CCSSI, 2022). While the standards do not explicitly include creativity in the standards, they stress critical thinking, problem-solving and analytical skills required for life outside the classroom. US teachers and teacher candidates create lessons based on these standards. California has deemed creative thinking important and includes it in its Teaching Performance Expectations, the standards for teacher candidates. Teaching Performance Expectations 1.5 states that teacher candidates must: 'promote students' critical and creative thinking and analysis through activities that provide opportunities for inquiry, problem solving, responding to and framing meaningful questions, and reflection' (CTC, 2016, p. 5). Further, the Application of the Content states that teachers are to 'engage learners in critical thinking, creativity, and collaborative problem solving related to authentic local and global issues' (InTASC, 2013, p. 8) as part of teachers' cross-disciplinary skills.

Purposely organising creativity and play into a pupils' education is critical to teacher candidate development in the United States. This chapter demonstrates how creativity could be incorporated into a teacher education programme in China as well as in the United States or other countries. The concepts discussed in this chapter are directly transferable to US teacher education programmes. A reflection on influential games from teacher candidates' childhoods links personal experiences with teaching. Articles with differing pedagogical models are read to construct teacher and learner roles during the instruction strategies. The thematic network map activity guides teacher candidates to think creatively as they discuss ideas for group activities. Candidates expand on their peers' ideas to develop a content-specific list of activities. Working together through this precise process permits teacher candidates to be creative, learn from each other and conduct research.

This process could be used to develop a list of activities for a classroom with unique identities. Culturally relevant activities could be developed through teacher candidate sharing of their own cultural play activities, researching play for their learners' cultural identities in their student teaching classroom, sharing and synthesising themes and sub-themes of activities, and individually lesson planning for their unique classrooms. Lesson planning can be a collaborative experience focused on a central theme with the goal of increasing creativity in teacher candidates and their pupils. As the chapter states, 'Before children can be creative, teachers need to improve the rich material preparation'. This process is not only applicable for preschool and kindergarten classrooms but also for elementary and secondary classrooms.

References

California Commission on Teacher Credentialing (CTC). 2016. 'California Teaching Performance Expectations'. Accessed 8 July 2023. https://www.ctc.ca.gov/docs/default-source/educator-prep/standards/adopted-tpes-2016.pdf.

Common Core State Standards Initiative (CCSSI). 2022. 'Preparing America's students for success'. Accessed 8 July 2023. http://www.corestandards.org/.

Interstate Teacher Assessment and Support Consortium (InTASC). 2013. 'Model Core Teaching Standards and Learning Progressions for Teachers 1.0'. Accessed 8 July 2023. https://ccsso.org/sites/default/files/2017-12/2013_INTASC_Learning_Progressions_for_Teachers.pdf.

7
Choreographic pedagogies: teaching creatively within dance-teacher education in Aotearoa New Zealand

Sarah Knox

Introduction to the educational context of tertiary dance in Aotearoa New Zealand

In Aotearoa New Zealand, dance is an increasingly valued subject within the school curriculum. Over the past 20 years, since it was introduced as part of the New Zealand Arts Curriculum, there has been substantial and sustained growth in the numbers of pupils choosing to study the subject at secondary school level. It has gained traction as an academically rigorous and legitimate area of study (Snook, Buck and O'Brien, 2014). Dance is considered a distinct way of knowing and being (Melchior, 2011) and dance education is a holistic 'way of understanding oneself and the world around us' (Koff, 2021, 71). The New Zealand Dance Curriculum is a location within which students explore transferable twenty-first-century skills such as collaboration, creativity and communication. Each pupil's culture, background and identity are valued and nurtured through engagement with the curriculum, aiming to provide opportunities for anyone to dance and have access to learning dance literacies (Ministry of Education, 2020).

It is important to note the bicultural context and multicultural society of Aotearoa. The New Zealand curriculum and teacher training are guided by New Zealand's founding document, Te Tiriti o Waitangi/the Treaty of Waitangi. Signed in 1840 as an agreement between Māori Rangatira (chiefs) and British settlers representing the Crown, this agreement governs the relationship and protects the rights of both Māori and Pākehā ('non-Māori'). The New Zealand Curriculum states that the Treaty of Waitangi is one of eight principles for education in New Zealand and specifies that, 'the curriculum acknowledges the principles of the Treaty of Waitangi, and the bicultural foundations of Aotearoa New Zealand. All students have the opportunity to acquire knowledge of te reo Māori me ōna tikanga' (Ministry of Education, 2000b, n.p). Te reo Māori me ōna tikanga means the Māori language and cultural practices. The Arts Curriculum in Aotearoa views dance through the lens of 'He atua, he tipua, he tangata – Dance is a descendant of culture' (Ministry of Education, 2020, n.p.). Learners have opportunities to explore their own and other's cultures, and to engage in mātauranga Māori ('Māori knowledge') and te ao Māori ('Māori worldview') (Ministry of Education, 2020).

In 2000, dance was introduced to the New Zealand primary (years 1–6 (children aged from five to 10 years old)), intermediate (years 7–8 (ages 11–12)) and secondary school (years 9–13 (ages 13–17)) curriculum, as a distinct subject of the Arts in the New Zealand Curriculum alongside drama, music and visual arts. It is possible to study dance in formal schooling, from year 1 through to year 13, as a university entrance subject, and as a specialisation within tertiary education, from diplomas and bachelor degrees through to doctoral study. Of this development, Hong (2002) says that 'Dance has been afforded the status of a conventional school subject and is now, at least in theory, equal to other academic subjects' (49). Secondary schooling in New Zealand sees pupils undertake the National Certificate of Educational Achievement Level 1, 2 and 3 qualifications in years 11–13. Within the National Certificate of Educational Achievement, students select subjects, of which dance is an option, to achieve credits. In some cases, the achievement of adequate credits is used to assess eligibility and admission to tertiary education courses.

Aspiring early childhood educators, and primary school teachers, undertake a three-year bachelor of education with specialisation in early childhood, primary teaching or Huarahi Māori. Māori are the indigenous people of Aotearoa New Zealand. Te Reo is the Māori language, one of New Zealand's official languages, alongside English and New Zealand sign language. The Huarahi Māori specialisation allows proficient Te Reo speakers, with knowledge of Te o Māori, which is the Māori worldview, to work in Māori immersion or bilingual Māori/English schools. Alternatively, students may complete a three-year degree in a subject related to the New Zealand Curriculum, followed by a one-year graduate teaching diploma. This is the same pathway required to become a secondary school teacher. Aspiring secondary teachers, within this fourth year of study, must select two subject areas to specialise in. Students wanting to teach dance are required to undertake teaching dance education courses, among other education papers. They also engage in two practicums, shadowing secondary school dance teachers, for 15 weeks through the year. Once employed as teachers, there is a two-year pathway to become a registered teacher in New Zealand.

There are a number of tertiary education providers in Aotearoa that specialise in dance. Predominantly, these are conservatoire style courses where students focus on performance and choreography. Courses with a focus on dance education are few.

Within the realm of recreational education, dance in New Zealand is learned by some 650,000 people each year (DANZ, 2014). In dance studios and community groups, teachers range from having no formal teaching qualifications to having completed degrees and further training in relevant educational or arts fields. While there are various national and international organisations that offer teacher training and student examination pathways for different dance styles in New Zealand (e.g. the Royal Academy of Dance), there is currently no overarching governing body for dance teachers in New Zealand. Essentially, anyone can open a dance studio or teach dance classes. There are a number of dance teachers who teach across both formal schooling and recreational dance training within Aotearoa.

The role of creativity in Aotearoa New Zealand

The New Zealand Curriculum states that one of its key values is 'innovation, inquiry, and curiosity' and pupils will do this 'by thinking critically, creatively, and reflectively' (Ministry of Education, 2015, 10). Further, 'thinking' is listed as a key competency. This is articulated as 'using creative, critical, and metacognitive processes to make sense of information, experiences, and ideas' (Ministry of Education, 2015, 12). However, how creativity might play out within formal education in New Zealand is somewhat unclear. There is research that suggests that creativity has been squashed within schooling in Aotearoa. The Creative Schools Index research project found that:

> the cultural and pedagogical environment of New Zealand schools fail to nurture playful, curious and innovative behaviours in children. Schools fail to help children realise their full human

> capacity through reinforcing environments where creative opportunities are less frequent and almost fade away by the end of compulsory education. (Te Rito Toi, 2020, 7)

This project also found that the lack of creative environments and opportunities impacts on imagination, risk-taking, curiosity and playfulness within learning. A further finding was that creativity is increasingly siloed into domain specific disciplines (Te Rito Toi, 2020).

The New Zealand Arts Curriculum appears to provide some clearer links to creativity as a key twenty-first-century skill (Partnership for 21st Century Skills, 2009). It recognises that pupils may 'pursue careers outside the arts using analytical, creative, co-operative, entrepreneurial, and problem-solving skills that have been enhanced through learning in the arts' (Ministry of Education, 2000a, 9). The aim of the arts curriculum is to develop participation, understandings and literacies including:

- explore and use its elements, conventions, processes, techniques and technologies;
- draw on a variety of sources of motivation to develop ideas and make art works;
- present and respond to art works, developing skills in conveying and interpreting meaning; and
- investigate the discipline and art works in relation to their social and cultural contexts (Ministry of Education, 2000a, 10).

Further to this, the arts curriculum aims to develop the following four strands of achievement:

- developing practical knowledge;
- developing ideas;
- communicating and interpreting; and
- understanding context (Ministry of Education, 2000a, 13).

Within the dance curriculum, where students learn in, about and through dance (Ministry of Education, 2000a), creativity lies in its most obvious and tangible form in the mode of choreography. This takes place within the developing ideas in dance strand and encourages pupils to create their own dances that express ideas, emotions or experiences. They learn about choreographic devices, processes and structures.

Tensions emerging in the teaching of the dance curriculum are that many teachers are not dance specialists. So, within the primary school curriculum generalist teachers may have limited confidence in teaching with dance (Snook, 2012). At secondary level, in some cases dance is taught by drama or physical education teachers who may lack expertise in all or some areas of dance or choreography. In addition, it has been proposed that the curriculum itself can both constrain and liberate creativity (Murphy, 2017). A further creative challenge noted by numerous teachers in informal conversations is the dilemma faced by many pupils who learn dance styles in recreational dance classes and who bring these values of product, physique and technique into the National Certificate of Educational Achievement dance curriculum and can be very challenged by the creative expectations.

Case study of teaching creativity in Aotearoa New Zealand

This case study reflects on my teaching practice, with a focus on teacher education within a first-year choreographic course in a liberal arts, research-led institution in Aotearoa New Zealand. The students are diverse in ethnic and cultural background, as well as dance history, ability and aspiration. Numerous graduates teach in formal education across New Zealand and internationally, as well as in recreational dance studios and community groups. Many build portfolio careers that may include teaching and facilitating dance in myriad contexts simultaneously.

Choreography is generally viewed as an imperative part of a well-rounded dance education (Risner, 2010) and necessary for diverse career pathways. Students work independently and collaboratively to create dance works for performance, and both process and product are assessed. The first-year choreographic course is a foundational programme of study focusing on the creative skills and steps that may be engaged in dance-making. Some students have choreographic experiences through the National Certificate of Educational Achievement Dance, but these can be extremely varied, and others have no choreographic background. Because of this, the course is designed to extend skills, but also to unify the groups' foundational choreographic understandings. Students are encouraged to develop their thinking towards making/teaching choreography in any context, including the professional dance industry, early childhood, primary and secondary schools, recreational dance studios and community groups.

About me

I am a former professional contemporary dancer, and now wear a collection of 'hats': choreographer, teacher, scholar, arts advocate. I began teaching somewhat reluctantly during my performing career when I gained employment with Footnote New Zealand Dance Company, which has an extensive national touring schedule. I presented dance education workshops to primary, intermediate and secondary schools. I do believe that I started out as a terrible teacher, but I quickly learned that my inherited pedagogies (Warburton, 2008), which were likely rather authoritarian, as historically they have been in dance (Lakes, 2005), served neither me nor my pupils. I was never taught to teach, or to teach teaching. Similarly, most choreographers had no focus on leadership or teaching as part of their choreographic education (Knox, 2013), even though these two skills are inherent in the choreographer's role. However, my collection of experiences within dance, choreography and teaching, accumulated over some 20 years, underpin the development of a creative pedagogy within the choreography class.

Methodology

This research engages self-study as a methodological approach to investigating my own teaching practice, within the educational context (Hamilton *et al.*, 2008) of a choreographic course. Self-study has been explained as 'intentional and systematic inquiry into one's own practice' (Dinkelman, 2003, 8) to excavate 'knowledge about practice' (9). Further, it is suggested that the aim of self-study is to improve oneself (Russell, 2002, 4) and to generate new understandings of both teaching and the world (Hamilton, 2004, 204). Within this case study, I ask: What am I doing? How am I doing it? Why am I doing it like that? What are the impacts? What are the possibilities for doing things differently?

In this case, an integrated form of self-interviewing (Keightley *et al.*, 2012) and journalling was used for critical reflection, whereby I provided myself with open-ended interview questions that I then responded to with a journal entry. This was for practical reasons, being a sole researcher, as well as to allow for an organic stop-start reflection process (Keightley *et al.*, 2012). These entries were then mined for deeper content with further questioning and refined for greater clarity. The narratives and critical reflections within this chapter are the products of this interfolding self-interview and journalling process.

What is choreography and how is it creative?

Within diverse Western contemporary dance contexts, dances are made through choreographic processes. Choreography can be defined as organising movement in space and time (Klien, 2007). Typically, the aim is to physically research conceptual themes, 'think[ing] things out not only in words, but also with . . . bodies' (Fournier, 2003, 2).

Creativity has been described as 'the emergence in action of a novel relational product, growing out of the uniqueness of the individual on one hand, and the materials, events, people, or circumstances of his life on the other' (Rogers, 1961, 350). This describes well the creative agency that choreographers and dancers have as active and imaginative collaborators within the dance-making process. Both roles require participants to engage their identities, life history, ideas and relationships to generate possibilities for the choreography. Dancer Lucy Marinkovich affirms this, stating 'the root of anything you create is some form of reflection of yourself and your experiences' (Knox, 2013).

Dance-making is also a complex and inherently social activity (Barbour, 2008) and can, in varying ways, be collaborative (Butterworth, 2004; Knox 2013; Newall and Fortin, 2012). This means that student choreographers (and their dancer peers) are navigating numerous interpersonal and sociocultural moments in relation to hierarchy, power, authority, leadership/followship, voice, agency, inclusion and contribution (Knox, 2013). But, in any creative process involving two or more participants, the relational aspect reveals more about how creativity unfolds. Stevens *et al.* (2000) argue for the 'complex dynamics and interactions among dancers and choreographers in this community of creative minds' (n.p.) to be recognised as a key part of how creativity emerges within collaborators' imaginations and actions. With relevance to this research, it may also be that the relationship between teacher and student impacts on how creativity emerges within the choreographic class.

In reflecting on the infinite creative moments of decision-making, imagination, trial and error, I have come to understand that teaching choreography is in itself a choreographic process. In any class I may be required to research, improvise, invent and refine my practice. And, although I may have a lesson plan prepared, classes are regularly derailed by a single creative question that deserves time and attention.

While there may be distinct or nuanced differences between processes and methods, it is possible that most steps fall into one of eight parts of the dance-making process. Each of these tactics engage myriad modes of creative thinking, problem-solving, decision-making, imagination, testing, experimenting, as well as discussion and collaboration. The following section considers a single choreography class filled with these eight micro-moments of the choreography process reimagined as pedagogical experiences: thematic research; improvisation; movement generation; manipulation of the movement language; structuring; rehearsing; performance; and reflection.

Thematic research

Thematic research commences with the choreographer selecting and researching a series of core ideas to explore:

> We start by exploring small and calm movements, moving with a partner, leaning, pulling, following, manipulating limbs, taking turns. I watch, giving the students space to discover which way wrists bend, how to support knees, how far necks tip back. They laugh when their estimations of weight and force are inaccurate, and they stumble and stagger. Occasionally I interject to adjust a connection for safety and briefly explain why a hand should go over or under a shin, or behind, not in front, of a knee. I am speaking 'off the cuff' in response to what I see, and the dancers never stop moving. I wander around the entire dance studio, weaving between the groups, feeding the class a sporadic commentary of reminders, questions, observations, and provocations.

As part of lesson planning, research does not stop once the class begins. As pedagogy, this feedback process could also be viewed as a choreographic thematic research process, also akin to a qualitative research methodology. Qualitative research aims to explore feelings, experiences and behaviours within a specific context, in this case, the students' experiences of choreographic discovery. Within a choreographic process, research can be ongoing and the material gathered will provide stimulus for the subsequent choreographic tactics. For me, the pedagogical 'research' moment above is rich with information to reflect on and decide the direction for the next steps of the class. As I observe, I garner information about how each individual is engaging with the class content. Information is revealed in the students' body language, facial expressions, as well as their improvised movements. As a 'connoisseur' (Eisner, 1975) of choreographic contemporary dance education and choreography, I can ascertain what and how a student knows or is yet to understand through observation. The nuances of what is not said, or not danced, is just as valuable as what I can see and hear. These encounters with the students also allow me to get to know them better as humans, students, dancers and future teachers.

A qualitative approach offers the potential for multiple themes to emerge (Ryan, 2006); bringing into focus what is important and relevant to the dancers' needs, mirroring what is sought by the research questions and aims, or, in the case of the choreography class, the lesson plan and stage of the choreographic process. The themes reveal themselves as I move around the class, in the way of common issues that the students have in their movement or creative decision-making. I may see, for example, that the class appears to be having trouble with how to position their hands in partnering, getting tangled at the peak of lifts. While each dancer may reveal their knowledge gaps differently, the teaching theme becomes clear. This is extremely useful as, at times, the challenge of teaching choreography is in assuming a place to start. I do not necessarily know what the students know until we begin. Creativity lies in deciding how to respond to both the individuals and the class cohort who may have different needs.

Improvisation

Improvisation is a tool used to explore, in real time, a movement vocabulary, provocation, partner or idea. While improvisation can be a skill in and of itself, typically within a choreographic process the aim is to research movement ideas that may be then formed into set phrases of movement:

> The dancers are working on a group task that requires them to slowly travel whilst supporting one member's movement entirely off the floor. 'Tell me how that felt to you' . . . 'heavy', 'difficult, uncoordinated' 'I don't like it!'. 'How did you hope it might feel?' 'Smooth' 'free as a bird!' 'fun!' 'hard work, but . . . more cohesive?' 'Yes, I think we can try a different way. Liftees, try moving much more slowly. The bigger your shapes are, the more opportunities you'll offer your lifters to support you, and you will also mind more useful ways to hold on' I demonstrate with one leg lifted into the air, slowly turning and stretching my body. The dancers begin again. I observe. It is better, but only a little. I wonder what else I can communicate that might help them. 'Let's pause again', I give them a moment to bring their partners to the floor. I walk to the group closest to me 'can I try with you?' They all stare at me nervously. 'I trust you!' I say and they laugh. I place my hands onto Sophia's

> shoulder and press down offering my bare foot to Thomas. He takes it. I push down, and I'm up. I slowly rotate my body and stretch my arms out in a wide V shape. I am falling in slow motion between Ricki and Athena. They catch me and I swing my right leg around. Someone I can't see catches it and instinctively helps me to complete the spiral, flipping me over, full circle. 'Wow' someone says. 'Pause I say' as I reach a sort of sitting position 'now I'm going to do the opposite feeling of what I just did, ok?' The students nod. I relax my whole body, slowly, so as to not shock them. I begin to move a little more erratically, smaller, faster and then not at all. The students are groaning at me, staggering. I laugh, 'ok, please put me down'.

There are several aspects of this teaching moment that warrant unpicking. First, I had to be careful, because in varying degrees they are all doing exactly what I initially asked them to do. Just not in the way that I had hoped they would. And, therefore, not engaging in the specific learning that I had hoped they would experience. I ask myself, what is it I want them to understand through this task and how can I get them to do that, rather than just doing the task itself? I remind myself that choreographic tasks I set are multipurpose, to 'make' the choreography, but also to *learn* how to make the choreography. There are also numerous practical skills that are hidden within each task; for example, elements of dance technique. So, rather than implying that they have not done it correctly, I try to draw their attention towards the specific way that I would like them to approach the activity. This is important within teacher education, as students are likely to model their own teachers when encountering such moments themselves (Hornbach, 2004).

Second, how a movement task develops in the choreography class is unpredictable. While the lesson plans are prepared, it is impossible to gauge the creative decisions that students will make as they improvise. This forces me to improvise in response, based on 'careful observation and diagnosis of student thinking' (Dezutter, 2012, 31). This filters through my teaching in moments, like the 'research' one above, as well as into my own improvised physical demonstrations. Teaching has previously been theorised as an improvisational practice (Donmoyer, 1983; Kelly *et al.*, 2000; Sawyer, 2004, 2012). Dezutter (2012) proposes that learning to improvise should be an important aspect of teacher education.

Improvising is not just 'doing', but an instinctual (Biasutti, 2013) sensing, feeling, considering, responding. Within the choreographic process we might improvise alone or socially, improvising with or in response to one another. The narrative above assumes the position of the latter two. Improvised teaching may be beneficial in this context due to the nature of choreographic learning; the course content is focused on learning *how* rather than learning *what*. Therefore, there are infinite ways that the class activities can be engaged in; there is never one finite choreographic response.

Regarding teacher education, Sawyer (2004) asserts that novice teachers may be more likely to engage in scripted teaching until they gain the necessary expertise to go 'off-script' and teach creatively. However, pre-service choreography teachers are required to move directly into improvised teaching/facilitation, within their education, and immediately within their first teaching employment opportunity. In support of this dilemma, the choreographic process is filled with numerous skills that are transferable to other contexts, of which improvising is only one. The role of the choreographer is inherently improvisational. While they may have an artistic vision and a plan, how the process unfolds requires swift decision-making and in-the-moment response. As the teacher education students learn to choreograph, they engage in multiple opportunities to practise their leadership, facilitation and teaching.

Movement generation

Movement generation is a collection of methods used to explore and invent a new movement vocabulary for the dance being made. The movement generation stage of the choreographic process may be entwined with improvisation, or it may appear later in the creative process as the needs of the dance emerge (Fournier, 2003; Lavender, 2006). *Tasking* is the most prevalently used method and engages the dancers as co-authors of the work being made. Tasking can include an infinite and diverse range of creative tasks, problems or questions that the choreographer poses to the dancers to solve through movement. Here, the dancer's aim is to transform the idea into 'a visible thought' (Stevens and McKechnie, 2005, 244) through drawing on their own movement tendencies, interests and ideas:

> I scanned the dance studio to see how the students were getting along with their movement invention task . . . Maggie, taking up as much space as possible, limbs flying and jutting, sweat forming a big circle on the back of her t shirt. She catches my eye and grins. Martin, intently repeating the same arm movement over and over and over in the mirror . . . smaller, bigger, faster, incomplete, in reverse. He is riffing, in his own world. Connie, sitting on the floor,

> hunched. Writing? I wander a little closer. Not writing? A few steps closer. Pretending to write? I sit down next to her. I smile. 'How's your movement going Connie? Are you having any challenges?' Connie looks at me 'I can't do this. I don't know what to do'. 'Sure you do! Can you tell me what is difficult today?' 'oh . . . it's just that . . . I'm just not creative!'

Perceptions of creativity pervade the choreographic process and can, at times, be detrimental to the dance being made. In the same way that I performed teaching (terribly) at the start of my career, I can see that the pressure of performing creativity well might hinder students' ability to engage in the task at hand. I wonder if Connie's perceptions about what 'good' creativity looks like in choreography are inhibiting her thought processes to translate ideas into her own movement. I am thinking about how too much freedom can actually cause fear within the creative process. Just like how we might be overwhelmed with choice if we could teach anything at all within our curriculum, Connie may be bombarded with all the possibilities that lie within movement.

> 'Yeah, I've definitely felt like that too, there were times in my performing career when I thought I was a complete creative fraud . . . How about we place some limitations on the task so it seems a bit more manageable?' 'Yeah ok, like what?' 'Well we start by facing away from everyone else!' I scoot around on the floor to sit facing the centre of the room, so that Connie has to swivel to face me and the wall. Now she isn't distracted by all the other students creating their movement phrases. 'Why don't you try pick only two body parts to use, there're too many choices when everything is available right? So, if we narrow it down I think that will help. The other thing that I know really helps me is to remind myself that what I make doesn't have to be any good – in fact it can be terrible – because the next step is to manipulate it, so it can only get more interesting from there!' Connie nods and laughs 'yeah!'

I can see that our students 'task' us through our interactions. Connie's statement, 'I'm just not creative', might actually be a provocation that she wants me to fill with a helpful response. As with choreographic tasking, I am invited to draw on whatever resources I have within myself to reply. I return to Rogers's (1961) suggestion that creativity develops out of one's identity, history and relationships. In this moment, I reflect on my own experiences of not feeling creative and reveal my experiences of trying to work through this to reassure and encourage Connie. It has been suggested that students welcome teachers sharing their personal experiences if they are related to the learning (Proulx, 2009, cited in Bélanger and Lussier, 2011). Further, 'the moments when teachers reveal their classroom practice, the degree of detail with which they allow others to "see" their work, and the aspects of practice they share or avoid sharing shape opportunities for learning' (Levine and Marcus, 2009, 394) within teacher education.

Manipulation

Manipulation processes aim to further develop the phrase material towards the unique world, mood or style of the piece being made. Movements may be complexified, edited, extrapolated or reordered; sometimes with choreographic devices such as repetition and level changes, or have emotional, textual or dynamic information layered onto it. This may take several experiments to find the most appropriate or interesting selection of devices:

> We are exploring layering text over movement and I ask for a volunteer. Erin puts her hand up. We make a circle around her and sit down. 'Ok Erin, I'm going to give you some random instructions . . . let's see what happens if you whisper your text as you do your movement. Find one word to shout loudly . . .' Erin nods and lays down. We can barely hear her as she begins. The atmosphere quickly condenses around us and there are a few murmurs of curiosity. 'You!' Erin exclaims. 'You, you!' She holds her finishing movement and we all exhale. Max says, 'that was awesome!' 'Ok, so that was interesting! Let's try another experiment . . . Erin, can you face the same direction the entire way through, and speak your text as if you are reading the news' Erin starts again. The group watches. Erin finishes. Pause . . . I speak for the group, 'Well that wasn't so interesting, was it?!' 'Yep, big fail!' Jonny tells me. I laugh and everyone agrees enthusiastically. 'Would anyone else like to offer a provocation?' They are avoiding eye contact with me now. 'So, as you can see it doesn't work all the time, my instructions weren't quite right, were they? But if we don't try we won't know what it looks like will we?'

As the choreographer leads the dancers through the dance-making process, they are manipulating the movement towards their preferences. However, the container within which the process takes place is just as malleable. This crafting considers how to best build relationships between the dancers for the creative task, or to transform the energy of the room conductively towards creativity. While I am not enthusiastic about the word 'manipulation', the process of movement manipulation might provide an interesting way to view the role of choreographer/teacher as leader. There are a series of decisions to undertake throughout about what, how, when, whom, how and why. In the case of teaching, it may be the students' attention, energy or discussion that require crafting.

The term 'climate' pertains to the atmosphere or mood of an environment (Morgan, 1997). It has been recognised that creativity is impacted on by the environment within which it transpires (Csikszentmihalyi and Sawyer, 1995). Choreographer and scholar Sarah Foster-Sproull stated 'anything that happens within the dance studio is a part of the work that is being made' (Knox, 2013), and therefore contributes to the creation of climate. Within the teaching and learning moment, we might understand that the teacher is paying careful attention to the climate and how to ensure this is safe, supportive and creative for everyone in the room. While I do believe that students are as responsible for a creative climate just as much as the teacher is, as facilitators we are able to craft the climate towards efficient and enjoyable learning. We can make the room fizz with energy through our use of space, crack tension with jokes or hone focus with the tone of our voice.

The narrative above also unveils a useful approach to dance-making, which I believe might be relevant to learning to teach. The notion of experimentation and the possibility of failure are valuable within dance-making. In this context, 'failure' might be defined as whether choreographic decisions are to the preference of the choreographer. Likewise, within teaching, a playful approach without worry of perfection or needing to know everything can be helpful. The narrative above combines these two points of manipulating the climate of the room and deliberately introducing failure as an option in order to learn more about facilitating the creation of choreography.

Structuring processes

Structuring processes begin once there are several chunks of movement material; the choreographer will begin to organise the dance (Fournier, 2003; Risner, 1992). The work may reveal gaps where new material needs to be created or sections can be repeated and the order may be changed several times. This process requires attention to be paid to questions of what, whom, when and where the parts of the dance take place:

> We are sitting in a circle on the floor surrounded by post it notes. The students have written the name, duration and dynamic of each short chunk of choreography they have created onto a coloured note. We discuss the possible dynamic arc of their works . . . should the choreography start slow and meditative and progress to powerful and energetic? Can it stay monotone in energy the whole way through? What do the micro dynamic shifts in each phrase offer the overarching journey for the dance? The students shuffle their post its around into various orders, taking photographs to document. They layer solo and group sections against each other and move them spatially around stage diagrams in their books. There are infinite possibilities of how their dances could progress, and ultimately, they need to decide what kind of experience they want the audience to have.

Choreography deals with energy, space and time. Attention towards these aspects aims to create a satisfying journey and rhythm for the work. Similarly, the choreographic class requires the same consideration of how to order and divide time to create the same sense of flow, cohesiveness and resolution. In a state of flow, classes can speed up; and in moments of challenge, time can slow down. A choreographer I worked with said, 'dancers can stretch time'. We wrangle with expanding a movement as long as possible, so that it lingers in space even as the next step begins.

I start each class by writing the macro-chunks of our class on the whiteboard, so the students have a 'map' to refer to. As with any piece of choreography, a class has a beginning, an end and multiple moments in between. The structure of the course, of a class and of an activity matters, especially when asking students to be creative, take a risk, work with someone new or share what they have made with the group. We are leading our students towards a revelation, an understanding or an experience. The 'book ends' of the introduction are where I have found rituals and protocols pervade and can really assist the students to dive into their creativity.

When teaching choreography, I am aware of two issues that emerge. The first is when progress slows to the point where it can stop completely. This is often due to students becoming too critical of their work, where every decision made is second-guessed and rejected. This can lead to the problem where they have no choreographic content to discuss, share and learn further from. This affects their choreographic comprehension, creates gaps in their learning journey and at times causes embarrassment within the class. The second issue is when the class works at differing speeds and some students or groups will fly through activities and others will stall. Depending on whether the task is solo or collaborative, and related to the spatial design, is how students might be grouped together. I have learned that these groupings can greatly affect the speed with which the class progresses through each activity. These moments force me to address the activity structure, creating more 'chapters' for some dancers to work with, and deleting some for others. Ensuring that everyone receives the key learning content is key and a challenge.

Creating speed activities where the students are encouraged to work as quickly as possible to make decisions can assist with their learning. My favourite speed task, '54321' forces students to make quick decisions and create choreographic content that can then be utilised. I set a timer for 5 x 1 minute, and feed one instruction to each pocket of time. Minute 1: to improvise and physically 'riff' on the idea; minute 2: to pluck out key movements from memory and place into a rough order; minute 3: to refine the phrase and commit to memory; minute 4: to add choreographic manipulations; minute 5: to rehearse. Minutes 6 and 7 are sometimes added to share and teach to a friend. This process always results in a fantastic sense of accomplishment from the dancers and provides an explicit structure for them to work within for the micro parts of their creative process. These methods become part of the students' own tool boxes for their own choreographic and teaching practices.

Consideration of the spatial design is also a key contribution to the structure of the class. The different ways to extrapolate or condense the students in space to introduce, chat, move, explore, connect or reflect. Like choreography, the formations we create direct attention towards or away from me, or to connect with or disconnect from one another. I can direct this explicitly, as a choreographer would say 'please come to this side of the room', 'make a circle and then change places with someone', 'find someone on the other side of the room with the birthdate closest to you' or 'everyone spread out'. Where I place myself in relation to them can mean that I distinguish myself as a clear leader with the central focus or disperse the focus and work within the group in a much more collaborative and constructivist manner.

Rehearsing and refining

Rehearsing and refining processes include practising and 'running' the work, in smaller sections, and from start to finish of the entire work, to polish the movement (Fournier, 2003). This process involves giving the performers feedback about the choreographic details, consolidating memories, altering certain moments and generally building fitness towards the performance. During this time, the dancers will also begin to create a 'personal artistic journey for themselves . . . This might incorporate the development of emotional content, characterizations and relationships with the other dancers' (Knox, 2013, 43):

> We are 'running' the final big dancing section for our end of semester performance. The dancers are flying and smudge sweat in streaks across the floor. The music is so loud I have to really raise my voice so I can be heard over it. We only finished structuring this section in yesterday's class, so I feed the group reminder about what come next, and directions to assist their spatial formations. There is a high risk of crashing as there are 28 of them, but this is an assessment criterion, so this is intentionally complex. Their ability to be consistent, professional and apply feedback at speed are also assessed as part of the course. This aims to prepare them for situations they may find themselves in within the profession. The music energises the dancers and they exert themselves through their fatigue. The last movement phrase ends . . . 'Hold it! hold it!' Then they explode into laughter, hugs and high fives as the last beat in the music fades away. This process feels familiar to me as both a choreographer and dancer and I am excited seeing the dance come together.

I have taught this first-year choreography course for seven years now. It is a favourite within my teaching portfolio because of the huge development I see the students make. I also truly believe that the choreographic process echoes life, in that there are valuable lessons we can learn about ourselves as humans. There are discoveries to be made about how to *be* with others, as well as the full spectrum of transferable twenty-first-century skills (Partnership for 21st Century Skills, 2009). Every class is an enjoyable adventure, even if the process can be extremely stressful as we progress towards the end of semester performance. Each year is an opportunity to refine the structure and content, and to rehearse how it can be communicated and explored in each class with a new and diverse student cohort. I can view the annual course as a rehearsal for the next year, using what I have learned about myself as a teacher, applying what I have discovered within my own choreographic practice. I look back to the first few years I taught and I realise how much was missing and how much I now want the students to experience. I catch myself using tried and tested vocabulary, phrases and tasks. I am amused when I hear that students from previous years have told the next year's group things that I teach every year, for example 'never will I ever partner someone's knee cap' and 'feel the door' (meaning to wait in improvisation until they feel the gut instinct to move). Other years, the way that I have explained something in the past simply doesn't connect with the current group and I flounder to find a new way, new words, new demonstrations and exploratory tasks.

Performance

Performance is the moment where the work is shown to an audience in its final form. However, performance is not static. The dancers still navigate feedback, memories of the creative process, learning more about their artistic journey in the work and refining these in each performance opportunity:

> I explain the task that the students will do next. Mid way through I begin to make my arm gestures bigger and bigger to emphasise how I hope the dancers will engage in the activity. I make my movements mimic the rhythm of the words I am saying. I flail and flap. It is movement nonsense. The dancers look amused and I see they understand the playfulness of the task. I find a dramatic finishing pose on the floor and hold this as I say 'any questions? Ok, begin . . .' I take a moment to turn the music up as the dancers start the task, and realise I am slightly out of breath. I am excited and feel a buzz in my body. It feels good to move and to remember that this is where I started – dancing is what brought me here.

Teaching has also been viewed as performance (Horning, 1979; Lessinger and Gillis, 1976; Pineau, 1994; Sarason, 1999; Sawyer, 2004; Timpson and Tobin, 1982). Sawyer (2004) proposes that the teaching as performance metaphor identifies teaching skills relevant to communication. He indicates that this metaphor maintains the teacher as the focus rather that the collective learning community of the classroom. Whereas, teaching as improvisation fosters a collaborative approach to learning (Sawyer, 2004). I propose that teaching is more complex than this dichotomy. Perhaps the teacher-focused teaching and performance metaphor, and collective focused teaching as improvisation metaphor might exist alongside one another. It is possible for teachers to flex between these two points on a scale depending on what students might need.

In the past, I was critiqued in a teaching review for deliberately minimising the demonstration element of my teaching practice. I did this to encourage students to find their own ways of inhabiting movement, rather than replicating what my dancing looks like. A peer encouraged me to 'be more aspirational' and suggested that students benefit from seeing expertise in motion. While I do not feel any need to impress my students, there are probably always going to be high expectations about my ability to evidence my professional experience. Like the ideas within the Movement Generation section above, performing in the choreography class might be a moment for students to get to know the idiosyncrasies and personality of their teacher a little better.

In reflecting on my teaching practice, I wonder what it really means to perform teaching, and when is performing simply sharing different parts of yourself. The notion of performing might imply being something different from yourself. There have been numerous classes when I was tired, emotional or frustrated as I walked into the dance studio. This is an important tension to be addressed when discussing students' present and future creative and teaching engagements. There is a pervading issue within the dance industry that dancers should 'leave their problems at the door'. While I understand what this one-liner aims to achieve, the issue that I see is that this might be detrimental to the choreographic process (Knox, 2013). If dance-making and artistry requires dancers to draw from themselves broadly – physically, emotionally, spiritually and intellectually – then 'bracketing' these off may work in opposition to what is useful. Teaching, like artistry, requires emotion, empathy and connection. I wonder how our 'problems' might actually enhance our teaching or choreographic journeys. How can we feel what we feel but also manifest our best energy to do good work? This topic has generated many conversations with my students: how we can shift our energy, how we can hold multiple complex emotions at one time, and how we can let our authentic selves infiltrate our artistic and pedagogical work?

Reflection

Reflection is the final step and may be done formally or informally. Reflection may be on how to improve the performance for the next one, or on learnings of the events of the process or nuances of the product:

> We close the class with discussion. 'Talk to the person next to you about a one way you would do today's class differently if you were teaching it'. Mako tells me about how she would have feed the instructions to our warm up game faster so the group could get moving into the more complex structures more quickly. 'Oh thanks! I didn't realise it was a bit slow for you. I really appreciate hearing that, I'll try doing that next time'. 'What would you do differently,

> Sarah?' It would be easy to turn the question back to Mako to see what other feedback she has for my teaching practice. But I think for a moment 'well I suppose there's always a lot I think I can improve in my teaching . . . and I guess I worry about whether I've done enough, if you all understood everything . . . I also think I probably don't give myself enough credit for what I do well. So actually, thinking about it, the thing I care most about is did you all have a good time in today's class. And today I think we did.'

This case study has promoted reflection of the pedagogical micro-moments within the creative context of dance-making and teacher education. In framing choreographic teacher education as a choreographic process my focus has been drawn to the sheer amount of decision-making, negotiating, sensing, feeling, observing, responding and 'making it up as I go along' I do within my teaching practice.

I review the times in class where I am offered minute moments of reflection. These moments might be in-between conversations, a fleeting facial expression after communicating a task, missing a raised hand, reading body language between two students. Relevant here, again, is the subtext of the room and how whatever happens in the studio becomes part of the choreography (Foster-Sproull, cited in Knox, 2013), or in this case, the learning moment. Russell (2002) notes that 'most teacher educators are acutely aware that their students can read every teaching move we make for an implicit message about how to teach' (3). How I deal with these moments gives these future teachers clues about how they might manage their creative classrooms in the future. The overarching question for me here is what parts of my pedagogy would I be comfortable for these students to inherit? And how can I foster the creation of their own pedagogies?

Critique of the creative approach presented

The choreographic process has provided eight useful pedagogical tactics for creative teacher education: research; improvisation; movement generation; manipulation; structuring; rehearsing; performance; and reflection. This case study has revealed to me much about the ways that I approach choreographic education, and my pedagogical values. I am reminded that authenticity and congruence are two values that underpin everything I do and what I hope to draw out of the students.

Returning to the questions I asked earlier – Why do I teach like that? What are the impacts? How could I do things differently? I see several issues with some of the strategies used. First, as was suggested, students can begin to teach how they have been taught. I do hope that my teaching might positively influence their practice. However, I do not want students to teach creatively just like me. I want them to develop their own creative pedagogies. The reason for this is something that I experienced early in my teaching career. In attempting to teach the way that I thought it should be done, I never felt comfortable teaching and was disconnected from my learners. Once I realised that I could be myself and I aligned my personal identity with my teaching identity, my teaching became enjoyable and connected. The choreographic course is filled with activities for the students to discover who they are as makers, but these tasks could be more explicitly geared towards the teaching aspect of choreography. This may encourage students to join the dots between their choreographic and teaching practices.

A second issue is that my students could perceive that I lack planning. This could be true. However, the course is new to the students but well-rehearsed by me. My approach to improvisation within teaching may lead them to believe that I am making everything up as I go along, but in reality this is underpinned by 20 years of professional experience. This is the potential to translate an ability to 'wing it' into their practice in that they may begin their teaching careers with a lack of preparation and struggle to teach well. This point reminds me to ensure I am exposing the pedagogical thinking as much as possible.

Contemporary dance choreographic processes within Aotearoa New Zealand are not unlike those you may find elsewhere in the world. Expanding these ideas within other dance forms that utilise different kinds of creative process may provide a stepping stone. Furthermore, I am quite sure that there may be elements of the eight choreographic tactics to be found in teaching and teacher education within any other setting. Therefore, the ideas within this case study may be easily applicable to other cultural contexts. Expanding these ideas within other dance forms that utilise different kinds of creative process may offer another stepping stone. Within other arts education contexts (e.g. theatre or music), there may be similarities of creative processes and/or ways to develop the eight choreographic steps found here.

This case study has presented a broad overview of the eight choreographic strategies. It could be of benefit to drill further into each tactic to more deeply understand how these can be articulated and developed. Furthermore, this case study has not ascertained the students' perspective of how this creative pedagogy is experienced, nor has it explored how it might be progressed by a future generation of teachers. A pertinent further area for future study might also be the teacher/student teacher relationship within the choreographic class, from a collaborative and constructivist perspective.

Summary of key elements and recommendations

- Key element 1: Playfulness is essential.
- Key element 2: Everything is an experiment.
- Key element 3: Being together trumps content.
- Recommendation 1: Consider how creativity can pervade the climate of your classroom.
- Recommendation 2: View each teaching and learning moment as an experiment to try something differently. Be bold.
- Recommendation 3: Get to know the humans in your classes. Share yourself with them.

References

Barbour, K. 2008. 'Sustainable dance making: Dancers and choreographers in collaboration', *BROLGA*, 41–51.

Bélanger, D. C., and Lussier, S. 2011. 'College student expectations for the first class in the term', *Péagogie Collégiale*, 24(2): 1–7.

Biasutti, M. 2013. 'Improvisation in dance education: teacher views', *Research in Dance Education*, 14(2): 120–40.

Butterworth, J. 2004. 'Teaching choreography in higher education: A process continuum model', *Research in Dance Education*, 5(1): 45–67.

Cancienne, M. B., and Snowber, C. N. 2003. 'Writing rhythm: Movement as method', *Qualitative Inquiry*, 9(2): 237–53.

Cheesman, S. 2009. 'Sustaining dance education in New Zealand: Some issues facing pre-service, primary teacher educators'. In *Dance Dialogues: Conversations across cultures, artforms and practices*, edited by C. Stock, Proceedings of the 2008 Dance Alliance Global Summit, Brisbane, 13–18 July. QUT Creative Industries and Ausdance. Accessed 8 July 2023. http://www.ausdance.org.au.

Csikszentmihalyi, M., and Sawyer, K. 1995. 'Creative insight: The social dimension of a solitary moment'. In *The Nature of Insight*, edited by R. J. Sternberg and J. E. Davidson, 329–63. Cambridge MA: MIT Press.

Dance Aotearoa New Zealand (DANZ). 2014. *Dance Facts*. Accessed 8 July 2023. https://danz.org.nz/dance+facts+the+popularity+of+dance.

Dezutter, S. 2012. 'Professional improvisation and teacher education: Opening the conversation'. In *Structure and Improvisation in Creative Teaching*, edited by R. K. Sawyer, 27–50. Cambridge: Cambridge University Press.

Dinkelman, T. 2003. 'Self-study in teacher education: A means and ends tool for promoting reflective teaching', *Journal of Teacher Education*, 54(1): 6–18.

Donmoyer, R. 1983. 'Pedagogical improvisation', *Educational Leadership*, 40(4): 39–43.

Eisner, E. W. 1975. *The Perceptive Eye: Toward the reformation of educational evaluation*. Stanford CA: Stanford University.

Fournier, J. E. 2003. 'Composing in dance: Thinking with minds and bodies'. Unpublished doctoral thesis, University of Washington.

Hamilton, M. L. 2004. 'Professional knowledge, self-study and teacher education'. In *International Handbook of Self-study of Teaching and Teacher Education Practices*, edited by J. J. Laughran, M. L. Hamilton, V. K. LaBoskey and T. Russell, 375–419. Dordrecht: Kluwer Academic Publishers.

Hamilton, M. L., and Pinnegar, S. 1998. 'Conclusion: The value and promise of self-study'. In *Reconceptualizing Teaching Practice: Self-study in teacher education*, edited by M. L. Hamilton, 235–46. London: Falmer Press.

Hamilton, M. L., Smith, L., and Worthington, K. 2008. 'Fitting the methodology with the research: An exploration of narrative, self-study and auto-ethnography', *Studying Teacher Education*, 4(1): 17–28.

Hong, C. M. (2002). *Dance in the School Curriculum of Aotearoa New Zealand*. Paper presented at the UNESCO Regional Pedagogical Conference on Arts Education in the Pacific in Fiji.

Hornbach, C. 2004. 'Response to Masafumi Ogawa, "Music Teacher Education in Japan: Structure, Problems, and Perspectives"', *Philosophy of Music Education Review*, 12(2): 201–4.

Horning, A. S. 1979. 'Teaching as performance', *The Journal of General Education*, 185–94.

Keightley, E., Pickering, M., and Allett, N. 2012. 'The self-interview: A new method in social science research', *International Journal of Social Research Methodology*, 15(6): 507–21.

Kelly, G. J., Brown, C., and Crawford, T. 2000. 'Experiments, contingencies, and curriculum: Providing opportunities for learning through improvisation in science teaching', *Science Education*, 84(5): 624–57.

Kirsh, D., Muntanyola, D., Jao, R. J., Lew, A., and Sugihara, M. 2009. 'Choreographic methods for creating novel, high quality dance'. In *DeSForM 5th International Workshop on Design & Semantics of Form and Movement Proceedings*, 188–95.

Klien, M. 2007. 'Choreography: A pattern language', *Kybernetes*, 36(7–8), 1081–8.

Knox, S. 2013. 'Dancer-centered dance-making: Five dancers' meanings and experiences of agency within choreographic collaboration'. Master's dissertation, ResearchSpace@ Auckland.

Koff, S. R. 2021. *Dance Education: A redefinition*. London: Bloomsbury Publishing.

LaBoskey, V. K. 2004. 'The methodology of self-study and its theoretical underpinnings'. In *International Handbook of Self-study of Teaching and Teacher Education Practices*, edited by J. J. Laughran, M. L. Hamilton, V. K. LaBoskey and T. Russell, 375–419. Dordrecht: Kluwer Academic Publishers.

Lakes, R. 2005. 'The messages behind the methods: The authoritarian pedagogical legacy in western concert dance technique training and rehearsals', *Arts Education Policy Review*, 106(5): 3–20.

Lavender, L. 2006. 'Creative process mentoring: Teaching the "making" in dance-making', *Journal of Dance Education*, 6(1): 6–13.

Lessinger, L., and Gillis, D. 1976. *Teaching as a Performing Art*. Dallas TX: Crescendo Publications.

Levine, T. H., and Marcus, A. S. 2010. 'How the structure and focus of teachers' collaborative activities facilitate and constrain teacher learning', *Teaching and Teacher Education*, 26(3): 389–98.

Melchior, Elizabeth. 2011. 'Culturally responsive dance pedagogy in the primary classroom', *Research in Dance Education*, 12(2): 119–35.

Ministry of Education. 2000a. *The Arts in the New Zealand Curriculum*. Wellington: Learning Media Limited.

Ministry of Education. 2000b. *Treaty of Waitangi principle*. Wellington: The New Zealand Curriculum Online. Accessed 8 July 2023. https://nzcurriculum.tki.org.nz/Principles/Treaty-of-Waitangi-principle.

Ministry of Education. 2015. *The New Zealand Curriculum*. Wellington: Learning Media Limited.

Ministry of Education. 2020. 'What is dance about?', *NCEA Education*. Accessed 8 July 2023. https://ncea.education.govt.nz/arts/dance?view=learning.

Morgan, G. 1997. *Images of Organizations*. Thousand Oaks CA: SAGE.

Murphy, C. 2017. 'What are New Zealand secondary school Dance teachers' meanings of teaching and assessing creativity?'. Master's dissertation, ResearchSpace@ Auckland.

Newall, P., and Fortin, S. 2012. 'The Montreal danse choreographic research and development workshop: Dancer-researchers examine choreographer-dancer relational dynamics during the creative process'. In *Fields in Motion: Ethnography in the worlds of dance*, edited by D. Davida, 191–217. Waterloo: Wilfrid Laurier University Press.

Partnership for 21st Century Skills. 2009. *A Framework for Twenty-First Century Learning*. Accessed 8 July 2023. http://www.p21.org/.

Pineau, E. L. 1994. 'Teaching is performance: Reconceptualizing a problematic metaphor', *American Educational Research Journal*, 31(1): 3–25.

Proulx, J. 2009. *Enseigner mieux. Réalité, réflexions et pratiques*. Trois-Rivières QC: Cégep de Trois-Rivières.

Risner, D. 2010. 'Dance education matters: Rebuilding postsecondary dance education for twenty-first century relevance and resonance', *Arts Education Policy Review*, 111(4): 123–35.

Rogers, C. 1961. *On Becoming a Person: A therapist's view of psychotherapy*. London: Constable.

Russell, T. 2002. 'Can self-study improve teacher education?'. In *Improving Teacher Education Practices through Self-study*, edited by J. Laughran and T. Russell, 3–9. London: Routledge.

Ryan, A. 2006. 'Post-positivist approaches to research'. In *Researching and Writing your Thesis: A guide for postgraduate students*, edited by S. H. Gilligan, 12–26. Kildare: MACE.

Sarason, S. S. 1999. *Teaching as a Performing Art*. New York: Teachers College Press.

Sawyer, R. K. (ed.). 2011. *Structure and Improvisation in Creative Teaching*, 27–50. Cambridge: Cambridge University Press.

Sawyer, R. K. 2004. 'Creative teaching: Collaborative discussion as disciplined improvisation', *Educational Researcher*, 33(2): 12–20.

Snook, B. 2012. 'Someone Like Us: Meanings and contexts informing the delivery of dance in New Zealand primary classrooms'. Doctoral dissertation, ResearchSpace@ Auckland.

Snook, B., Buck, R., and O'Brien, P. 2014. 'A historical overview of dance in the New Zealand school curriculum', *Brolga: An Australian Journal about Dance*, 39: 9–19.

Stevens, C., and McKechnie, S. 2005. 'Thinking in action: Thought made visible in contemporary dance', *Cognitive Processing*, 6(4): 243–52.

Stevens, K., McKechnie, S., Malloch, S., and Petocz, A. 2000. 'Choreographic cognition: Composing time and space'. In *Proceedings of the 6th International Conference on Music Perception & Cognition*, 1–8. Keele: Keele University.

Te Rito Toi. 2020. *Replanting Creativity During Post-normal Times*. Research report by the Centre for Arts and Social Transformation. Auckland: University of Auckland.

Timpson, W. M., and Tobin, D. N. 1982. *Teaching as Performing: A guide to energizing your public presentation*. Englewood Cliffs NJ: Prentice-Hall.

UNESCO. 2006. *Road Map for Arts Education*. The World Conference on Arts Education: Building Creative Capacities for the 21st Century, Lisbon.

Warburton, E. C. 2008. 'Beyond steps: The need for pedagogical knowledge in dance', *Journal of Dance Education*, 8(1): 7–12.

A response from the perspective of the United States

Karen Ramlackhan

This chapter reports on creativity in education in dance and choreography, which is less conventional within primary and secondary education contexts. The use of movement and the body inform creative thinking, being and doing. Embedded within particular spaces, times and structures, dance and choreography are experiential, application-based and founded on creative capacities.

Experimentation, problem-solving, leadership and decision-making can be used to inform and engage in the creative processes of applying aspects of dance and choreography where students and educators can learn from and with each other. It is a process that is interpretive and reflective of different understandings and experiences from individual and collective perspectives. The incorporation of students' cultures, backgrounds and identities demonstrates that each person is valued, belongs to the class community and is integral to the dance-making process. It is collaborative process, an interpretative process, a resounding demonstration of creativity and risk-taking. What a fantastic form of creative representation through the interconnection of body, mind and spirit.

Dance-making in the context of teacher education not only resonates within the arts, but also in subject areas such as mathematics, language arts, science and social studies. Drama, music and visual arts courses and curricula are well-suited for the inclusion of dance and choreography. Theatrical plays and musical performances provide an open forum – a space to play, to push boundaries, to imagine and to create.

From early childhood to primary and secondary schooling, and even to tertiary education, this approach can be instilled within programmes, processes and instruction to build creative capacities of educators, student teachers and students, along with using creativity in teaching leading and learning contexts. There would be much value in using dance-making processes, such as the choreographic pedagogies described, in education programmes and practices in the United States.

In our neoliberal context, education is ensconced in standardisation through narrowed curricula, high-stakes testing learning environments and accountability-driven professional development (Au, 2011; Slater and Griggs, 2015). Through twenty-first-century skills, the focus of education can be shifted to address the most meaningful of social issues that affect communities around the world. Twenty-first-century skills espouse critical thinking, problem-solving, creativity and collaboration through adaptability, self-direction, leadership and responsibility (Trilling and Fadel, 2009).

In the United States social issues related to race and racism, xenophobia, homophobia, gender and immigration continue to pervade politics, policies and even directions and practices in schooling institutions. The promotion of critical thinking and problem-solving the challenges relevant to these social justice matters in schools is particularly useful in this context (Darling-Hammond, 2017). Consequently, it is of utmost importance to prepare educators to create and maintain schooling communities that regard the twenty-first-century skills as important to the development of pupils and students for a future that rests on their shoulders. Equally, the preparation of teachers to use creativity in instruction and pedagogy as well to grow their creative capacities to do so, is necessary, so they can encourage and develop that within their learners. Critical thinking fosters creativity in problem-solving entrenched issues and challenges that require imagination, and creative capacities to envision new directions and not otherwise tried solutions.

Using dance-making and choreography as a mechanism that enhances critical thinking and creativity representation in teaching and learning will encourage collaboration, communication and self-direction. The demonstration of understanding topics and content related to social issues through dance, individually and collectively, can be used as a non-traditional method of assessment, which would typically take the form of tests and quizzes with pre-determined answers and structures to follow.

The choreographic pedagogies that the author explained in the chapter can be integrated into alternative schooling, such as so-called 'charter' and 'magnet' schools in the United States that have focused specialisms such as the arts, STEM, environment and provision for the gifted and talented. The pedagogies can also be integrated into university-level education programmes and in traditional early childhood, primary and secondary schools. Not all aspects may be utilised but some can be threaded to develop critical capacities and to use creativity in leading, teaching, learning and assessment.

Imaginative theatre practices emphasise a person's social situation, limitations, sociopolitical standing and cultural aspects (Boal, 1993). As such, the practices can be used in multiple ways to address issues in education. This has been done to help with understanding intersectionality and student and teacher identities in classrooms focused on preparation of teachers to use culturally relevant pedagogy (Powers *et al.*, 2015). Thus, dance-making and choreography with theatre illuminate experiences and highlight expressions of marginalised understanding and oppressed being. This ties with the choreographic pedagogies of improvisation and movement, along with manipulation and structuring processes. Choreography involves leadership and teaching, decision-making and problem-solving, which are all necessary for the twenty-first-century learner. More broadly, this approach can be used to contemplate, 'Should art educate, inform, organize, influence, incite to action, or should it simply be an object of pleasure?' (Boal, 1993, xiii).

References

Au, W. 2011. 'Teaching under the new Taylorism: High stakes testing and the standardization of the 21st century curriculum', *Journal of Curriculum Studies*, 43(1): 25–45.

Boal, A. 1993. *Theatre of the Oppressed*. New York: Theatre Communications Group.

Darling-Hammond, L. 2017. 'Teaching for social justice: Resources, relationships, and anti-racist practice', *Multicultural Perspectives*, 19(3): 133–8.

Powers, B., and Duffy, P. B. 2015. 'Making invisible intersectionality visible through theater of the oppressed in teacher education', *Journal of Teacher Education*, 67(1): 61–73.

Slater, G. B., and Griggs, C. B. 2015. 'Standardization and subjection: An autonomist critique of neoliberal school reform', *Review of Education, Pedagogy, and Cultural Studies*, 37(5): 438–59.

Trilling, B., and Fadel, C. 2009. *21st century skills: Learning for life in our times*. San Francisco CA: John Wiley & Sons, Inc.

A response from the perspective of Brazil

Klesia Garcia Andrade

Considering the improvement of teaching practices, Sarah Knox highlights the challenges and possibilities of dance-teacher education through the creative and collaborative process in the construction of choreographies. How can we train teachers capable of developing their own creative pedagogies? Where do we begin? What content and materials need to be explored? The chapter presents eight pedagogical tactics that contribute to broaden our reflections on the theme. In the description and analysis of the eight tactics, Knox reveals the expectation of teacher education for teachers that are capable of developing their own pedagogies.

From my experience in music teacher education and research on creativity developed in my doctoral research (Andrade, 2019), I understand that exercising autonomous and creative teaching practice can begin on conscious contact with meaningful teaching and learning proposals. These can support the elaboration of unique procedures that are appropriated to the context of action. In dialogue with the field of psychology (Alencar, 2009; Beaudot, 1975; Lubart, 2007), the transition between knowing consolidated approaches and exploring new possibilities can be based on the balanced stimulation of convergent and divergent thinking.

Through the stimulation of convergent thinking, which is characterised by knowledge, processes and pedagogical proposals built throughout history, among others, we can master a set of skills that can support the exercise of teaching, in Knox's case, that of choreography. Divergent thinking, on the other hand, turns to multidimensional research. From a generating viewpoint we seek unusual ideas that are remote, far from conventional standards and already known in society. In divergent thinking there is no right and wrong, only countless possibilities (Santos, 1994, 24). Thus, articulating Novaes's (1980, 116) ideas with Knox's perspectives, the creation of creative pedagogies presupposes the establishment of new and original, divergent, relationships in dialogue with previous knowledge and the mastery of specific, convergent, skills.

This chapter highlights the dilemmas present about the lack of creative practices in both teacher training courses and basic schooling in Aotearoa New Zealand. Despite knowing some initiatives by peers in the area, which seek to break with the traditional and 'scripted' standards of teacher education, I have observed this lack in the field of Brazilian music education. Lubart (2007, 8) criticises formal teaching contexts that, in general, follow pre-established procedures instead of promoting learning that would allow the individual to face day-to-day situations in a more creative and less limited way. One of the 10 educational maxims written by composer and musician-educator Murray Schafer states that 'the first practical step, in any educational reform, is to take the first practical step' (Schafer, 2011, 265). If we aim to train teachers with sufficient autonomy to develop their own creative pedagogies, we need to take this step towards the exploration of new possibilities. Knox does this by describing and discussing scenes from this process. Teaching creatively, whether in teacher education or in other educational contexts, requires a willingness to take risks, as well as courage and daring to expose, restart, modify, experiment, observe and evaluate: would there be (an)other way(s) of walking the paths of creativity?

Studies and practices aimed at understanding creative processes reveal the similarity of pedagogical procedures and conceptions. Exploration, improvisation, collaborative work and refinement of ideas, such as the eight tactics listed by Knox, seem to be inherent in all creative practice, regardless of whether the artistic language is visual arts, dance, music or theatre. In general, the teacher in training has opportunities to know traditional and contemporary teaching methodologies, in addition to developing the ability to adapt them to the most different contexts of action. However, what experiences/knowledge are essential to train a creative teacher?

In the Brazilian educational-musician field, we have seen some proposals that articulate, in one way or another, some elements that refer to the tactics listed by Knox. The 'Re-arranging' (Penna and Marinho, 2012), the 'Creative Choir' (Andrade, 2019), the models of improvisation and communication games by Hans Joachim Koellreutter (Brito, 2011), and the proposal '1, 2, 3, 4 Ra!' (Kater, 2012, 238–9) used in the context of teacher education in Brazilian universities, are proposals that contribute to pedagogical-creative education.

The thematic research process, the first tactic presented by Knox, highlights the importance of expressive elements and nuances of what is not said, or danced. In the field of music education, many sound activities can start from the discovery of the body as the first instrument. There is no shortage of resources if we conceive our body as the richest of musical instruments. In the percussive experience and in the use of the voice, the articulations with dance (e.g. movement and sound) can reveal potentialities and limitations, instigating us to think about what is not sung, perpetuated or expressed. Thus, awareness about exploration and thematic research can follow complementary paths – paths directed to the personal experience of the teacher in training: how they feel and express themselves, what is fluent and where their limitations are. The teacher who works in this training collaborates to expand the repertoire of movements, sounds and ways of artistically expressing ideas. Another path is driven to the possibilities of dealing with the various situations in the exercise of teaching practice: ways to solve the impasses and for the divergent perspective to collaborate so that teachers in training feel encouraged to deal with the risks and unpredictability of the creative process. Thus, the discussions and data presented by Knox, originating from a specific context, provide indications that may be useful for the expansion of studies on the training of critical, autonomous and creative teachers.

References

Alencar, Eunice M. L. Soriano de. 2009. *Como desenvolver o potencial criador: um guia para a liberação da criatividade em sala de aula.* Petrópolis: Editora Vozes.

Andrade, Klesia Garcia. 2019. 'Creative choir: An action research on musical creation in practice coral', 262. Doctoral dissertation, Universidade Federal da Paraíba.

Beaudot, Alain. 1975. *A criatividade na escola.* São Paulo: Ed. Nacional.

Brito, Teca Alencar de. 2011. *Koellreutter educador: o humano como objetivo da educação musical.* São Paulo: Peirópoles.

Kater, Carlos. 2012. '1 2 3 4 Rá!'. In *A música na escola*, Gisele Jordão *et al.*, 238–9. São Paulo: Vale.

Lubart, Todd. 2007. *Psicologia da criatividade.* Porto Alegre: Artmed.

Novaes, Maria Helena. 1980. *Psicologia da criatividade.* Petrópolis: Editora Vozes.

Penna, Maura, and Marinho, Vanildo Mousinho. 2012. 'Ressignificando e recriando músicas: a proposta do re-arranjo'. In *Música(s) e seu Ensino*, Maura Penna, 173–207. Porto Alegre: Sulina.

Santos, Regina Márcia Simão. 1994. 'A natureza da aprendizagem musical e suas implicações curriculares: análise comparativa de quatro métodos'. *Fundamentos da educação musical*, 7–112. Série Fundamentos 2.

Schafer, Murray. 2011. *O ouvido pensante.* São Paulo: Ed. Unesp.

Conclusion: future directions for creativity in education

Karen Ramlackhan, Amanda Ince and Nicole Brown

When we originally drafted the idea for an edited book on creativity in education, we could not have foreseen how drastically our world would change. In a short space of time there has been a worldwide pandemic and a war in Ukraine that has affected economies, energy and nations. These have had and continue to have a huge impact and influence on societies and education worldwide, and our contributors have acknowledged and recognised aspects within this book. This concluding chapter continues the discussion framed within creativity for the future.

If the emergence of the Covid-19 pandemic with its distancing rules, travel restrictions and pivot to online learning has shown us anything, it is how important creativity is in education. Using creativity within learning and teaching requires risk-taking and adaptability. But, more importantly, we must reconsider our traditional delineations of what it means to teach and learn. For example, the chapters focused on New Zealand, South Korea and Qatar quite openly disrupt the conventional conception of learning spaces. The contributions from Chile and the United States connect current issues of social justice and equity with the preparation of educators and school leaders through critical thinking. The chapters on teacher education in Sweden and China highlight the importance of building creative abilities in pre-service teachers to create learning environments that encourage creativity in student teachers within early childhood environments. In this concluding chapter we argue that using case studies as transformative practice, these examples of creativity in education and the lessons drawn out in the responses from international colleagues, will provide an antidote to some of the key concerns around the marketisation of education.

Creativity as a sociocultural phenomenon

Creativity as action and creative work as activity emphasise a sociocultural perspective (Glăveanu, 2018). Situated and contextual dynamics are crucial when addressing issues and challenges that require creativity in problem-solving. This is because these matters are positioned within larger social, political, cultural, historical and/or economic systems, and they are contingent on the time, place and space in which they have developed. Consequently, critical thinking, collaboration, creative action and risk-taking are required for generating solutions (Massie *et al.*, 2022). To ensure that educators and learners can handle this kind of thinking and acting, creative capacities must be developed through teacher and leadership preparation programmes, through educational policies and through educator actions within learning spaces. This, in turn, necessitates conditions across all phases of education that facilitate creativity, foster creative expression and actively promote creative capacities.

Educational systems should foster creativity in classrooms through creating educational policies that support creativity, teacher training and research that encourages creativity (Makel, 2009). The understanding that creativity is a relational intersubjective phenomenon, and that creative action happens between actors and their environments (Glăveanu *et al.*, 2013), provides insight into the utility of creativity in education. The sociocultural construction of creativity is tied to our understanding of creative potential. Creativity associated with the arts focuses on spontaneity, originality and divergent thinking. Yet, creativity also connects with science and discovery with a focus on problem-solving, technology and utility. Creativity can rethink everyday life and emphasise mastery and apprenticeship. Each of these distinctive ways of understanding creativity is related to human actions, activities and society (Glăveanu, 2018). The cultivation and conception of creativity as a sociocultural phenomenon mark the conceptual shift necessary for understanding creativity research and practice in education. For example, during the Covid-19 pandemic school systems needed to configure new directions in teaching, leading and learning within a virtual learning space. Parents, caregivers and community members were integral to these new processes and reimagined the notion of 'teacher' and 'educator'. With the shift to online learning and remote attendance, disabled people were suddenly able to participate more fully using virtual tools that had not been readily available in the traditional workspace environment. Flexibility, autonomy, care and wellbeing were at the centre of the new directions in education. But the mechanism for finding these innovative solutions was creative thinking.

Dominant discourses

The chapters in this book offer a portraiture of the use of creativity in educational spaces in various countries. With the help of case studies educators around the globe demonstrate their approaches to developing learning communities – whether within preschool, primary, secondary or tertiary education – centring the development and application of creative capacities. There is one prominent thread that links all chapters: pushing boundaries. That is, going against the neoliberal discourse (Gair *et al.*, 2021; Tight, 2019), a prevalent notion of teaching and learning in education.

Against the backdrop of neoliberalism and globalisation, education in a twenty-first-century context is framed as a competition, and success is constructed through quantifiable scores on standardised tests (Ramlackhan, 2019; Roberts-Holmes and Moss, 2021; Slater and Griggs, 2015). In this context, national and local polices stipulate the standardisation of learning through norms, curricular approaches and assessments, all of which drive what happens in schools and systems to demonstrate effectiveness. The professionalism of teachers is sidelined, and the teacher becomes a performative worker (Perryman and Calvert, 2020) within this market-driven environment. The accountability mechanisms that govern teaching and learning, normalise the 'marketized teacher, the managed teacher, and the performative teacher' (Holloway and Brass, 2018, p. 361). This has changed the teaching profession enormously. Teacher performance evaluation, student retention, graduation decisions and school incentives, are all tied to high-stakes test scores. Within a neoliberal global context where high-stakes accountability assessments determine students' trajectories, there is an understanding of the formidable pressures of standardised teaching and learning (Slater and Griggs, 2015) focused primarily on tested subjects (Eisenhart and Allen, 2016). Tested subjects vary according to context and the cultural and political importance placed on them by the policies, aims and values of each country or continent. Yet, these subjects – most often mathematics, language arts and science – are afforded dedicated time and resources, reflecting the perceived value according to assessment regimes and the consequential nature of the scores. This domination of time and focus may result in narrowed learning experiences that delimit students' knowledge acquisition and engagement. It also impacts on teacher autonomy and agency as well as on curriculum and pedagogical approaches. In many countries, 'teaching to the test' is used by researchers to describe this phenomenon (e.g. Adesope *et al.*, 2017; Ali and Hamid, 2020; Volante, 2004). For instance, Au (2011), argues that teaching to the tests influences teachers' choice of pedagogical strategy to align knowledge and content from these high-stakes assessments in relation to content and curricular form. Thus, teachers adopt more didactic or teacher-centred pedagogies, such as lectures to meet the demands of these tests. The resulting limited pedagogical control, in turn, prevents teachers from readily adopting student-centred learning practices. Therefore, critical thinking and problem-based collaborative approaches to learning that centre learners' capacities and interests may be replaced with more structured and individualised learning methods because of the consequences of high-stakes testing.

Social justice and inequality

There are intended and unintended consequences of policies and curricula (van den Akker, 2010). The current educational accountability systems that rely heavily on high-stakes standardised testing may be detrimental to learners (Roberts-Holmes and Moss, 2021). For example, learners from populations that are commonly marginalised because of race/ethnicity, social class, language, dis/ability or gender have different, often lower outcomes (Jones, 2009; Li *et al.*, 2018; Strand, 2014). Issues of equity, inclusion and social emotional wellbeing illuminate the importance of addressing the impacts of accountability systems grounded on neoliberal ideologies. These issues also direct attention to how educators can work within existing constructions to develop critical thinkers, risk-takers and innovative problem solvers for the twenty-first century.

School systems do not exist in a vacuum. They are enmeshed in and developed through societal, political, economic, cultural and environmental discourses. Polarising politics, fake news and other propaganda, therefore, do not leave the educational settings unscathed. Recent societal developments and movements such as #MeToo and #BlackLivesMatter, which have a significant impact on marginalised communities, have entered educational contexts and consciousness (e.g. Alexander *et al.*, 2020). These discourses put educators and school leaders into positions where they face moral dilemmas and concern over losing their jobs due to differences in values and beliefs. For example, in the state of Florida in the United States, ideology and politics drive the enactment of policies that restrict the curricula – what is discussed, taught and assessed – and the pedagogy or instructional approaches that are used in classrooms and schools. This has potential implications, as in some quarters what happens in the United States may be perceived as the way forward.

Currently, there is much volatility taking place in countries around the world. The war in Ukraine, the exodus of refugees crossing the Mediterranean from African and Middle Eastern countries, refugees from Haiti, Myanmar, as well as south and central America and other disenfranchised communities, along with climate change from global warming, are examples of urgent matters that need addressing. These pressing humanitarian issues require innovation to generate solutions that push boundaries and upend traditional ways of problem-solving. The Covid-19 pandemic also created a lightning rod for controversary politics and policies. It made glaringly evident issues of inequity that disproportionately impact on communities of colour, individuals of low socio-economic backgrounds and people who are disadvantaged by gender and disability. It highlighted issues of access and equity. For example, children in some rural and low-income communities had no access to resources and technology at home. Not all schools had capacity to remain open for children of key workers. Wi-Fi and broadband connectivity became crucial, not just for working from home but for health, education and society as a whole, exacerbating existing inequalities across the whole world. In education, there was an immediate need for school leaders to enable learning in virtual learning environments with minimal training or capacity. What happened throughout the world was that educators, family, community members, students and pupils used creativity and critical thinking to problem-solve the challenges of teaching, leading and learning during a pandemic. They found creative ways to communicate with colleagues, parents, learners and communities, to teach in virtual learning spaces and to bridge school and family relations. The pandemic may yet be seen as a small silver lining in the cloud, as although challenges continue and are evolving, for a twenty-first-century learner the pandemic has increased awareness and brought changes in education for more inclusivity and equity orientation.

Educational inequity is an enduring global challenge. UNESCO's 2030 Agenda for Sustainable Development includes Education for Sustainable Development and is considered a driver for the achievement of all 17 Sustainable Development Goals. Specifically, Education for Sustainable Development:

> empowers everyone to make informed decisions in favour of environmental integrity, economic viability and a just society for present and future generations. It aims to provide the knowledge, skills, attitudes, and values necessary to address sustainable development challenges. (UNESCO, n.d.)

These are pressing challenges that require critical thinking, problem-solving and collaboration to develop creative and innovative solutions. The education sector is highly important in this endeavour. It prepares pupils, students and student teachers for a future enmeshed in technology and advancements that links humans and artificial intelligence with professional and personal spaces.

A focus on equity, inclusion and social justice leads to research and practice about the inclusion of epistemologies and methodologies in higher education institutions that are emerging, such as indigenous education practices (Smith, 1999), Black creative educational experiences (Patton *et al.*, 2022), hip hop pedagogy, coloniality and its shaping of educational systems that sidelines non-Western perspectives (Mehta and Henriksen, 2022). Sahlberg and Cobbold (2021) argue for a focus on equity of educational outcomes and provide five principles to improve equity in education:

- Education policies must proceed in conjunction with economic, social and health policies designed to reduce inequality.
- Education policies must be directed at providing the financial, human and physical resources to achieve an adequate education for all and investing in greater social equity in education outcomes.
- The design of curriculum, pedagogy and assessment must recognise and reflect the cultures of disadvantaged students and minority groups, as well as provide access to the broad range of knowledge and skills for all learners.
- Parent participation in schooling and the learning of their children is fundamental to improving attendance at schools and outcomes for students from disadvantaged backgrounds.

- Enhancing learners' active role in planning, implementing and evaluating teaching and learning leads to positive engagement in education and can contribute to all learners' wellbeing.

This can happen through developing creative capacities in teachers, leaders, student teachers, students and pupils by embedding creativity within pedagogical strategies, instructional practices and assessments. For example, the relationships of schools with local communities are bounded by shared values, beliefs, languages and cultures that can be harnessed. Principals and headteachers as cultural and curriculum leaders should create a learning community that values all (Lucas *et al.*, 2021). School administrators, teachers and educators should also focus on social justice issues and create learning environments where all learners belong by using culturally responsive and sustaining pedagogies and practices (Paris and Alim, 2017).

Future possibilities for creativity in education

A more dramatic approach is a reorientation or rethinking of the purpose of educational institutions in the twenty-first century and the utilisation of creativity and the development of creative capacities. The key to transforming systems for equity and inclusion (Ramlackhan and Catania, 2022; Showunmi *et al.*, 2022) is the criticality of educators as deep thinkers, as leaders, as change agents (Lopez, 2016; Sahlberg and Cobbold, 2021).

Technological advancements such as artificial intelligence, virtual reality, augmented reality and mixed reality, among others, must continue to be focused within science, technology, engineering and mathematics in schools. Yet, we also need to integrate arts-based subject areas such as music, dance, theatre and chorus, to enhance innovative and creative education practice. This can be done via synchronous and asynchronous online teaching, through hybrid models and traditional in-person structures. These exciting developments take education beyond the historical constructs that still influence the organisation and structure of education systems across the world and offer new opportunities and challenges. However, there remain places that lack basic resources necessary for survival. There are multiple issues affecting the world, including the impacts of climate change, refugee/immigration crises, racialised and minoritised groups' performance in education, access to education, wars and polarising politics.

Creativity has an important role to play in problem-solving, as well as in interdisciplinary and transdisciplinary collaborations. Dissolving barriers between the industry and academic spaces to develop partnerships will aid addressing the global and local consequences of these challenges. In short, globalisation and knowledge exchange go hand in hand. The complexity of educational settings and the dynamism of these environments call for new approaches to teaching, leading and learning that prepares learners for an interconnected global community with skills, strategies and capacities to handle issues creatively. In turn, to prepare the next generation as twenty-first-century learners, we need to use creativity to rethink, restructure, recreate and reimagine solutions for a wide range of problems. Teaching and learning in educational settings and beyond need methods and approaches that align with the constructs of creativity, adaptability, risk-taking and problem-solving.

A reform in education that propositions the interrelationships between education and the political, cultural and social spheres is essential. The case studies in this book offer vignettes to demonstrate various ways in which educators push boundaries to make this happen in different contexts around the world. We hope that in its entirety this text offers a step towards a greater recognition of the value of creativity for the future.

References

Adesope, O. O., Trevisan, D. A., and Sundararajan, N. 2017. 'Rethinking the use of tests: A meta-analysis of practice testing', *Review of Educational Research*, 87(3): 659–701.

Alexander, C., Fox, J., and Aspland, T. 2020. '"Third wave" politics in teacher education: Moving beyond binaries'. In *Teacher Education in Globalised Times*, pp. 1–21. Singapore: Springer.

Ali, M. M., and Hamid, M. O. 2020. 'Teaching English to the test: Why does negative washback exist within secondary education in Bangladesh?', *Language Assessment Quarterly*, 17(2): 129–46.

Au, W. 2011. 'Teaching under the new Taylorism: High stakes testing and the standardization of the 21st century curriculum', *Journal of Curriculum Studies*, 43(1): 25–45.

Cumming, J. J., and Dickson, E. 2013. 'Educational accountability tests, social and legal inclusion approaches to discrimination for students with disability: A national case study from Australia', *Assessment in Education: Principles, Policy & Practice*, 20(2): 221–39.

Eisenhart, M., and Allen, C. D. 2016. 'Hollowed out: Meaning and authoring of high school math and science identities in the context of neoliberal reform', *Mind, Culture, and Activity*, 23(3): 188–98.

Gair, S., Hager, T., and Herzog, O. 2021. 'Tackling difference in a neoliberal classroom'. In *Compliance and Resistance Within Neoliberal Academia*, pp. 83–114. Cham: Palgrave Pivot.

Glăveanu, V. P. 2018. 'Educating with creativity?', *Thinking Skills and Creativity*, 27: 25–32.

Glăveanu, V. P., Hanchett Hanson, M., Baer, J., Barbot, B., Clapp, E. P., Corazza, G. E., Hennessey, B., Kaufman, J. C., Lebuda, I., Lubart, T., Montuori, A., Ness, I. J., Plucker, J., Reiter-Palmon, R., Sierra, Z., Simonton, D. K., Neves-Pereira, M. S., and Sternberg, R. J. 2020. 'Advancing creativity theory and research: A socio-cultural manifesto', *Journal of Creative Behavior*, 54(3): 741–5.

Glăveanu, V. P., Lubart, T., Bonnardel, N., Botella, M., De Biaisi, P. M., Desainte-Catherine, M., Georgsdottir, A., Gouillou, K., Mouchiroud, C., Storme, M., Woytczuk, A., and Zenasni, F. 2013. 'Creativity as action: Findings from five creative domains'. *Frontiers in Psychology*, 176.

Holloway, J., and Brass, J. 2018. 'Making accountable teachers: The terrors and pleasures of performativity', *Journal of Education Policy*, 33(3): 361–82.
Jones, B. D. 2007. 'The unintended outcomes of high-stakes testing', *Journal of Applied School Psychology*, 23(2): 65–86.
Jones, S. R. 2009. 'Constructing identities at the intersections: An autoethnographic exploration of multiple dimensions of identity', *Journal of College Student Development*, 50(3): 287–304.
Li, C., Kruger, L. J., Beneville, M., Kimble, E., and Krishnan, K. 2018. 'The unintended consequences of high-stakes testing on English-Language learners: Implications for the practice of school psychology', *School Psychology Forum*, 12(3): 79–90.
Liebowitz, D. D., and Porter, L. 2019. 'The effect of principal behaviors on student, teacher, and school outcomes: A systematic review and meta-analysis of the empirical literature', *Review of Educational Research*, 89(5): 785–827.
Lopez, A. 2016. *Culturally Responsive and Socially Just Leadership in Diverse Contexts: From theory to practice*. New York: Palgrave Macmillan.
Lucas, B., Spencer, E., and Stoll, L. 2021. 'Creative leadership to develop creativity and creative thinking in English schools: A review of the evidence'. London: Mercers' Company.
Makel, M. C. 2009. 'Help us creativity researchers, you're our only hope', *Psychology of Aesthetics, Creativity, and the Arts*, 3(1): 38–42.
Massie, M. H., Capron Puozzo, I., and Boutet, M. 2022. 'Teacher creativity: When professional coherence supports beautiful risks', *Journal of Intelligence*, 10(3): 62.
Mehta, R., and Henriksen, D. A. 2022. 'To democratize, first decolonize: Approaches beyond Eurocentric and colonial epistemologies in creativity', *Review of Research in Education*, 46(1): 105–33.
Paris, D., and Alim, H. S. 2017. *Culturally Sustaining Pedagogies: Teaching and learning for justice in a changing world*. New York: Teachers College Press.
Patton, L. D., Jenkins, T. S., Howell, G. L., and Keith Jr, A. R. 2022. 'Unapologetically Black creative educational experiences in higher education: A critical review', *Review of Research in Education*, 46(1): 64–104.
Perryman, J., and Calvert, G. 2020. 'What motivates people to teach, and why do they leave? Accountability, performativity and teacher retention', *British Journal of Educational Studies*, 68(1): 3–23.
Ramlackhan, K. 2019. 'Restricting social justice practices in public education: The neoliberal stronghold'. In *Handbook on Promoting Social Justice in Education*, edited by R. Papa. Cham: Springer.
Ramlackhan, K., and Catania, N. 2022. 'Fostering creativity, equity, and inclusion through social justice praxis', *Power and Education*, 14(3): 282–95.
Roberts-Holmes, G., and Moss, P. 2021. *Neoliberalism and Early Childhood Education: Markets, imaginaries and governance*. London: Routledge
Sahlberg, P., and Cobbold, T. 2021. 'Leadership for equity and adequacy in education', *School Leadership & Management*, 41(4–5): 447–69.
Showunmi, V., Moorosi, P., Shakeshaft, C., and Oplatka, I. 2022. *The Bloomsbury Handbook of Gender and Educational Leadership and Management*. London: Bloomsbury Academic.
Slater, G. B., and Griggs, C. B. 2015. 'Standardization and subjection: An autonomist critique of neoliberal school reform', *Review of Education, Pedagogy, and Cultural Studies*, 37(5): 438–59.
Smith, L. T. 1999. *Decolonizing Methodologies: Research and indigenous peoples*. Dunedin: University of Otago Press.
Strand, S. 2014. 'Ethnicity, gender, social class and achievement gaps at age 16: Intersectionality and "getting it" for the white working class', *Research Papers in Education*, 29(2): 131–71.
Tight, M. 2019. 'The neoliberal turn in higher education', *Higher Education Quarterly*, 73(3): 273–84.
UNESCO (n.d.). *Sustainable Development Goals: Resources for Educators*. Accessed 7 July 2023. https://en.unesco.org/themes/education/sdgs/material/.
van den Akker, J. 2010. 'Building bridges: how research may improve curriculum policies and classroom practices'. In *Beyond Lisbon 2010: Perspectives from research and development for educational policy in Europe*, edited by S. M. Stoney, 175–95. Slough: CIDREE.
Volante, L. 2004. 'Teaching to the test: What every educator and policy-maker should know'. *Canadian Journal of Educational Administration and Policy*.

Index

www.ingramcontent.com/pod-product-compliance
Lightning Source LLC
LaVergne TN
LVHW010731020926
846742LV00029B/42
9781800080645